BREAKING THE
LEADERSHIP
MOLD

BREAKING THE LEADERSHIP MOLD

An Executive's Guide to Achieving Organizational Excellence

ROSIE STEEVES

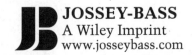

JOSSEY-BASS
A Wiley Imprint
www.josseybass.com

Library and Archives Canada Cataloguing in Publication Data

Steeves, Rosie, 1957-
    Breaking the leadership mold : an executive's guide to achieving organizational excellence / Rosie Steeves.

Includes index.
ISBN 978-0-470-67766-7

1. Leadership.   2. Executive ability.   3. Corporate culture.   I. Title.

HD57.7.S7258 2010   658.4'092   C2010-901767-6

Production Credits
Cover and Interior Design: Michael Chan
Typesetter: Thomson Digital
Front Cover Image: ©istockphoto.com
Printer: Friesens Printing Ltd.

Editorial Credits
Editor: Don Loney
Production Editor: Pamela Vokey

John Wiley & Sons Canada, Ltd.
6045 Freemont Blvd.
Mississauga, Ontario
L5R 4J3

Printed in Canada

1 2 3 4 5 FP 14 13 12 11 10

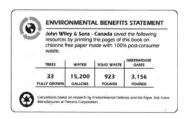

ENVIRONMENTAL BENEFITS STATEMENT

John Wiley & Sons - Canada saved the following resources by printing the pages of this book on chlorine free paper made with 100% post-consumer waste.

TREES	WATER	SOLID WASTE	GREENHOUSE GASES
33	15,200	923	3,156
FULLY GROWN	GALLONS	POUNDS	POUNDS

Calculations based on research by Environmental Defense and the Paper Task Force. Manufactured at Friesens Corporation

CONTENTS

PREFACE

Do you want your legacy to be a mediocre organization? Are you passionately striving to disengage employees, alienate the senior team from the rest of the organization, limit communication, and create huge inefficiencies? Have you made it your life's work to create a dysfunctional and unprofitable organization?

These are silly questions, I know. No one purposely wants to achieve mediocrity or unprofitability. Every leader worth his or her salt strives to create a great organization. Too bad it's not working out that way for most companies. Mediocre organizations dominate business today, while great ones are few and far between.

What do I mean by a great organization? In simple terms, I consider it to be an organization that is competitive and sustainable. Let's be clear: in today's world, profitability and competitiveness are key. But these goals must be attained in a manner that does not threaten the organization's very existence—short or long term. In other words, the organization must be sustainable. Furthermore, I believe (and hope you do too) that organizational success must not be achieved at any cost. Ethics and values *must* be taken into consideration. We must value and respect the people we interact with, because it is the right thing to do. This is the hallmark of a healthy (or great) organization. It's nice to know that such an attitude also makes good business sense, as you'll discover throughout this book.

Unfortunately, many leaders focus solely on profitability and competitiveness, paying little attention to the "people" aspect of the business. They assume their human resources (HR) department takes care of this for them. "Hard" takes precedence over "soft" in every facet of organizational life, whether it is resources invested in development, the focus of the strategic planning process, or how individual decisions are made. The irony is that such a myopic view works against the very thing they so anxiously seek—great margins.

While close attention to the bottom line is clearly necessary, such a single-minded focus fails to account for the fact that organizations are groups of people who collectively strive to produce a product or service. Thus, it is the people and the way they feel and interact that make or break an organization.

The increasing focus on people mirrors the change in organizational paradigms that has occurred in recent years. In the past, a mechanistic world-view suggested that organizations are best thought of as machines and employees as interchangeable parts. In such organizations, employees' output on a production line is believed to be driven by the production process and not the employees' sense of engagement or well-being. The idea of empowering or engaging employees to take the initiative was not seen to be of any value. Indeed, such efforts were to be avoided, as they were believed to negatively impact the bottom line.

Those days are now gone, replaced by a more organic and humanistic approach to organizations. Today, we understand that the quality of relationships, leadership, and people practices all have a direct impact on the bottom line. Despite this, mechanistic thinking pervades every aspect of organizational life. Senior leaders, many of whom began their career under traditional "command and control" managers, are often unaware of how these practices negatively impact the bottom line.

Make no mistake: many senior leaders are failing to acknowledge the human element of business. The numbers we see regarding the level of employees' engagement and satisfaction are appalling, pointing to serious problems in many organizations. For example, on average, less than 30 percent of employees are engaged at work and only 6 percent believe that senior management treats them as though they are the organization's "most valuable asset."[1] These figures are astounding when we know that the level of employee engagement is directly linked to an organization's profitability. Something is clearly wrong.

The responsibility for these terrible numbers lies, I believe, fairly and squarely on the shoulders of senior management. Not because we need these individuals to be larger-than-life charismatic leaders, but because they are simply not doing what must be done to create an engaged workforce, and along with it a healthy, sustainable, and, yes, profitable organization. They have not adapted their leadership style or their organizational people practices to the present reality and, instead, remain firmly embedded in the model of mechanistic thinking, despite what many may preach. Senior management are in a position to be able to effect an organization's transformation, but unless they open their eyes to alternative paradigms and changing roles, their organization will continue to disengage employees and be a fine example of mediocrity. Organizational greatness will remain simply a pipe dream.

We know what to do. Organizational greatness is not some unattainable nirvana. It simply requires those at the top to do the following:

- Ensure their own leadership behavior is relevant for today's organizations. Organizations have changed, but unfortunately, many senior leaders continue to rely on the behaviors that got them to the top. It's just not working. For example, a recent study revealed that only 38 percent of employees believe that senior management communicates openly and honestly.[2] A hierarchy does not exclude executives from the need for ongoing development. Rather, it demands it. Yet a willingness to take a long hard look at one's leadership practices is a rare phenomenon at the top of the management ladder. It seems like everyone's just too busy "leading."
- Develop a collaborative and effective senior leadership team. The rapidly changing environment in which organizations now operate means that the leadership of an organization must fall into the hands of not one all-powerful CEO, but the team at the top. Unfortunately, most executive team members fail to fully comprehend the dynamics of the executive team. As a result, executive team dysfunction is rampant. One study suggested that only 6 percent of organizations could boast that the executives in their C-suite were a well-integrated team.[3]
- Purge the organization of all remnants of mechanistic thinking. It can be found everywhere, from how we implement change, to how we recognize and reward employees. Many times, we are not even aware that commonly accepted practices come from a long-gone era of a mechanistic world-view.

In the chapters that follow, I offer some clear guidelines for any leader who wishes to create a great organization. While written primarily for those at the top, the lessons outlined in the following pages are relevant for all who are no longer willing to tolerate organizational mediocrity.

In Part One, I propose that those at the top who want to create a great organization first need to increase their understanding and appreciation of how modern organization life has failed to evolve in parallel with our increased knowledge of what makes for an effective organization. The first four principles are as follows:

- Principle #1: Face the Facts
- Principle #2: Break the Mold
- Principle #3: Define a Better Way
- Principle #4: Figure Out if You Have What It Takes

Despite their best intentions, many executives continue to operate using outdated paradigms. The net result of this is employees who are disengaged and organizations that are fractured, creating silos and a gulf between senior management and employees. Executives would be well advised to reflect on, and clarify, their own personal beliefs regarding organizational leadership and to define for themselves what they want. More than motherhood statements, wishful thinking, and lists of competencies, those at the top need to ensure that they can clearly articulate a leadership brand that links behavior and results. They also need to understand how such behavior is only possible by those who have achieved a certain level of personal development. All leaders need to accept that the developmental level of those at the top is a "show-stopper." In other words, organizational transformation is simply not possible unless a sufficient number of senior leaders have attained a sufficiently high stage of developmental maturity. And few have.

The first four principles demand some deep reflection and a willingness to let go of old paradigms and the belief that all is well. Once this occurs, an individual is able to explore new ways of leading the organization. As they embark on this journey, they will acquire a deeper understanding both of themselves as a leader and their organization, which will, in turn, impact their organizational change efforts. Thus, the cycle continues.

In Part Two, I suggest that prior to embarking on organizational transformation efforts, executives first consider *how* they are leading. The four principles that embody this concept are these:

- Principle #5: Give Yourself a Leadership Reality Check
- Principle #6: Conduct a Personal Leadership Audit
- Principle #7: Embark On a Leadership Makeover
- Principle #8: Put Yourself First

One of the vestiges of the outdated, mechanistic model of leadership is that those at the top rarely have a good sense of how they are leading. Worse, they convince themselves that a senior position in the organizational hierarchy is clear evidence of leadership effectiveness. Yet despite good intentions, many executives are using methods that do not meet the needs of their employees, with the net result an ineffective and unhealthy organization.

Any executive who wishes to create a great organization must ensure that their own personal leadership skills and capacity helps, rather than hinders, their organization. Although many at the top may acknowledge that development is a never-ending journey, their behavior suggests something quite different. Once they reach the upper echelons of the hierarchical pyramid, their development efforts take a back seat to what they perceive to be the more important needs of the organization.

Such leaders would do well to recognize that the organization first needs them to lead more effectively. In trying to do the right thing, they are actually accomplishing the opposite. For example, many executives try to meet the needs of their organization by assuming ridiculous workloads with little, if any, down time. They fail to realize that such work habits are counterproductive to their efforts to create a great organization.

In Part Three, I explore the importance of developing a highly functioning executive team. Prior to focusing on the entire organization, leaders must first get their own house in order, whether this be with respect to their own personal leadership or the leadership and behavior of their peers and colleagues. The four principles presented in Part Three are these:

- Principle #9: Understand What Could Be Amiss with Your Top Team
- Principle #10: Recognize How Executive Team Dynamics Promotes Mediocrity
- Principle #11: Get the Top Team Working
- Principle #12: Get the Board on Board

It is in the area of the senior leadership team effectiveness where much work is required. Many paradigms exist in organizations about the team at the top. In most cases, this mythology stems more from actions in the past, rather than present-day reality, yet stories still persist of arrogant, grossly overpaid, and out-of-touch senior executives.

Given this persistent negative image, great effort must be taken by the senior team, not only to enhance their effectiveness, but also to create a different story about the team at the top. This is not an easy task given the powerful dynamics present in any senior team. As many executives are unaware of these dynamics, senior team mediocrity is rampant. Furthermore, with all the pressures on their time, rarely do executives make senior team development a priority.

Executives would be well advised to avoid this trap and spend the time that is necessary to develop a highly functioning senior team. By doing so, not only will better decisions be made for the organization, but also all employees will understand the expected standards of communication and collaboration. The senior team can, in effect, model through their actions the type of organizational culture that they are trying to create. This also means ensuring relationships with board members are equally productive, open, and healthy.

Once personal and team leadership have been developed, a senior leader has then earned the right to focus on transforming the organization. The four principles presented in Part Four are these:

- Principle #13: Develop Everyone's Leadership
- Principle #14: Get Other Executives on Board (Or Out of the Way)
- Principle #15: Figure Out Communication
- Principle #16: Create Communities

One of the most effective strategies for transforming an organization to greatness is to develop the leadership of everyone within the organization. This requires an investment in everyone, regardless of their position in the hierarchy. While the format of leadership development will vary depending on an employee's role, there must be a personal investment in every employee. Those at the top should not naïvely assume that the more senior leaders have the skills or capacity to develop the leadership of those who report to them. Furthermore, influential senior executives must be committed to and supportive of all leadership development initiatives.

Organizations will transform when the individuals who make up that organization are connected to each other. This requires that those at the top pay close attention to communication and adjust their communication strategies to the needs of employees. Technology is opening up new avenues in this regard. In addition, a wide range of employees can be connected through communities. Such communities can be effective structures to ensure that organizational boundaries are spanned. The net result will be an organization that develops the capacity to learn, grow, and change.

In Part Five, I discuss the need for an ongoing focus on improvement, which demands an effective feedback system that incorporates all aspects of organizational life. The four principles presented in Part Five are these:

- Principle #17: Tell People How They're Doing
- Principle #18: Promote for the Future
- Principle #19: Integrate the Hard and the Soft
- Principle #20: Never Stop

An organization is a system and all parts of that system must be aligned and integrated. Behaviors that are advocated through leadership development initiatives or senior leadership communication must be rewarded and supported. Those individuals who are the "early adopters" should be recognized and placed into positions where they can have the most influence. Action must also be taken with those who struggle with these changes.

The responsibility for these organizational systems does not reside solely with the HR department. All senior executives should be intimately involved with talent management processes and must recognize that the enactment of these systems sends a loud message to the organization regarding what is expected. They are, in effect, powerful communication tools.

The same applies to many other internal processes that tend to separate out the hard and the soft elements of organizational life. Senior leaders would be well advised to continually consider how integration, rather than separation, can occur in processes such as leadership and management development, strategic planning, and decision-making.

The shift to organizational greatness never ends. Those in the C-suite must dispel the myth that they and their organization have "arrived." Change is an ongoing process that must be normalized within any organization.

If you follow the guidelines outlined in this book, your organization will indeed make the shift to greatness. Oh, and it will also be profitable, healthy, and sustainable. But if you read and don't act, rest assured you will be a champion of mediocrity.

The choice is yours.

ACKNOWLEDGMENTS

A number of people were instrumental in seeing this book through to fruition. I'd like to thank John Hoover, who got me started on the right path and gave me the tools and assurance I needed to move ahead. Don Loney from Wiley proved to be my greatest supporter. I thank him for having faith in me from the outset and the unwavering confidence he has shown in me every step of the way. To Carol Bonnett, who with eagle eyes did an incredible editing job, and to everyone at Wiley for welcoming me in ways I never imagined. I must thank the clients who have allowed me into their inner organizational sanctuaries and who have been courageous enough to make changes and, in doing so, made a difference to so many. And finally, to my family, who have put up with a restless Mom and the crankiness that not enough outdoor time produces. You guys are the best!

Dedication

This book is dedicated to Kelly and Megan, who have taught me more about leadership than anyone; to Bob, who has always been there for me; and to Tatlow, for her constant companionship.

PART ONE

FACE THE FACTS

The vice president of operations of a mining company recognizes that the leaders in his organization are too focused on short-term tactics to be able to lead the organization into an anticipated aggressive growth phase. The director of human resources (HR) of an engineering company believes her organization's leaders are technical experts, but they are sorely lacking in people skills. Following the merger of three separate companies, the CEO of a gaming company recognizes a key opportunity to create a corporate identity and ensure the consistency of people practices. A government assistant deputy minister has a strong desire to improve engagement. The manager of organizational development of a credit union sees a need to revamp and implement the organization's talent and performance management system.

All of the case studies above are examples of people in positions of responsibility attempting to effect change in different situations, and one thing unites them. They all require an organizational intervention that necessitates changing the behaviors of individuals within the organization, which, in turn, demands an investment in developing people skills.

If these executives act boldly and aggressively to develop the "people" side of their respective businesses, not only will they create great organizations, but they will leave their competition far behind. However, as we will see in this book such executive action is rare or, at best, limited. Let's be clear: this inaction is not due to bad intentions, but a simple lack of awareness of the lost opportunity. The net result is disengaged, inefficient, and uncompetitive organizations, simply because executives are not doing what is required.

What *should* executives be doing? As I will outline in future chapters, there are numerous things that they should do. But first, it is important to set the scene—and face the facts.

THE LINK BETWEEN ENGAGEMENT AND THE BOTTOM LINE

Regardless of who initiates change, regardless of who drives it, and regardless of what form it takes, the very acknowledgment of the need to change the behavior of people assumes that the effectiveness and efficiency of an organization is driven by the manner in which people behave. Any "people" intervention consumes resources, most notably time and money. Thus, implicit in the acknowledgment that this consumption is necessary is the assumption that such an investment will, ultimately, yield a better bottom line.

Increasingly, research is confirming that there is indeed a direct correlation between behavior (in particular, the behavior of leaders) and results. Managers who create motivating and energizing climates have been found to deliver double the margins of those who create neutral or de-motivating climates.[1] Furthermore, the average five-year annualized returns of the 20 companies with the best leaders beat the S&P 500 over the same period by 3.53 percent.[2] Another study determined that, on average, 14 percent of a firm's performance is dependent on its leader.[3]

The term "engagement" is often used to describe the behavior leaders are endeavoring to facilitate. We know results are positively impacted when leaders create engaging environments and do not act in ways that cause employees to become disengaged. However, while the concept of engagement is increasingly gaining popularity as a way to define the desired employees' behavior, a myriad of definitions exist that only adds to the degree of confusion for a manager trying to create a more engaged organization.

In a recent study, Towers Perrin defined engagement as employees' willingness and ability to contribute to company success. They measure engagement based on employees' connections to the organization across three dimensions:

- Rational: How well employees understand their roles and responsibilities (the "thinking" part of the equation).
- Emotional: How much passion and energy they bring to their work (the "feeling" part of the equation).
- Motivational: How well they perform in their roles (the "acting" part of the equation).[4]

In 2008, Hewitt & Associates advocated that employee engagement is best defined as

- Say—consistently speak positively about the organization to co-workers, potential employees, and customers.
- Stay—have an intense desire to be a member of the organization despite opportunities to work elsewhere.
- Strive—exert extra time, effort, and initiative to contribute to business success.[5]

Another consulting group, BlessingWhite, suggests that full engagement represents an alignment of maximum job satisfaction (I like my work and do it well) with maximum job contribution (I help achieve the goals of my organization).[6]

In his book *Getting Engaged: The New Workplace Loyalty*, Tim Rutledge proposes that truly engaged employees are attracted to, and inspired by, their work (I want to do this), committed (I am dedicated to the success of what I am doing), and fascinated (I love what I am doing).[7]

And so it goes on. There's no shortage of definitions or theories when it comes to engagement, but it's clear that an engaged organization is one in which all employees, regardless of where they work or the position they hold, care passionately about the future of the company and are willing to invest the discretionary effort necessary to ensure the organization succeeds. It's more than just working hard—it's doing what must be done for success. It's going above and beyond, not because someone tells you to, but because you care.

Not surprisingly, studies are confirming the link between engagement and the bottom line. For example, organizations in the top quartile on engagement have revenue growth that is 2.5 times higher than that of organizations in the bottom quartile.[8] Towers Perrin determined that companies with high employee engagement had a 19 percent increase in operating income and almost a 28 percent growth in their earnings per share. Conversely, companies with low levels of engagement saw their operating income drop more than 32 percent and their earnings per share decline more than 11 percent.[9] Gallup found that public companies ranking in the top quartile for employee engagement had earnings per share growth that was 2.6 times the rate of those that were below average. Conversely, it is estimated that disengaged employees cost U.S. companies as much as $350 billion annually in lost productivity.[10] Likewise, Hewitt's 2008 research has confirmed that employee engagement at double-digit-growth companies exceeds employee engagement at single-digit-growth companies by over 20 percent.[11]

TODAY'S ORGANIZATIONS: A FAILING GRADE

Clearly, good leadership and effective people practices can positively impact the bottom line. To many, this is akin to stating the obvious. However, as obvious as it may be, organizations appear to be failing miserably when it comes to fully utilizing their greatest asset. The current numbers emerging from various studies on engagement are astounding and disturbing. For example,

- After surveying 90,000 employees worldwide, Towers Perrin found that only 21 percent were fully engaged. A worrying 38 percent were partially or fully disengaged. And in Canada, 32 percent of employees were found to be disengaged.[12]
- BlessingWhite determined in a 2008 study that just 29 percent of North American employees were fully engaged.[13]
- In 2008, the American Society for Training and Development found that just 34 percent of U.S. workers were engaged.[14]
- In 2007, Ott and Killham found that just 26 percent of employees were engaged.[15]

So, although we know that engagement is clearly linked to successful financial performance, many organizations appear to be doing a less-than-stellar job in engaging their employees and, as a consequence, are losing a lot of money for their organization.

The problem lies, I believe, in the fact that our philosophy regarding people practices and the "softer" side of organizational life has not kept up with the times. Over the past few decades, the environment in which organizations operate has changed dramatically. This, in turn, has precipitated some radical changes in organizational design. Yet vestiges of our past philosophy regarding the required investment in people have not evolved in parallel. Despite what they may preach, the extent to which organizations invest in and value people is more akin to days gone by. Simply put, there is a huge disconnect between our investment in people and relationships, and the associated job expectations.

In order to understand the origins of this problem, a brief history lesson is in order.

ORGANIZATIONAL EVOLUTION (OR LACK THEREOF)

Prior to 1500 in Europe, most people adopted an organic world-view. Society, communities, and individuals were defined by relationships.

The nature of medieval science was to understand the meaning and significance of things—control was deemed to be in the hand of the creator.

The scientific discoveries by Copernicus, Galileo, and Newton radically changed this world-view. With increased understanding, a desire to describe the workings of the world as mechanistic developed. If the world was a machine, the thinking went, then surely prediction and consequently, control, were possible. This, in turn, would allow emancipation from such things as prejudice, superstition, and unjust authority. This belief soon took hold and the age of enlightenment emerged.

As a consequence of these developments, a Cartesian/Newtonian world was developed, which was defined by the following beliefs:

- The universe is a mechanical system composed of a series of building blocks.
- The universe can best be comprehended by understanding the individual building blocks (reductionism).
- The purpose of science is prediction and control.
- Reality and truth are absolutes that can be uncovered.
- Valid knowledge is obtained only through the positivistic scientific method that emphasizes the rational, mathematical, objective approach. Intuitive wisdom is not scientific and must, therefore, be discounted.

Events such as the Industrial Revolution solidified the Cartesian/Newtonian world-view as the "correct" way to regard the world. Despite the fact that it was developed in the seventeenth century, the design of our modern organization is still derived from philosophies aligned to this mechanistic viewpoint.

A mechanistic world-view suggests that organizations are generally thought of as machines. Organizational charts depict the workings of a machine. As Margaret Wheatley points out in her book *Leadership and the New Science*, there is an emphasis on structure and parts, responsibilities are organized into functions, people are organized into roles, numerical data is gathered and valued, decisions are made on the basis of mathematical rationalizations.[16]

Reductionism is evident in the way groups focus on improving their own efficiency, having little concern for their relationships to other groups. Mechanistic organizations are driven by a belief that if every business unit and individual employee works effectively, then the organization will be effective. We understand organizations by reducing, describing, and separating people and departments into little boxes and lines. The emphasis on parts has led to a tendency to focus on the tasks and functions of individuals, rather than the relationships individuals have with each other.

The mechanistic organization was further consolidated in the early twentieth century with the development of the scientific management method. The father of this methodology, Frederick Winslow Taylor, believed that the application of the scientific method to the management of workers could greatly improve productivity. Rather than work being performed by skilled craftsmen who made their own decisions about how their job was to be performed, supporters of the scientific management method suggested that better productivity could be achieved by taking away much of this autonomy. Skilled tasks were converted into a series of simplified jobs that could be performed by unskilled workers easily trained to perform these tasks efficiently.

Taylor argued that even the most basic, mindless tasks could be planned in a way that would dramatically increase productivity and that scientific management of the work was more effective than the "initiative and incentive" method of motivating workers. The initiative and incentive method offered an incentive to increase productivity, but placed the responsibility on the worker to figure out how to do it.

The scientific method soon gained popularity in organizations where mass production and cost efficiency were the primary goals. Employees performed unskilled tasks and had no special status. Management's goal was to extract maximum output while minimizing their cost, and in this regard, employees were viewed in the same way as other inputs such as raw materials. Employees were considered expendable commodities; in effect, they were interchangeable parts of a machine.

With this philosophy of management, the idea of empowering or engaging employees to take the initiative was not seen to be of value. Indeed, such efforts were to be avoided, as they would negatively impact the bottom line. An employee's output on a production line was driven by the production process and not their sense of engagement or well-being. Given the design of the organization, employee satisfaction was irrelevant to productivity. Furthermore, such satisfaction was seen as a measure of poor productivity, as it occurred only when employees were overpaid or underworked, both of which are detrimental to shareholder value.

Mechanistic organizations work well in a stable and predictable environment, but a rapidly changing environment demands a different type of organization. Today's world is full of unknowns, rapid change, and disappearing boundaries. This different world demands a different organization. While many organizations still bear vestiges of the mechanistic organization, the organic organization has taken root.

Organic organizations are characterized by decentralization, flexible and broadly defined jobs, interdependence among employees and units, and multi-directional communication. Employees are required to think creatively and take the initiative. Employee satisfaction and participation in problem solving and decision-making are seen as essential to organizational success. As a consequence, typically there are relatively few, broadly defined rules, regulations, procedures, and processes. In organic organizations, the emphasis is on effectiveness, problem solving, responsiveness, flexibility, adaptability, creativity, and innovation. Such an organization is able to respond in a timely manner to environmental changes because employees are empowered to be creative, to experiment, and to suggest new ideas. The process of innovation is triggered by employees throughout the organization in a "bottom-up" manner.[17]

Clearly, in such an organization employees are not simply expendable or interchangeable commodities, but unique individuals who can directly impact the success of the organization. Human relations theorists such as Maslow or McGregor supported this belief by suggesting that employees are best viewed as key organizational assets who can create substantial value by inventing new products or building client relationships. These theories suggest that satisfaction can improve employee retention and motivation, benefiting the shareholders. Relationships, effective leadership, and people practices become key to improving the bottom line.

Our organizations have, fundamentally, evolved from mechanistic to organic (although vestiges of the old world order exist). With this shift, a change has come in the extent to which employees and their sense of satisfaction can impact profitability.

In a mechanistic organization, efforts are focused on ensuring the systems and processes are effective and efficient. Few, if any, resources are spent on people initiatives such as creating environments where employees are content in their work and have great relationships with each other and their manager. After all, productivity is driven by the process, and employees have little discretion in their work. Time is spent educating the future workers on the technical aspect of their job.

But in the organic organization, the manner in which profitability is achieved is different. The quality of relationships within the organization, an employee's happiness, sense of engagement, and satisfaction will all determine the extent to which they are willing to give discretionary effort. This, in turn, directly impacts profitability.

Let me offer an example. Several years ago I was working with the maintenance crew of a lumber mill. Because of different shifts, this crew reported to two supervisors—one whom they respected and one whom they didn't. The supervisor they detested treated them with disdain and no respect. At times, each of these supervisors would have to phone the crew, asking them to come and deal with a problem at the mill. When the well-liked supervisor phoned, the crew instantly put down their coffee cups, picked up their tools, and hurried over to the site. Conversely, when the other supervisor called, the crew responded in a much more leisurely way. In both cases, the crews were doing what was asked of them. However, the degree of effort was discretionary and this was due solely to the behavior of the different supervisors.

It wasn't always this way. Years ago, when direct orders came from supervisors to fix a problem, a timeline was set and everyone's roles were spelled out clearly. But with the increasing complexity of technology, more decision-making license is given to employees. In the case of the maintenance crew, they were required to solve complex problems, take the initiative, and have input into the decisions. Thus, the crew could no longer be viewed as simply part of a machine, but as a critical asset to the organization. One of the supervisors understood this, while the other did not. The net result was a variance in productivity on the part of the crew.

CHANGING ORGANIZATIONS DEMANDS A CHANGE IN LEADERSHIP

The advent of organizations that are dependent on the quality of relationships requires that we do not concern ourselves solely with systems and processes, but instead pay attention to the human side of organizations. In order to do this, we must ensure managers are well versed in the complexity of human behavior with a deep and rich understanding of leadership, motivation, and engagement.

Unfortunately, much of the focus in the area of development of people remains embedded in the era of scientific management. The manner in which we prepare and continually develop workers in organizations has not yet changed to reflect the current reality. For example,

- While training for a profession, little, if any, time is spent learning the complexities of human nature. The emphasis continues to be on our learning the technical aspects of the job, whether it is engineering, accounting, marketing, or some other profession. This emphasis on the technical continues to dominate, despite the fact that an individual's ability to work with people will likely make or break a person's career.
- When an organizational initiative to develop people skills is proposed, it is frequently viewed with mixed support. While it may be recognized as a good thing for an organization, all too often people question the value to the bottom line. Those

in charge demand metrics such as the return on investment (ROI). There is no doubt that people skills development is judged by a different standard than the so-called harder skills. For example, when employees take a computer skills course it is assumed that this is a necessary part of their job. There is rarely any follow-up to see if they are using the skills acquired on the course and the ROI is not discussed. The same cannot be said for people skills courses.

- Those whose organizational responsibilities lie in the realm of people are often not valued to the same extent as those who are responsible for systems, processes, and numbers. Even today, it is not uncommon to see HR "missing in action" from the executive table. Although some progress has been made in recent years, I know of many large organizations that relegate the HR function to a low level within the organizational hierarchy. One organization I work with has placed the person in charge of all leadership development four levels below the CEO—at the lowest supervisory level.

- When times get tough, the investment in people is typically one of the first things to be cut. Rather than recognizing that it is the people who will help the organization survive, those in charge revert to a more mechanistic mindset, and focus instead on tightening up systems and processes.

- Organizations continue to promote people into leadership positions based on their technical expertise. Furthermore, they give them limited, if any, training as they assume this new role. The assumption continues to be that the technical skill set is similar to the leadership skill set. This holds true only if those who fall under the leader's responsibility are viewed as part of a machine, rather than as emotional humans.

These paradigms are holdovers from the days when relationships mattered less, employee satisfaction was seen as irrelevant to profitability, and there were limited opportunities for discretionary effort. But today's organizations call for a different approach. The numbers we see concerning employee engagement (or lack thereof) are clearly a symptom that something is wrong with our organizations.

A new paradigm is required. People practices must no longer be synonymous with a mechanistic organization, but instead reflect that which is required in an effective organic organization—and when they do, profitability will increase dramatically.

* * *

A few years ago, a friend of mine was cooking a ham. Prior to putting it into the oven, she cut the end off. Her husband, who was sitting across the counter casually chatting with her, suddenly asked her why she did this. She stopped and looked at her husband. "I have no idea. My mom always did it." She then phoned her mother and asked why she cut the end of a ham. Her mother's reply? "I have no idea. My mom did it." My friend then phoned her grandmother and repeated the same question. Her grandmother was finally able to shed some light on the mystery. "Oh, that was because we had a really small oven and a large ham would never fit in!"

All too often we fail to see what is wrong or what needs changing simply because it is familiar. This is also true with the value we place on people within organizations. We say employees are our biggest asset, yet only 6 percent of employees believe that managers act in a way that truly demonstrates this to be the case.

This is why your first task in *Breaking the Leadership Mold* is to determine the extent to which your organization is governed by outdated paradigms and beliefs regarding your people practices. And that starts with an examination into your organization's leadership practices.

Chapter One Takeaways

1. Executives who act boldly and aggressively to develop the "people" side of their businesses will not only create great organizations, but will leave their competition far behind.

2. There is a direct correlation between behavior (in particular, the behavior of leaders) and an organization's bottom line. Results are positively impacted when leaders create engaging environments and do not act in ways that cause employees to become disengaged.

3. The majority of organizations have a failing grade when it comes to employee engagement, despite the fact that engagement is clearly linked to successful financial performance. Recent estimates suggest that a lack of employee engagement in U.S. organizations costs approximately $350 billion per year.

4. The root of this problem is the failure of most organizations to change their people practices from those best suited for a mechanistic organization to those that support the more relevant and effective organic organization.

5. Despite the fact that it was developed in the seventeenth century, the design of our modern organization is still derived from
   philosophies aligned to a mechanistic viewpoint. In a mechanistic organization, employees are viewed as interchangeable
   commodities. An employee's output on a production line is
   believed to be driven by the production process and not the
   employee's sense of engagement or well-being. The idea of
   empowering or engaging employees so that they take the
   initiative is not seen to be of value. Indeed, such efforts are to
   be avoided, as they negatively impact the bottom line.

6. Organic organizations are characterized by decentralization,
   flexible and broadly defined jobs, interdependence among
   employees and units, and multi-directional communication.
   Employees are required to think creatively and take the initiative. Employee participation (and satisfaction) in problem solving and decision-making is seen as essential to organizational
   success. Relationships, effective leadership, and people practices are critical to improving the bottom line.

7. Unfortunately, much of the focus regarding people and relationships remains embedded in the era of the mechanistic organization. The manner in which we prepare, develop, and value
   those who work in organizations has not yet changed to reflect
   the current reality. As a result, engagement levels are low,
   employee dissatisfaction is high, and organizations are failing
   to achieve their full potential. Executives who fail to appreciate
   this fact are losing money for their organizations.

8. An executive's first task in "breaking the leadership mold"
   is to determine the extent to which his or her organization is
   governed by outdated paradigms and beliefs regarding their
   people practices. The advent of organizations that are dependent on the quality of relationships requires that senior leaders
   concern themselves not just with systems and processes, but
   also with the human side of organizations.

PRINCIPLE #2:

BREAK THE MOLD

Given that the design of organizations has evolved during the previous decades, it would be safe to assume that the way organizations are led has also changed. The mechanistic model of organizations demands a certain style of leadership. The organic model demands something else.

For as long as humans have inhabited the world, there have been leaders. Leadership is not some man-made construct, but rather, it is deeply embedded in who we are as social beings. It is seemingly in our DNA. Whenever a group of people is faced with a task, whether it is now or back in the days of hunters and gatherers, successful accomplishment typically required at least one individual to take on a different coordination-type of role from the rest of the group. Unless this occurs, the chances of the task being successfully and efficiently completed are slim to none.

The same is true in organizations. Groups of people, sometimes numbering in the hundreds of thousands, are required to complete tasks. And this is possible only if some individuals assume different roles from others. But the question we must ask is: What is the nature of these different roles and how can these roles be best leveraged in order to ensure that the work to be done is completed effectively, efficiently, and in a sustainable manner? In other words, what is effective leadership? Before we can answer this, we must first understand what the term "leadership" means.

WHAT IS LEADERSHIP?

There is no shortage of information on leadership. A simple browse through the shelves of a local bookstore or an Internet search can easily become overwhelming. Yet despite the abundance of literature, or perhaps because of it, there is no clear, universally accepted, definition of leadership. As Bass and Stogdill noted in *Bass & Stogdill's Handbook of Leadership*, "There are almost as many different definitions of leadership as there are persons who have attempted to define the concept."[1]

In order to make some sense of the wide range of definitions of leadership, it becomes necessary to classify them in some way. While some researchers define leadership in terms of the traits of the individual leader, others focus more on the behaviors of that individual. Other definitions may focus on interaction patterns between leaders and followers, role relationships, hierarchical positions, power relationships, and influencing strategies.

Yet all of this is of little use to the senior executive trying to run his or her organization. Indeed, while leadership research may be intriguing and fascinating (at least to some), much of it is, unfortunately, of little practical use to today's leaders.

J. Kotter, in an article in *Harvard Business Review*, states that leadership involves (1) establishing direction, (2) aligning people in terms of that direction, and (3) motivating and inspiring people to move in that direction.[2] H. Knowles and B. Saxberg, in their book *Personality and Leadership Behavior*, suggest that leadership involves gaining another's cooperation through the communication process. They emphasize the nature of the helping relationship defined by leadership and propose that leaders are change agents.[3] Hogan, Curphy, and Hogan believe that "leadership involves persuading other people to set aside for a period of time their individual concerns and to pursue a common goal that is important for the responsibilities and welfare of a group."[4]

A. Bryman wrote that leadership involves three main elements—influence, goal, and group. By recognizing the role of the group, Bryman acknowledges that followers may influence the leadership process.[5] While E. Locke proposes that leadership is "the process of inducing others to take action towards a common goal,"[6] J. A. Conger states that "leaders are individuals who establish direction for a working group of individuals, who gain commitment from these group members to this direction, and who then motivate these members to achieve the direction's outcome."[7] Thus, the realm of influence may vary greatly.

While there is some difference in these definitions, some similarities are evident. R. Smith provides a simple consolidation of these ideas: (1) there are at least two people involved, the leader and the follower; (2) leadership happens where given, implied, or even unconscious goals or objectives are established; and (3) leadership is a process about influencing.[8]

Thus, in simplistic terms, leadership is best defined as the process of influence through which followers achieve goals. Note that this is not defined by hierarchical position. It also suggests that leadership inherently involves interaction with others. The use of the word "leader" to identify an individual who is an expert, but acts independently of others, is an adaptation of the primary concept.

The manner in which goals are set, influence occurs, and followers are defined is known as the leadership style. Leaders who do not clearly know what their goals are or the process by which to set them, who are unaware of who considers them to be their leader, and who only have limited means to influence others' behaviors, will, in all likelihood, be poorly regarded as leaders.

An effective style is one that best matches the environment and situation. And it is in this arena of style that things have changed over the past decades. What was seen as effective in the past is, more often than not, now seen as outdated or inappropriate.

TWO EXTREMES OF LEADERSHIP

When organizations first came about in the era of the Industrial Revolution, the "great man" theory of leadership was alive and well. Also known as heroic leadership, command-and-control, or autocratic leadership, this style has been prevalent throughout history. Leadership was seen as the domain of those strong enough, charismatic enough, tall enough, and from a suitable genetic background. These men (and yes, they were men) were the ones to whom we looked to lead and guide us. Whether in organizations, politics, or the military, the success or failure of any undertaking lay in the hands of these great men. They willingly shouldered the huge responsibilities and we willingly let them.

This style of leadership is characterized by confidence, decisiveness, and strength. It is the leader who sets the goals, makes critical decisions, assigns the tasks, and holds the power. Input may be sought from others only to inform the leader's decision-making process. As Richard Nixon once stated, "I would not think of making a decision by going around the table and then deciding on the basis of how everyone felt. Of course, I like to hear from everyone, but then I go off alone and decide. The decisions that are important must be made alone."

The leader must, at all times, be confident, self-assured, and strong. Vulnerability, doubt, or "humanness" is a sign of weakness and, therefore, ineffective leadership. Any self-doubt must be masked and buried at all costs. The heroic leader is firmly convinced that any display of genuine openness or hesitation will be viewed by others as a failing in their leadership.

This model of leadership was in place well before the age of the Industrial Revolution. Leaders throughout history have been seen as strong, decisive, and heroic. It was, therefore, only natural that as organizations formed, this style of leadership was adopted. Furthermore, the lack of focus on the human element of followers that goes hand in hand with the heroic model of leadership was an ideal fit for the mechanistic organization. Those who were technical experts were promoted into leadership positions. Given the fact that people were viewed to be interchangeable parts of a machine, the skills required to lead were not that dissimilar from the skills required of a technical specialist, making such promotions generally successful. In addition, those new to a leadership position did not need a great deal of specialized training on how to deal with people. The command-and-control style of leadership does not require an adjustment to the nuances of followers.

For many years, this style of leadership prevailed. It proved to be seemingly ideal for those leading in mechanistic organizations that operated in a stable environment. Those in leadership positions were able to make good decisions as they had previously encountered similar situations. Unknowns were few, and problems, while they may have been complex, could be resolved through determination and a well-thought-out plan of attack.

As clear and unambiguous as it is, this style of leadership brings with it some serious shortfalls. While there is no doubt about who is ultimately responsible, great man leadership effectively abdicates others of responsibility. When things go well, the leader takes much of the credit. Conversely, when things do not go as planned, the leader shoulders the blame. Such a model does little to develop future leaders and, therefore, has a tendency to lead to succession problems.

The great man model assumes that those in charge are familiar with the situation and have encountered something similar in the past. If this is the case, then naturally their decision-making abilities can be trusted. However, in a changing world, this situation does not occur often. The notion that the leader has the answer is folly. Many of those currently leading organizations learned to lead in a time when the Internet did not exist and such things as e-mail or social networking sites were considered the domain of science fiction.

This changing environment demands a different leadership style in the same way that organizations need to move away from a mechanistic to an organic model. As our world has become more complex and faster paced, increasingly we have come to believe that collective wisdom is more appropriate than a single, all-powerful, and all-knowing individual. As a result, the heroic model has fallen out of favor. It no longer seems appropriate in today's world that we could, or indeed should, rely on a single individual. In a world of unknowns, the notion that one individual has all the answers is, at best, wishful thinking. And younger generations demand a different style—a style in which they have a say in the future.

Martin offers a simple breakdown of these two forms of leadership.[9]

Old World Leader	New World Leader
Heroic	Collaborative
Enforcer	Context setter
Heads a hierarchy	Builds a community
Decisions are made at the top	Decisions occur in a choice cascade
Organization structure is rigid, fixed	Organization is organic
Communicates to give instructions	Communicates to generate dialogue
"Sells the solution"	Values authentic employee input
Command and control	Collaborate and consult
Formulators versus implementers	Everybody is a leader within their sphere of expertise
Employees need to be motivated	Employees are cherished partners

This shift to a more organic organization has required a change to a more collaborative or adaptive leadership style in which the leader is primarily a facilitator assembling a great team, facilitating dialogue and solutions. As the leadership scholars Ron Heifetz and Don Laurie state, "Instead of looking for saviors, we should be looking for leaders who can move us to face the problems for which there are no simple, painless solutions—the challenges that require us to learn new ways."[10] We have shifted from the leader as hero to the leader being a facilitator of others. Followers are no longer seen as passive spectators wishing to be led, but active participants in their future.

The collaborative leader is very different from the heroic leader. The heroic leadership style is primarily a task orientation whereby leaders believe they get results by consistently keeping people busy and urging them to produce. Conversely, the collaborative leadership style has more of an employee orientation in which leaders are concerned about the human needs of their employees. They build teamwork, help employees with their problems, and provide psychological support. When they do this, results are forthcoming.

Many traits that are considered to be weaknesses in heroic leaders are seen to be strengths by collaborative leaders. For example, vulnerability, self-doubt, friendliness, approachability, and humanness are traits valued by collaborative leaders and are often viewed as either weakness or wasted effort by those operating in the heroic model. Conversely, confidence, decisiveness, and a lack of collaboration are characteristics that are sometimes viewed as arrogance by those who have a more employee-centric model of leadership.

In many ways, the emergence of collaborative leadership from heroic leadership parallels the emergence of the organic organization from the mechanistic. When we consider the design of organizations or the prevalent form of leadership, we see that one is based on the belief that tasks can be completed most efficiently by clear and unambiguous structure and direction, while the other is based more on a humanistic philosophy in which an environment is created to allow employees to work to their full potential.

THE RISE OF EMOTIONAL INTELLIGENCE

Along with this shift in leadership style has come some changes in what we look for in our leaders. In the past, intelligence was viewed as an important trait. And while this hasn't changed, we know that on its own, intelligence is not enough. To be effective, leaders not only need a high intelligence quotient (IQ), but also a high emotional intelligence (EQ).

Like leadership, a myriad of definitions abounds regarding emotional intelligence. In simple terms, it can best be thought of as the ability or capacity to perceive, assess, and manage the emotions of one's self and of others. This is a key leadership skill in any organization that has moved beyond the concept of a mechanistic organization. Indeed, this shift away from the importance of IQ towards an appreciation of the importance of EQ in many ways parallels the shift from a mechanistic organization to an organic, humanistic one.

If we accept that organizations are made up of humans whose behavior is driven by emotion, then clearly an understanding and recognition of these emotions is key. This is true for both one's self and for others. As Cherniss and Goleman suggest, "The most effective bosses are those who have the ability to sense how their employees feel about their work situation and to intervene effectively when those employees begin to feel discouraged or dissatisfied. Effective bosses are able to manage their own emotions, with the result that employees trust them and feel good about working with them. In short, bosses whose employees stay are bosses who manage with emotional intelligence."[11]

Research also suggests that the farther up the hierarchical ladder one climbs, the more EQ becomes of greater importance for success. As executives face increasing complexity at the same time as becoming increasingly distant from many parts of the organization, they must rely on their emotional intelligence to navigate the complexities and ambiguities of the senior leadership role.

THE CURRENT STATE OF LEADERSHIP AFFAIRS

In the work I do with senior leaders, I rarely encounter any resistance to the notion that leaders should adopt a collaborative style, should engage their employees, should seek input, and should listen and value all that their employees have to offer. All agree that leaders who exhibit a command-and-control style of leadership tend to disengage employees and, consequently, have a negative impact on their organization's financial performance. Without a doubt, the command-and-control, heroic style of leadership is considered passé.

Yet, despite this, we see disturbing numbers regarding employee satisfaction and engagement as discussed in the previous chapter. This data suggests that there continues to be a mismatch between employees' expectations and the leadership style they encounter. With just 10 percent of employees feeling as though they really are their organizations' most valuable asset (despite the rhetoric they hear), 38 percent believing they are just another part of the organization to be managed, and a disturbing 15 percent feeling as though they don't matter to their leaders, something is clearly amiss.[12]

WHAT IS THE PROBLEM?
Outmoded mental models and paradigms

Leadership is all around us. From our earliest days, we have been exposed to information about what makes a leader. Whether it was from elementary school history lessons or politicians in the media, time and time again the heroic leader has taken center stage. And through this, we have developed our own mental models and paradigms around leadership. Many of those currently leading organizations likely had this paradigm reinforced by their first experience of organizational leadership, when the mechanistic organization and the command-and-control style of leadership dominated. So, while we may, on the one hand, say we support a more collaborative form of leadership, this contradicts much of what we have learned to be true and our deep imprinting about leadership.

Failure to see weaknesses as strengths

At the rational level, few would argue that for the most part greater collaborative leadership would not benefit organizations. Gone are the days when we had to justify employee involvement in decision-making. It is now assumed that this is a necessary part of organizational life. However, this is the rational side. The emotional side of leadership finds the new way to be more challenging. To adopt a collaborative style, individuals must be willing to admit they do not know the answer to a particular problem. They must be human, they must be real, and they must not put on false bravado. Yet these are the very things that in the old days were considered weaknesses. Many individual leaders, particularly those in senior positions, find such humanness and vulnerability to be exceptionally difficult. While they certainly have no expectations that those around them know the answer to a particular problem, they apply different standards to themselves. Until they recognize that the things they previously considered to be weaknesses are, in fact, strengths, they will remain stuck in the past.

Going boldly where no one else has gone

For many leaders, the world of the organic collaborative organization is a new one, understood only through theory or case studies. Leaders in organizations often become insulated and know of experiences only within their own organizations. As a result, few have actually witnessed and experienced firsthand the type of organization they are trying to create. Simply put, they just don't know what an organic collaborative organization should look like.

A while ago, I was with a group of senior executives as they toured one of their operations. The general manager at the site was new to the organization and, therefore, had not yet adopted the cultural norms of reverence to the executive, avoidance of negativity, and guarded conversation. During the tour, the general manager spoke openly, honestly, and passionately about his operation and the relationship with the corporate office. He did not hold back from stating his truth and offered both criticism and suggestions for the senior executive.

The executives were stunned, yet invigorated by the conversation. Although some of them had worked for the organization for well over 20 years, never before had they witnessed such an honest conversation. Although I had been working with this group for close to two years, teaching them the skills to have authentic conversations, until this point they did not know what that sounded like. Following the conversation with the general manager, they at last had a clear sense of what open dialogue could be. From then on, they did whatever they could to re-create such a conversation with others.

Finding the balance

The challenge of leadership is to be able to integrate opposing views. Rather than focus on black and white, an effective leader must be able to create and live in shades of gray, with all its paradoxes. So it is with the two foci of leadership. A focus on task does not mean ignoring people any more than a focus on people does not mean ignoring task. However, unfortunately there is a danger of overreacting to a history of authoritarian leadership by becoming too collaborative.

An organization with whom I've worked for a number of years clearly illustrates the danger here. For many years, the CEO epitomized the command-and-control style of leadership. He was strong, was unapproachable, and enforced a rigid hierarchy. Executives remained on the executive floor and rarely interacted with employees. While for the most part, the organization was successful, employees lived in fear. Certainly there was not an environment of innovation, openness, or creativity. After several years, this CEO retired and a senior vice president was promoted into the position of CEO. This individual had experienced working under such a rigid, dictatorial leader and was determined to change the culture of the organization. He began leading with a collaborative leadership style, insisting that decisions be made collectively. At first glance, one could assume this was a smart decision. Unfortunately, the pendulum soon swung too far the other way. Collaboration was taken to the extreme and no decision was ever made without extensive consultation. The organization started to grind to a halt and become overly "nice." Decision-making was slow, no one was willing to challenge anyone, and innovation did not flourish—not because people were fearful of speaking up, but because it was seen as disrespectful in this new collaborative culture.

THE LEADERSHIP MOLD THAT MUST BE BROKEN

The problems identified above could easily be addressed by an organic organization. An organization that values relationships and people will be led by those who have a collaborative leadership style. However, this is a case of chicken and egg. A collaborative leader will ensure organic organization is in place, yet it is the organic organization itself that produces collaborative leaders.

Most executives assume they are good leaders because of the title on their business cards. Too busy, too outwardly focused, and too oblivious to the obvious, in reality, they are largely unaware of how they're actually perceived as leaders. A study by The Refinery Leadership Partners in 2008 reported that 75 percent of executives believe they are performing better as leaders than their competitors; the balance believes their performance is at least equal to their competitors.

Organizations and leadership are in trouble. Despite what we know, money is being lost through disengaged employees, younger generations are disaffected with corporate life, and, all too often, senior leaders are viewed as overpaid, out of touch, and arrogant. Employees are not getting what they want from their senior leaders. The result is inferior organizational performance. The future does not look good.

Yet there is a solution. We know how to develop leaders and we know how to change organizations. It is not easy, but it can be done by anyone who has an appetite for it.

The starting point is to recognize what outdated leadership styles we are clinging to. We still rely too much on the scientific management method and the heroic leader. This mold must be broken. Organizations cannot perform to their maximum potential unless the vestiges from the past are truly purged and replaced with the new philosophies and humanistic values that lead not only to great satisfaction and engagement, but superior financial performance.

In order to be effective, it is essential that every leader is clear on his or her personal philosophy of leadership. Rather than dismissing one over the other, it is more important to gain clarity of one's fundamental beliefs concerning leadership. And this requires understanding personal leadership paradigms and aligning actions with beliefs.

While an understanding of history is important, particularly with respect to how it holds us back, what is more important is creating a sense of what we want in terms of personal and organizational leadership. Only then is it possible to act on these commitments and truly break the mold.

Chapter Two Takeaways

1. The mechanistic model of organizations demands a certain style of leadership. The organic model demands something else.
2. Leadership is best defined as a process of influence through which followers achieve goals. It is not related to hierarchical position.
3. The great man, heroic, command-and-control, or autocratic leadership style, has been prevalent throughout history. It is characterized by confidence, decisiveness, and strength. The leader sets the goals, makes critical decisions, assigns the tasks, and holds the power.

4. This style of leadership brings with it some serious shortfalls. It abdicates others of responsibility and, therefore, it disengages employees and does little to develop future leaders. It also assumes that those in charge are familiar with the situation and have encountered something similar in the past. However, in a changing world the notion that the leader has the answer is folly.

5. Today's constantly changing environment demands a different leadership style in the same way that organizations need to move away from a mechanistic to an organic model. As our world has become more complex and faster paced, collective wisdom is more appropriate than a single, all-powerful, and all-knowing individual. Thus, an effective leader is primarily a facilitator who assembles a great team and facilitates dialogue and solutions.

6. Emotional intelligence (EQ)—the ability or capacity to perceive, assess, and manage the emotions of one's self and of others—is a key leadership skill in any organization that has moved beyond the concept of a mechanistic organization. To be effective, leaders need not only a high IQ, but also a high EQ, particularly as they enter the ranks of senior leadership.

7. Executives today typically accept that they should adopt a collaborative style, engage their employees, seek input, and listen and value all that their employees have to offer. Many executives believe they are effective in this regard. However, data suggest that there continues to be a mismatch between employees' expectations and the leadership style they encounter. With just 10 percent of employees feeling as though they really are their organization's most valuable asset while 38 percent believe they are just another part of the organization to be managed and a disturbing 15 percent feel as though they don't matter to their leaders, it appears as though a heroic, mechanistic style of leadership is alive and well. Many executives are unaware of how their employees view their leadership.

8. The prevalence of ineffective leadership styles at the top is due to a number of factors, including outdated mental models and paradigms, a struggle to accept that vulnerability and humanness are strengths and not weaknesses, a lack of decent examples, and an inability to embrace every element of leadership.

9. The net result is that organizations and leadership are in trouble. Money is being lost through disengaged employees, younger generations are increasingly disaffected with corporate life, and, all too often, senior leaders are viewed as overpaid, out of touch, and arrogant.

10. Organizations cannot perform to their maximum potential unless the vestiges from the past are purged and replaced with the new philosophies and humanistic values that lead not only to great satisfaction and engagement, but superior financial performance. Organizational "people practices" must catch up with changes in organizational environments. This demands changes by those at the top.

DEFINE A BETTER WAY

LEADERSHIP BRAND

The starting point for any senior leader who wishes to create a great organization is to understand what behaviors are required (for both themself and others within the organization) to best meet the desired results.

The clarification and articulation of the behaviors necessary to achieve organizational results can be thought of as the definition of an organizational leadership brand. Branding is most commonly thought of with respect to marketing and not necessarily leadership. A product or service is branded so that it can be differentiated from other similar products or services. The branding process facilitates communication about a product or service that in turn facilitates marketing. Ultimately, a position is created in the marketplace that is much more difficult for the competition to poach.

Leadership branding is similar. Leadership in an organization is branded when the unique attributes and specific business results are integrated for all leaders within the organization.[1] Leadership branding occurs when leaders at every level are clear about which results are most important and how they need to behave in order to achieve these results.

The concept of a leadership brand allows the development of an organizational culture that is focused on leadership and permeates the entire organization. It allows for a linkage between behavior and results. Done properly, it can pull together both the task and the people side of the leadership equation.

More importantly, a clearly defined leadership brand can create a language of leadership. As discussed earlier, leadership is a complex and, for some, confusing topic. The word "leadership" is used in many contexts and, more often than not, is simply used to refer to the behavior of individuals with an organization. Yes, confusion abounds about what some words actually mean, which means people are unclear about organizational behavior expectations.

Let me offer an example. A short while ago I was working with several groups of leaders from a large organization. When I asked each group how they thought they should behave as leaders, the idea that they should be "open and honest" was typically given a high priority. Yet these same leaders often withheld critical information from each other and failed to rise to the challenge of having what they considered to be difficult and awkward conversations. "Open and honest" did nothing to guide them in how they should lead.

After I worked with these leaders for some time and taught them the skills to fully disclose and have difficult conversations, the word "authenticity" was introduced into the corporate leadership vocabulary. All leaders understood what this meant and gave each other permission to say what was on their mind, regardless of how uncomfortable this might be. As a result, they started having unfiltered conversations. This behavior soon became embedded and normalized in the organization. In effect, the language of leadership (in this case, related to authenticity) created a leadership brand.

Unfortunately, all too often leadership is described through overused, trendy, and meaningless buzzwords that cause employees to roll their eyes and ignore the message. However, when the required leadership behaviors are clearly defined and articulated in a realistic and relevant manner and then linked together through a leadership brand, this confusion and skepticism can be overcome. A leadership brand can give all employees, regardless of their level within the hierarchy, a clear sense of how to behave in order to achieve the desired results.

A strong leadership brand not only helps employees internally, but can help to position the organization externally. Research by Ernst & Young has shown that between 30 percent and 45 percent of investors' decisions may be linked to the market's perception of the quality of management.[2] As Intagliata, Ulrich, and Smallwood point out in their seminal work *Leveraging Leadership Competencies to Produce Leadership Brand*, "Investors are more confident in (and more willing to pay a premium price for) companies that have a track record for delivering results and that also have branded leaders who instill confidence in their ability to deliver again in the future."[3]

Further, Ulrich, Smallwood, and Snyder have noted eight characteristics that are present when an organization possesses a strong leadership brand. They suggest that the organization can do the following:

1. Express the importance of leadership for business success.
2. Craft a clear statement about what makes an effective leader.
3. Translate statements of effective leadership into measures for both behaviors and results.
4. Invest resources to build leadership capability and a leadership system.
5. Ensure clarity about how a leadership brand relates to a firm brand.
6. Align the human resource systems to ensure they sustain the brand.
7. Have positive and negative consequences for leaders who do or do not embody the brand.
8. Ensure that leadership brand permeates the organization.[4]

These characteristics offer some insight into how organizational leadership should be articulated, reinforced, supported, and enacted throughout the organization. These elements will be discussed further in the book. However, the starting point is to be able to articulate the leadership brand throughout the organization. This is done through the clarification of (a) personal leadership vision; (b) values; (c) definition of competencies; and (d) the effective use of storytelling.

Personal leadership vision

On an individual level, you must have personal clarity on how you want to lead—in other words, how you want to show up for work every day. This means gaining clarity on how you wish to interact with and influence others in order to achieve the desired results. Without personal clarity, authenticity, and consistency, any attempt to articulate an organizational leadership brand will be viewed with skepticism by others in the organization.

Typically, the development of such a personal leadership vision is something that occurs when responsibilities change. Remember the time you were first promoted to a leadership position? Or perhaps the time you first became an executive? At that point, you likely thought ahead, imagined yourself in that role, and pictured how you wished to lead. For example, at the moment I'm working with an individual who, in a matter of months, will be appointed as a vice president in his company. Every conversation we have is focused on how he wishes to lead once he assumes the role. There is a great deal of personal leadership visioning taking place.

We therefore often use a change in personal circumstances to create a vision for our leadership. However, once we assume the role, our behaviors soon become normalized and *we tend to assume that the style we have adopted is the correct one.* I fully expect that in a year's time my conversations with the individual I am currently working with will be focused on specific challenges or problems, rather than his personal vision of leadership.

Yet, as described in the previous two chapters, a change is needed. Business as usual, leadership styles developed in the era of the mechanistic organization, and the heroic leader are no longer working. Given this, the challenge for those within organizations is to start afresh, to create a vision for their leadership that is based not on current practices, but rather personal beliefs. In fact, no personal leadership vision can be developed without clarity of personal leadership philosophy.

To that end, let me challenge you to consider the following questions and through reflection develop a picture of the type of leader you want to become in future years. Be careful not to base this on current reality or on what you believe is possible in your present organization. The time for rationalization is later. At this point, determining what you truly believe in is more important. If you find that these questions make your head hurt, they should. What is important is that you have clarity in your beliefs. Some deep reflection on the following questions will help you get there. Find a quiet spot and formulate your answers at a relaxed pace.

1. What does leadership mean for you? What qualities do you believe a leader should possess?
2. To what extent do you value the traits of mechanistic or organic organizations? What does this tell you about you and your leadership beliefs?
3. Where are you on the command-and-control versus collaborative style of leadership continuum? What does this tell you about yourself and your leadership beliefs?
4. To what extent do your personal paradigms and mental models hold you back from being an effective leader? How might you overcome this?
5. What makes some people "better" leaders than others? What are the implications of this for you?
6. When does leadership happen for you? For others within your organization?
7. Does a leader need power? How can a leader avoid being corrupted by power?
8. How might you lead so that others will follow? How would you like your relationship to be with those whom you lead?
9. What traits must you demonstrate to build effective teams?

10. For you, what is the most important thing about leadership? How might this differ for others in your organization?

These reflections, when considered with sufficient intensity, are not meant to be easy, but then neither is leadership. Yet they are important for any leader who wishes to create an effective, healthy, profitable, and sustainable organization. Ultimately, the goal is to be able to extensively and clearly articulate the following: What I believe about effective leadership. (Part Two of this book will guide you in exploring the personal implications of such a statement in more detail.)

The development of a personal leadership vision is the starting point for setting the leadership expectations for everyone in the organization, regardless of their level. Put simply, defining leadership means defining the behaviors that are acceptable or unacceptable in an organization in a variety of circumstances. It starts with you, but then soon it must progress to others within the organization.

Values

At its most basic level, leadership is about people interacting with one another. While this interaction must have a purpose in the form of goals and results, ultimately, it is about how humans interact and build relationships. The standard that you hold yourself to, in regard to these relationships, is driven by your personal philosophy of leadership. For example, the extent to which you believe employees are best managed as technical experts with a specific skill set versus unique human beings with individual personalities will define the manner in which you enact leadership.

Such beliefs are embodied and articulated in the form of organizational values. Values are traits or qualities that are considered worthwhile. At an organizational level, they define how people want to behave with each other in the organization. They are statements about how the organization will value customers and suppliers, as well as the internal employee community.

Given this, it is impossible, and also completely inappropriate, to define a leadership brand without a clear understanding of the values upon which this brand will be based. *The desired future values must be identified and aligned to the philosophy of leadership.*

Just the identification of values can dramatically increase engagement. Collins and Porras in their book *Built to Last* suggest that a critical element of high-performing companies is "a core ideology—core values and sense of purpose beyond just making money—that guides and inspires people throughout the organization and remains relatively stable for long periods of time."[5] Berry notes in his book *Discovering the Soul of Service* that leading with values can provide an effective alternative to the traditional organizational command-and-control model and thereby enable employees to make better decisions and to have higher job satisfaction in service institutions.[6] Kouzes and Posner suggest, "Values enable people to know in their own minds what to do and what not to do. When values are clear, they do not have to rely upon direction from someone in authority."[7] Harmon proposes that "values are the vibrant core of institutional life in all for-profit and not-for-profit enterprises. . . . Commitment to values lifts performance—personal and corporate."[8]

Are there two sides to your organizational coin?

To reiterate, the concept of organizational values is not new. However, unless such values are supported, acted upon, and aligned to leadership, they may actually do more harm than good.

Every organization has values. What many fail to realize is that in reality, organizations have two sets of values—those that are in play during daily organizational life and those that are articulated as the reality, but in truth bear little resemblance to employees' daily experiences.

Within any organization, there are norms of behavior and unspoken codes of conduct that form the culture. These real values define what is, and what is not, acceptable in how employees go about doing their job and interacting with others, whether these be internal or external relationships. And then there are the official, espoused values—those statements in which values are articulated, published, and endorsed by senior management.

Many companies, have value statements framed and hanging on the lobby wall. Unfortunately, many senior leaders do not recognize that these formal, espoused values are often very different from the ones that actually guide the organization. For example, how often do we hear organizational values focused on trust and respect? Yet these same organizations are mechanistic in nature and embody the command-and-control style of leadership. The last thing that employees think they have is a voice that will be respected and trusted. Senior leaders make naïve assumptions about what they want, authorize formal plaques on a wall, and assume that these values reflect reality. The gap between the real and espoused values is often the cause of skepticism and a lack of confidence in senior management, all of which leads to a sorry state of engagement.

The reason for this disconnect is due to a failure to connect values with behavior. Despite the fact that leadership and the manner in which relationships are formed are inexorably intertwined within the organization, values and leadership are separated in a way that is reminiscent of the mechanistic organization. Thus, the idea that leadership and values can be separated is folly. Values are enacted through leadership.

All too often, senior leaders create values with no consideration of their leadership philosophy. Yet I contend that the starting point must be the philosophy itself. From leadership philosophy, values can be articulated. And from this, leadership behaviors can be defined. Senior leaders must ask themselves what is the organization's collective belief about leadership and what does this say about what must be valued within the organization? In all likelihood, these values will be different to the reality and, therefore, an organizational culture change will be required.

This type of change can be driven only by senior leaders whose behavior embodies the desired values. Throughout the course of this book, you will learn how to do this. But you must first define your personal and organizational leadership stand and the behaviors that support it.

Leadership competencies

Often when organizations attempt to define leadership, they endeavor to define a series of behaviors they call leadership competencies.

Typically, competencies are general descriptions of the abilities needed to perform a role in the organization, described in terms that can be measured. Whereas job descriptions may list the tasks or functions and responsibilities for a role, competencies list the abilities needed to conduct those tasks or functions. Lucia and Lepinger define a competency model as "a descriptive tool that identifies the skills, knowledge, personal characteristics, and behaviors needed to effectively perform a role in the organization and help the business meet its strategic objectives."[9]

The definition of leadership competencies is important as it allows an organization to define the requirements of its leaders and measure and develop them accordingly. As Intagliata, Ulrich, and Smallwood (2000) suggest, "Most fundamentally, competencies provide organizations with a way to define in behavioral terms what their leaders need to do to produce the results the organization desires and do so in a way that is consistent with and builds its culture. They should provide the 'North Star' by which leaders at all levels navigate in order to create synergy and produce more significant and consistent results."[10]

However, leadership is both contextual and situational. The notion that it is possible to describe the exact behavior of a leader regardless of circumstances fails to take into account the reality of leadership.

There is no one simple prescription for leadership and all too often a desire for logical, rational thinking leads us to regard competencies as absolutes, as distinct from paying attention to the general intent they are designed to portray.

The competency modeling process itself requires a level of expertise that is typically found within the HR community. As a result, senior leaders abdicate this task to those in HR. Yet defining what behaviors are required of leaders obviously needs a clear articulation of the organizational leadership philosophy, an interpretation of the values, and the definition of the language of leadership, which will define the culture of the organization. In other words, this is important strategic work that must be "owned" by the most senior leaders within the organization. Although it is important to leverage the expertise that lies within HR, senior leaders must be intimately involved not only with the process but also in all strategic decisions.

While senior leaders must stay involved and champion the development of competencies, and HR can lend expertise and facilitate the process, those who actually do the work must also be included. The inclusion process must start here—without their participation, adoption of the competencies will be a struggle. Through a well-designed and thoughtful process there will be an opportunity for senior leaders to have dialogue with others within the organization about leadership—what it means for the organization, what it means for individuals, and what is needed in the future. These conversations will start the process of creating an engaged organization. Just as it is essential that all senior leaders have a clear sense of what is important in their own personal leadership, it is also important with others. Such dialogue can enhance leadership and, therefore, organizational performance.

After all is said and done, while a competency modeling process is useful for creating benchmark performance plans, it does little for creating a vision of organizational leadership that can engage and direct others. This requires something entirely different—storytelling.

Storytelling

Time and time again I have witnessed executives attempting to articulate organizational leadership through motherhood values and uninspiring competencies. Not surprisingly, the audience receives such monologues in a lukewarm manner. As their eyes glaze over, many wonder when they will be able to get back to their "real" job. While there is nothing wrong with what these executives are saying, such a rational and logical analysis of leadership behavior really misses the point of what leadership is all about.

It stems once again from the notion that we are not parts of the machine, but instead are emotional beings. If we were indeed unfeeling, unemotional beings, undoubtedly a list of competencies would suffice. Senior leaders would simply have to tell people how to behave when they interact with others and it would be done. However, as we now know, such a model is no longer relevant. Senior leaders must now be able to articulate the vision of leadership in a manner that excites and inspires those they are attempting to influence.

According to Stephen Denning, effective storytelling can accomplish something that logic and analysis fail to do in today's business world: "It offers a route to the heart. And that's where we must go if we are to motivate people not only to take action, but also to do so with energy and enthusiasm. At a time when corporate survival often requires disruptive change, leadership involves inspiring people to act in unfamiliar, and often unwelcome, ways. Mind-numbing cascades of numbers or daze-inducing PowerPoint slides won't achieve this goal. But effective storytelling often does. . . . Storytelling can translate dry and abstract numbers into compelling pictures of a leader's goals."[11]

Noel Tichy also supports the notion of storytelling. He suggests that "the best way to get humans to venture into unknown terrain is to make that terrain familiar and desirable by taking them there first in their imaginations."[12]

Why stories? As Edward Wachtman of StoryTellings ™ Consulting (www.storytellings.com) tells us,

> To be human is to have a story. Story is the structure that gives meaning and order to our lives. Instead of trying to make sense of the literally millions of independent events that comprise our lives, we intuitively organize them into an orderly sequence of events. Stories are how we convey our deepest emotions and talk about those things that we value the most. It is through the stories we tell that we are most able to portray the fullest array of human emotion. Stories 'speak' to us at a number of levels. They appeal to our reason and intellect by providing evidence and information to bolster arguments and help us make informed decisions. Emotionally, they bond us to others who share the same story and give us a sense of belonging and community. And finally, they are the connection to a long-forgotten past that is the rich source of the images and symbols that unconsciously motivate our behavior today.[13]

The ability to tell the right story at the right time is emerging as an essential skill for senior leaders. It is one that had no place in a mechanistic organization, but is of supreme importance in the organization of today. The telling of stories can overcome limitations of our language and can connect with people in a human and emotional manner.

The articulation of leadership within an organization, whether it is the organizational leadership brand, your personal vision of leadership, organizational values, or leadership competencies, can be accomplished in no other way than through the telling of stories. Thus, the challenge now is to look for, capture, and create your own book of stories. Find those events that best capture the behaviors you are attempting to articulate. Learn how to describe these events in a compelling and emotional manner. And repeat them often. See yourself more as a storyteller than a leader.

Chapter Three Takeaways

1. The starting point for any senior leader who wishes to create a great organization is to develop a clear picture of what superb leadership looks like at both a personal and an organizational level. Simply put, this requires understanding what behaviors are required (by both one's self and others within the organization) that will best meet the desired results.

2. This is best done through a clearly articulated leadership brand that links behavior and results. A well-defined leadership brand can pull together both the task and the people side of the leadership equation and create a language of leadership. It allows leaders at every level to be clear about which results are most important and how they need to behave in order to achieve these results.

3. All leaders, but most importantly those at the top, must be able to picture how they want to lead. This means developing a personal leadership vision that provides clarity on how they wish to interact with and influence others in order to achieve the desired results. Without such personal clarity, any executive's attempt to articulate an organizational leadership brand will be viewed with skepticism by others in the organization.

4. The desired future values must be identified and aligned to the leadership brand. Organizations have two sets of values—those that are in play during daily organizational life

and those that are articulated in an organizationally endorsed manner, but in truth, bear little resemblance to employees' daily experiences. Many senior leaders do not recognize that the formal, espoused values are often very different from the ones that are actually present within an organization. The reason for this disconnect is due to a failure to connect values with behavior.

5. The definition of leadership competencies allows an organization to define what is required by the leaders and to measure and develop their leaders accordingly. However, the notion that it is possible to describe the exact behavior of a leader regardless of circumstances fails to take into account the reality of leadership. There is no simple prescription for leadership and, all too often, the desire for logical, rational thinking leads us to regard competencies as absolutes, as distinct from paying attention to the general intent they are designed to portray.

6. Senior leaders must be able to articulate the vision of leadership in a way that excites and inspires those they are attempting to influence. This is done through storytelling. The ability to tell the right story at the right time is emerging as an essential skill for senior leaders. It is one that had no place in a mechanistic organization, but it is an ability of supreme importance in the organization of today. The telling of stories can overcome the limitations of our language and can connect people in a human and emotional manner.

PRINCIPLE #4:

FIGURE OUT IF YOU HAVE WHAT IT TAKES*

Once you have developed and articulated a clear vision of your personal leadership and organizational leadership brand, it is time to consider how you and others might develop into the type of leaders you have envisioned. If you intend to heal a sick organization or take your organization from good to great, you will need certain personal competencies—outlined in this chapter—that will enable you to spearhead organizational transformation. These are not simple skills—they have much to do with maturity (which is not the same as age) and how you make sense of the world around you. Unfortunately, few adults have matured sufficiently to access these competencies and, thus, most leaders simply "do not have what it takes" to lead organizational change.

Leadership development means development as a person. Those who fail to recognize that change must happen at a profound personal level, choosing instead to take an ad hoc approach focused simply on "fixing" a few ineffective behaviors, will not acquire the quality of leadership that today's organizations demand. Worse, they will convince themselves that they have done what it takes to be an effective leader, while in reality, they have likely become even more disconnected from how others see them as leaders and, therefore, will be less effective. Such behavior inevitably leads to rolling eyes and skepticism.

Leadership is best developed through a holistic and deep process that takes into account not only who you are as a person, but also

---

* I am indebted to David Rooke and Jackie Keeley of Harthill Consulting (www. harthill.co.uk) for their suggestions and contributions to this principle.

how you make meaning of the world. The most effective leaders are those adults who have matured to the later stages of development. This has little to do with age and more to do with how, as adults, we see and make sense of the world around us.

A DEVELOPMENTAL FRAMEWORK FOR LEADERS

For years we have come to recognize that as children mature, so they pass through clearly defined developmental stages. As Piaget showed us, these stages bring with them an ever evolving and broadening understanding of the world and the individual's role in it.[1]

However, the notion that once adulthood is attained development ceases is folly. Adults continue to mature, albeit at a somewhat slower pace than they experienced as children. With this continued development come changes in how they make sense of, and interpret, the world around them. As with children, we now know that adults can progress through a series of clearly defined stages, each of which impacts an individual's ability to problem solve, interpret, and interact with their environment.

A number of researchers—including Loevinger, Torbert, Cook-Greuter, and Kegan, along with Jackie Keeley and David Rooke of Harthill Consulting[2]—have been instrumental in developing these ideas in a way that is profoundly relevant for all leaders within organizations, but particularly those who are in senior positions and wish to transform their organization. In fact, they have found that unless the CEO and some other members of the senior executive team attained a later developmental stage (or at the very least the CEO partners with a consultant who can offer that perspective), positive organizational transformation efforts are doomed to fail.

Developmental theory suggests that how we behave as leaders is determined to a great extent by our perception of the world around us. Consider a time when two people had entirely different interpretations of the same event. Perhaps one thought that a supervisor was trying to impose his own agenda on his direct report, while the other thought that the supervisor was being helpful in attempting to provide some coaching to this direct report. The same event, two different interpretations. And it is these differing interpretations and perceptions that in turn likely governed these individuals' reaction to, and behavior with, their supervisor. How we perceive reality and how we make sense of the world around us (our meaning-making capacity) will, therefore, tend to determine how we relate with other people, what we think about, and, ultimately, how we behave and lead.

As we develop and grow as children, we see the world in increasingly complex ways. This process continues into adulthood. Developmental theory suggests that children and adults pass through a number of distinct stages. Each stage represents a qualitative and unique frame of reference through which we make sense of and understand our world. For instance, at one stage we "are" our impulses, while at the next, we can observe our impulses and decide whether it is in our interests to express them. Thus, individuals at different stages will be objective about different things and will, therefore, define reality in significantly different ways. This, in turn, suggests that an individual's character, behavior, and, consequently, leadership style will be directly related to his or her stage of development. Indeed, developmental theory offers the deeper understanding of leadership that many leadership theories appear to lack.

This is important for senior leaders. As David Rooke tells us, "This theory has profound implications for managers. In a nutshell, a manager is constrained by the self-generated framework within which he or she makes meaning."[3] How we interpret or "make meaning" in our world determines the action we choose to take.

This capacity to develop a meaning-making framework has been shown by the aforementioned researchers to develop through distinct stages (action logics), in which each stage encompasses the capacities of the previous stage. These sequential stages describe how a person interprets events, or makes meaning, which in turn determines their thinking and the action they then take.

Rooke and Torbert and their colleagues at Harthill Consulting have identified nine action logics, seven of which are described below. Together, they form Harthill's Leadership Development Framework, which offers "a way of understanding how a leader or manager is likely to interpret situations and thus how they may act."[4] Note that while I have included both the Impulsive and Ironist action logics, these two frames are rarely, if ever, found in managers, so they are not included in the discussion that follows.

As one moves through each progressive action logic, new behaviors become available. As this takes place, individuals also gain the capacity to choose to employ the behaviors of earlier stages, should they decide this is appropriate. Thus, a progression through the action logic stages results in an increased behavioral repertoire, as well as an increase in control over these behaviors. For example, an Achiever can choose to consciously act from a Diplomat perspective, should circumstances demand it. However, if a conflict needs to be resolved, an Achiever will have the capacity to handle it with relative ease, but it may be beyond a Diplomat's ability to take a confrontational stance.

	Action Logic	Characteristics
Increasing maturity, ability to make sense of complexity, time horizon.	Impulsive (Earliest stage)	Concerned with safety and the gratification of basic needs. Other people seen primarily as a source of need gratification or supply.
	Opportunist	Wins any way possible. Self-oriented; manipulative; "might makes right."
	Diplomat	Avoids overt conflict; wants to belong; obeys group norms; rarely rocks the boat.
	Expert	Rules by logic and expertise. Seeks rational efficiency.
	Achiever	Meets strategic goals. Effectively achieves goals through teams; juggles managerial duties and market demands.
	Individualist	Interweaves competing personal and company action logics. Creates unique structures to resolve gaps between strategy and performance.
	Strategist	Generates organizational and personal transformations. Exercises the power of mutual inquiry, vigilance, and vulnerability for both the short and long term.
	Alchemist	Generates social transformations. Integrates material, spiritual, and societal transformation.
	Ironist (Latest stage)	Experiences ambiguity as the creative, ongoing element of all experience. Can take multiple points of view and shift focus effortlessly among many states of awareness.

Although people can choose to see the world and then act through a lens of action logics earlier than their current one, the reverse is not generally true. That is, it is usually impossible for people to act through the lenses of action logics that are later than their present one. For example, while a Diplomat can act in the manner of an Opportunist, he or she cannot act in the manner of a Strategist should the situation call for such behaviors.

Furthermore, while most individuals have a primary action logic, some may be in a process of transition and operate from two frames.

Others may have a dominant frame, yet in stressful circumstances revert to old behaviors more akin to a previous action logic.

It is important not to pass a value judgment on which of the various action logics are supposedly "better." As Harthill Consulting tells us, "It is important to understand that this framework is not a guide to increased happiness (or even wealth). Each action logic has its own merits and difficulties, beauties, and shadows. There is no evidence that later stages bring more joy or greater satisfaction from life, only that the nature of what delights and what causes suffering changes."[5]

Having said that, when we view these various action logics through a leadership frame, it does become possible to comment on how each will impact one's effectiveness as a leader, in the context of attempting the difficult task of leading organizational transformation.

ACTION LOGIC AND LEADERSHIP EFFECTIVENESS

An individual's dominant action logic is inexorably intertwined with one's leadership capacity. As Harthill suggests, "Your primary action logic has a profound impact on your leadership approach and capability because it affects where you place your attention, your underlying assumptions, what inferences you draw and, crucially, what actions you take."

Rooke and Torbert suggest that the manner in which individuals perceive and act on events is the primary driver of their leadership abilities. "Most developmental psychologists agree that what differentiates leaders is not so much their philosophy of leadership, their personality, or their style of management. Rather, it's their internal 'action logic'— how they interpret their surroundings and react when their power or safety is challenged. What we found is that the levels of corporate and individual performance vary according to action logic."[6]

Therefore, while you may have a crystal-clear vision of how you would like to lead, your action logic may not have progressed to a level of maturity that would enable you to conduct yourself in the way you envision. For example, I have worked with many leaders who have an Expert action logic, who know that it is important that they delegate more often, but they are simply incapable of doing so (as compared to the realm of the Achiever). When they give tasks up to another, their whole sense of self is threatened by the fact that others may do things less than perfectly. Simply telling these leaders that they must delegate more is wasted effort. Instead, a much deeper developmental intervention is required.

Each action logic has an associated leadership style as outlined in the following table.

Action Logic	Leadership style associated with each action logic	Strengths
Opportunist	Short-term horizon; focus on concrete things; deceptive; rejects feedback; externalizes blame; distrustful; fragile self-control; possibly hostile humor or "happy-go-lucky"; views luck as central; views rules as loss of freedom; punishes according to "an eye for an eye" ethic; treats what they can get away with as legitimate. Seeks personal advantage: takes an opportunity when it arises.	Good in emergencies and in sales opportunities.
Diplomat	Observes protocol; avoids inner and outer conflict; works to group standard; speaks in clichés and platitudes; conforms; feels shame if they violate norm; avoids hurting others; seeks membership and status; face-saving essential; loyalty is to immediate group, not distant organization or principles. Attends to social affairs of group and individuals.	Good as supportive glue within an office; helps bring people together.
Expert	Is immersed in the self-referential logic of their own belief system, regarding it as the only valid way of thinking. Interested in problem solving; critical of self and others based on their belief system; chooses efficiency over effectiveness; perfectionist; accepts feedback only from "objective" experts in their own field; dogmatic; values decisions based on the incontrovertible facts; wants to stand out and be unique as an expert; sense of obligation to wider, internally consistent moral order. Consistent in pursuit of improvement. Strong individual contributor.	Good as an individual contributor.

Achiever	Effectiveness and results oriented; long-term goals; future is vivid, inspiring; welcomes behavioral feedback; feels like initiator, not pawn; begins to appreciate complexity and systems; seeks increasing mutuality in relationships; feels guilty if does not meet own standards; blind to own shadow, to the subjectivity behind objectivity; seeks to find ways around problems in order to deliver, may be unorthodox.	Well suited to managerial roles; action and goal oriented.
Individualist	Focus on self and less on goals; increased understanding of complexity, systems operating, and working through relationships; deepening personal relationships; takes on different role in different situations; increasingly questions own assumptions (part of rise in self-absorption) and assumptions of others; attracted by change and difference more than by stability and similarity; increasingly aware of own shadow.	Effective in venture and consulting roles.
Strategist	Recognizes importance of principle, contract, theory, and judgment—not just rules and customs; creative at conflict resolution; process oriented as well as goal oriented; aware of paradox and contradiction; aware that what one sees depends upon one's world view; high value on individuality, unique market niches, particular historical movements; enjoys playing a variety of roles; witty, existential humor (as contrasted to prefabricated jokes); aware of dark side of power and may be tempted by it—may misuse their own abilities and manipulate others.	Effective as a transforma-tional leader.

(Continued)

| Alchemist | Seeks participation in historical/ spiritual transformations; creator of events that become mythical and reframe situations; anchoring in inclusive present, seeing the light and dark in situations; works with order and chaos; blends opposites, creating "positive-sum" games; exercises own attention continually; researches interplay of institution, thought, action, and effects on outside world; treats time and events as symbolic, analogical, metaphorical (not merely linear, digital, literal), involved in spiritual quest, often helps others in their life quests. | Good at leading society-wide transfor- mations. |

The table below provides comparative data for two population samples. The first is a mixed group consisting of leaders, managers, supervisors, and students taken between 1980 and 1995, predominantly in the U.S. The second group consists mainly of leaders, managers, and consultants who were profiled by Harthill Consulting between 1993 and 2010, predominantly in the U.K.

	Sample A	**Sample B**
Action Logic	4,510 students, managers, and supervisors	2,890 consultants, managers, and executives
Impulsive and Opportunist	4%	0%
Diplomat	11%	1%
Expert	37%	12%
Achiever	30%	46%
Individualist	11%	27%
Strategist	5%	11%
Alchemist	2%	3%

As the consultants at Harthill point out, Sample A contains relatively fewer people in positions of seniority and the average age is younger than in Sample B. However, Sample B is highly selective— managers, executives, and consultants who have been profiled because they are engaged in personal or organizational development. Thus,

Sample B is atypical, with many people profiling at the later action logics of Individualist to Ironist.

The distribution shows, thankfully, that individuals with Opportunist and Diplomat action logics are certainly in a minority within organizations. Given that these are the least effective action logics for leadership, it is gratifying to see that among the group of consultants, managers, and executives these action logics are very rare.

However, both samples indicate that the majority of the population has an Expert or Achiever action logic. Certainly, within organizations those who are hardworking, goal oriented, and problem solvers are welcomed. As highlighted above, Experts are strong individual contributors, while Achievers are well suited for managerial roles. All good. Correct?

Not so. The problem is, while Experts and Achievers are valued by organizations, these individuals lack some crucial aspects of meaning-making capacity—in particular, the ability to engage with the multi-layered complexity necessary to lead organizational transformation.

GREAT ORGANIZATIONS NEED STRATEGISTS

Great organizations are constantly growing, adapting, and evolving. They have completed the transformation from a mechanistic to an organic organization, and in so doing, organizational transformation will have become normalized and integrated into the very fabric of the organization.

Any senior leader who wishes to create a great organization must, therefore, have the leadership capacity to embrace change. And this requires that they are, *at a minimum*, at the Individualist stage and preferably at the Strategist meaning-making frame. As Rooke proposes, "Only managers at the post-conventional stages, Individualist and later, can steer transformational culture change in organizations. Managers at earlier stages would either not see the need or seeing it, would not have the inclusive frame-making ability to realize it."[7]

Only when leaders have matured to the Strategist action logic do they have a deep awareness that all people, including themselves, understand, make sense of, and interpret their individual worlds differently. Strategists recognize and appreciate at a deep level (rather than only intellectually) that there is no absolute reality, but just different perspectives. The Strategist not only understands this, but also endeavors to understand the world-views of others and to engage in participative, rather than unilateral, meaning making. As Rooke points out, "This in turn leads to an inclusive way of operating in the world based upon inquiry. This gives rise to an important agility for those at the Strategist stage. If 'reality' is constructed, then any current framing of a situation is merely one of many possible framings. Strategists can equally quickly re-frame circumstances in order to transform action."[8] Individualists are developing this capacity, but cannot apply it as consistently as Strategists.

Any senior manager seeking to transform his or her organization is, thus, much more likely to succeed if they make meaning from the Strategist action logic. While Achievers will focus on enhancing performance within a given system, true organizational transformation requires strong leadership from the action logic of the Strategist.

Research and analysis by Rooke and Torbert support this assertion. In studying organizational development efforts in 10 organizations for an average of four years per organization, they observed that those organizations in which the senior leaders recognized that there are multiple ways of framing reality were able to implement inclusive, mutual, and voluntary initiatives. Of the 10 organizations, seven changed for the better. In five of these organizations, the CEO was found to be at the Strategist stage. In the remaining two, although the CEO was pre-Strategist, he chose to partner with an outside consultant and one or more team members, all of whom measured as Strategists.[9]

In contrast, the three remaining organizations that did not transform positively were led by a pre-Strategist CEO who was unwilling to partner with others who had a higher action logic.

Such data suggest that significant organizational change cannot take place without some, or all, of the senior management group being at the Strategist stage. Yet, at best, only 11 percent of executives have attained this stage. Perhaps this explains why so many change initiatives fail, why there is such a high degree of disengagement among employees, and why, all too often, employees believe that those who are at the top lack the required leadership capacity.

Does this mean that the Strategist action logic is the "best" or the "ideal"? Not necessarily. As suggested earlier, simply being at a higher stage does not imply greater happiness. However, if you are attempting to fulfill your role as a senior leader and transform you organization to greatness, then you need to be making sense of your world from the Strategist action logic, or partner closely with an outside consultant or team members who have this frame. It is, in effect, a necessary precondition for your job. Unfortunately, only about one in 10 senior leaders has what it takes to transform their organization.

THE STARTING POINT: DISCOVERING YOUR OWN ACTION LOGIC

To create a great organization, you must first hold your concerns about the organization at some distance and focus on yourself. While you cannot forget the organizational context, you will simply be unable to do that which is demanded of you until you have developed your personal capacity for complexity. It is essential that you understand, accept, and endeavor to grow beyond your present conventional action logic frame. To effect change, you must ultimately develop the strengths and characteristics of a Strategist.

How do you identify and appreciate your action logic framework? Three options are available to you:

1. Take a "best guess" based on the description in this chapter and in other literature.
2. Complete the brief simplified assessment accessible with the purchase of this book.
3. Commission your own comprehensive Leadership Development Profile (LDP) *and* debrief. This process begins with the completion of a Sentence Completion Form (SCF) found at www.harthill.co.uk/harthill-leadership-development-profile.html. The SCF is used to generate your profile. This, combined with a one-to-one debrief, will provide rich insight into your meaning-making frame, ways to consolidate it, and grow beyond it—if that is your imperative.

Best guess

At first blush, you may believe that it is possible to identify your present action logic stage though some simple reflection. Perhaps you have been doing exactly that as you have read this chapter. But beware: any self-determination of your stage of action logic is tricky. While those at the earlier stages may confidently believe they are at the higher stages, it is the very fact that they are at an earlier stage that clouds their judgment. In other words, they don't know what they don't know.

Simplified assessment

The simplified assessment accessible through this book offers some help in overcoming this issue and offers an indication of whether you are above or below the critical Individualist stage of action logic. This assessment is a simplified form of the full Leadership Development Profile described below. While it is a more effective form of assessment than that produced by self-refection, please be aware it offers just a brief window into your possible stage of action logic. As such, accuracy cannot be assured in the same way as is possible with the full Leadership Development Profile. (To access the assessment, please go to www.breakingtheleadershipmold.com and follow the instructions.)

Leadership Development Profile (LDP)

Realistically, the only way to accurately understand your action logic framework is to commission an LDP produced through the completion of what is known as the Sentence Completion Form. First developed by Loevinger and later refined by Torbert and colleagues at Harthill Consulting, this process requires participants to complete 36 unfinished sentences. Analysis of the content and structure allows a profile to be drawn up giving insight into the sense-making behind your actions, which enables your central action logics to be identified. The Sentence Completion Form is a highly validated instrument and has been used with thousands of people from diverse cultures, as well as having been rigorously researched for internal and external validity by both academics and practitioners.

This third-party assessment not only offers an accurate assessment of your present action logic frame, but also presents a personalized commentary giving insight into your meaning-making frames. This is written specifically for you from your sentence completions and will provide indications for actions you might experiment with to consolidate within a frame and/or move to later frames.

Any leader who wants to create a great organization must first determine if they have what it takes to lead organizational transformation. The LDP will provide this insight. It offers deep and rich insight into how each person acts in the world. This can open up unseen perspectives that often generate the impetus for transformational change in the individual, their teams, and the wider context they inhabit both at work and beyond. To commission your profile and debrief, go to www.harthill.co.uk/harthill-leadership-development-profile.html.

Developing to later stages of action logic

As we have seen, Strategists are required to enact organizational transformation. Unfortunately, leaders holding this stage of action logic are few and far between. Completion of an LDP will determine how close you are to having the capacities of a Strategist.

The good news is that it is possible to develop through the various action logics to attain the sorely needed Strategist stage. This can happen either through a conscious effort at development or through unconscious interactions with challenges that require later stage responses. But it is not easy, nor can it happen quickly. The gap between the Achiever to the Strategist is a huge one. Torbert has proposed that this transition often requires a minimum of two years and usually much longer. Given this, there is no easy "fix," no simple recipe for development. In my experience, it takes some, or all, of the following:

- A willingness to engage in some deep self-reflection. Much "heavy lifting," playfulness, and inquiry required in this regard.
- The availability of a coach or mentor, preferably one who is at a later action logic than your own, with whom one can explore alternative frames.
- A series of experiences that challenge current frames and offer alternative ways of meaning making.
- Significant life changes such as the death of a loved one, birth of a child, divorce, or traumatic world events (not that I would wish personal trauma on you for the sake of your development!).

Ultimately, the most effective development efforts are those that are customized to your individual needs. Every action logic offers a number of developmental possibilities, each more complex than the last. However, progression through these action logics is far from certain.

The LDP is invaluable in this respect. When you commission your LDP, you will have two choices: a straightforward LDF profile or an LDF profile with an interpretive/coaching session from a trained coach. I strongly recommend the latter, since this will provide deeper insight and a conversation that will open up new horizons for you.

Through the knowledge gained through the completion of the LDP and conversations with a coach who deeply understands not only the developmental framework, but also how leaders can develop the capacity of later action logics, you can consciously and deliberately evolve your leadership capability.

As we have seen, you may have the best intentions for your organization. However, unless you are leading in ways that facilitate organizational transformation, intentions will remain just that. Worse, you will lose credibility as you articulate a vision for organizational greatness that you are unable to enact due to the limitations of your own meaning-making system.

All organizational transformation starts with personal development. This fact is often lost on executives who believe they have "arrived," simply because they are at the top of their organization. Rather than focus on their own growth they instead choose to direct development efforts to others within the organization. Let me be blunt: if you chose to do this you might as well stop reading now. And rest assured your organizational transformation efforts will fail.

However, if you are truly interested in creating a great organization, then the following chapters will show you how. Be patient, for as I have pointed out, you must first work on yourself.

Chapter Four Takeaways

1. Leadership is best developed through a holistic, deep process that takes into account who you are as a person. The most effective leaders are those adults who have matured to the later levels of development. This maturity has nothing to do with age, but more to do with how, as adults, we see and make sense of the world around us.

2. Developmental theory suggests that how we behave as leaders is determined, to a great extent, by our perception of the world around us. How we perceive reality and how we make sense of the world around us will tend to determine how we relate with other people, what we think about, and, ultimately, how we behave and lead. Both children and adults pass through a number of distinct stages. An individual's character, behavior, and consequently leadership style will be directly related to their stage of development.

3. The most effective leaders in terms of leading transformations are those who make meaning at the later action logics. The majority of the population has an Expert or Achiever action logic. These individuals are hardworking, goal oriented, and problem solvers. Experts are strong individual contributors, while Achievers are well suited for managerial roles.

4. Although Experts and Achievers are valued by organizations, they lack some crucial aspects of meaning-making capacity, in particular, engaging with multi-layered complexity to lead organizational transformation.

5. Any senior manager seeking to transform an organization must be, at the very least, in the Individualist stage. While Achievers will focus on enhancing performance within a given system, true organizational transformation requires the action logic of, at a minimum, the Individualist and, ideally, the Strategist.

6. Research suggests that significant organizational change cannot take place without some or all of the senior management group being at the Strategist stage. Yet, at best, only 11 percent of executives have attained this stage. This helps explain why so many change initiatives fail and why, all too often, employees believe that those at the top lack the required leadership capacity.

7. It is important that all leaders charged with organizational transformation have a deep and rich understanding of their present stage of action logic. The starting point to determine one's current action logic is to complete and debrief Harthill's Leadership Development Profile.

8. It is possible to develop through the various action logics to attain the required Strategist stage. This can happen either through a conscious effort at development or through unconscious interactions with challenges that require later stage responses.

PART TWO

GIVE YOURSELF A LEADERSHIP REALITY CHECK

Self-awareness. Today, this concept is enshrined in almost every book and course about leadership. However, as Rooke and Torbert point out, "Relatively few leaders try to understand their own action logic, and fewer still have explored the possibility of changing it. They should, because we've found that leaders who do undertake a voyage of personal understanding and development can transform not only their own capabilities but also those of their companies."[1]

Executive self-awareness often takes a back seat to organizational issues that are perceived to be more pressing and urgent and, thus, more important. Indeed, as I will discuss in this chapter, there are many barriers to enabling executives to become more self-aware. But regardless of the obstacles, developing and nurturing a deep and profound self-awareness is essential for any executive who wishes to create a highly effective organization. Self-aware executives who understand their strengths, values, blind spots, and limitations, as well as the impact they have on others, will have the organizational credibility to effect significant change. In addition, as we saw in the previous chapter, only when this self-awareness has matured to the Strategist level—where they can comprehend other world-views—will they have the leadership capacity required to implement meaningful organizational change.

Those executives who are not self-aware and do not work on this key element of leadership will be viewed with skepticism by others within the organization, finding it hard to gain the organizational commitment required to create a competitive organization. They will be seen as out of touch and perhaps arrogant by others within the organization. It is also quite likely that they will not even realize this as they naïvely equate effective leadership with a hierarchical position.

Simply put, executive self-awareness is not an option for those who wish to create effective and successful organizations.

WHAT IS SELF-AWARENESS?

What do we really mean by this concept of self-awareness? All too often, the term gets bandied around without truly understanding what it really is and how it impacts the quality of leadership—both at a personal and organizational level. I believe there are three elements embraced in the concept of self-awareness: who I am, how I impact others, and how I manage myself.

Who am I?

Any individual who interacts with others needs to have an acute sense of awareness if the relationship is to be successful. If this person is in a leadership position, this awareness becomes even more critical.

Real awareness means not only understanding your values, default behaviors, and mental models, but also knowing and appreciating how these elements developed and evolved as you grew as a person and leader. In other words, true and deep self-awareness requires "peeling back the onion" and understanding the very source of who you are today. For example, you may be well aware that you tend to get frustrated more than others around you. But why is this? What were the events in your past that caused you to develop a rapid access to anger? And what does this mean for you today?

The reality is that we are shaped and formed by our past experiences. Likewise, what happens today will shape who we become in the future. We know this to be true for our children. However, we are sometimes slow to acknowledge that the same thing holds true for us as adults. We can only develop to the later stages of action logic through an ever-cycling process of experience and reflection.

Life experiences change who we are and how we lead. And these experiences are by no means limited to work. For many of us, advancement to a later stage of action logic occurs when significant events happen in our lives, such as marriage, having children, losing someone close to us, or having a significant adventure or experience. Yet life itself, with all its twists and turns, also changes us—less dramatically and less perceptibly—but just as the world around us transforms, we respond to these different circumstances by also changing. Whether we experience a significant event or continue our daily life with a "business as usual" approach, these changes demand a level of reflection to ensure deep and relevant self-awareness.

A while ago, I was working with a senior leader in an organization (I'll call him Mike) who, three years previously, had lost his wife to cancer, leaving him with two young children to raise on his own. He regarded himself as an outstanding leader and very self-aware. I remember him thrusting his 360 assessment in front of me as evidence of this fact. However, an EQ assessment revealed, not surprisingly, that Mike had an extraordinarily acute ability to feel sadness. Indeed, this is what I had observed in my interactions with him. He effused sadness, had quite a negative outlook and a very limited emotional expression. He was difficult to get to know and was so glib with his comments, it led you to wonder what he was hiding.

Was Mike self-aware? On one hand, you could argue that he was. His 360 assessment showed a definite alignment between the extent he believed that he exhibited some behaviors and what others saw in him. But the 360 focused only on some specific behaviors and did not address how his lack of emotion impacted others. At the deeper (and I would argue more pertinent) level, he was out of touch with his own emotions and sense of self. Ultimately, it became apparent that this impacted his relationships with those around him and his leadership. He was coping—his 360 revealed no major issues or problems. However, I could see that his direct reports trod carefully around Mike and were regularly making allowances for "poor Mike"—something he had no idea about. Without a doubt, Mike was a long way from being a self-aware leader.

How do I impact others?

All too often in my work with leaders and organizations, I come across individuals who have a good sense of who they are as a person and as a leader, yet they fail to recognize how they impact others. For example, one senior executive with whom I work (let's call her Janet) is confident and bright and has strong views on many things. She knows this and, rightly so, likes this about herself. However, what she fails to realize is that her willingness to quickly and confidently state her opinions intimidates and shuts down those around her. I know Janet is more than willing to hear alternative views and frequently asks for others' opinions. Unfortunately, few people are willing to share or challenge her and so she rarely receives contradictory comments. Janet's lack of awareness of the impact she has on others significantly limits her scope of leadership—and she has no idea this is the case.

Another CEO (I'll call him Jim) with whom I work was raised in a very traditional British household. He learned as a young boy that the expression of emotion showed a weakness in character. Not surprisingly, as a leader Jim has frequently struggled to show others his more human and personable side. He's been working on this for years and is well aware of the fact that the expression of emotion is not something that comes easily or naturally to him. However, while Jim knows this is an issue, he consistently fails to realize the impact it carries. His somewhat distant nature causes others to withdraw, suppressing their own emotions.

No leader I know *intends* to be a poor leader. Yet all too often they are unable to distinguish between intention and impact. Janet does not intend to be an intimidating person any more than Jim intends to be cold, yet this is often how others perceive them. What they have failed to do is take what they know about themselves and to truly reflect on how others perceive them. They see things only through their own eyes, leading to a distorted picture and the sense that others perceive them to be out of touch. Clearly, they have not progressed to the Strategist stage of action logic.

How do I manage myself?

As discussed, leaders must understand, at a very deep level, who they are, where they came from, and how circumstances shaped them in the past and continue to shape them in the present. Furthermore, they must have an acute awareness of how their persona impacts how others perceive them. Having these foundational pieces of self-awareness in place enables leaders to manage themselves to best fit the circumstances of any given moment. But there is another quality beyond self-awareness and the awareness of the impact one has on others—self-management.

Several years ago, I worked with a leader who possessed a fiery temper. He was well aware of this, he knew where it came from, and he knew how it impacted others. However, when we talked about it, his response to me was "Well, that is who I am. You want me to be an authentic leader? This is what you get."

Not good enough. Inappropriate behavior cannot be masked under the guise of authenticity or genuineness. Those who either choose or are chosen to lead others must develop the discipline and self-management skills to do so in a way that respects and brings out the best in others. If they are either unwilling or unable to do this, then it is time to return to a process of reflection and to consider what kind of a leader they are striving to be.

Self-management does not mean putting on an act—being someone who you are not. Rather, it means developing to a later action logic stage, which will allow you to have control over those things by which you define yourself. It does not mean fundamentally changing who or what you stand for.

SENIOR LEADERSHIP AND SELF-AWARENESS

Senior leaders are no different from those lower down the organizational hierarchy when it comes to the importance of developing a deep and rigorous self-awareness. However, while those who are in the earlier stages of their career often have a strong desire to grow and learn as leaders, the same cannot always be said for those who hold positions of greater responsibility or are in mid-career. As a result, executive blind spots are rampant.

These executive blind spots can, for the most part, be attributed to the fact that there are a number of barriers to becoming a self-aware executive.

Personal reluctance

Those lower down the organizational hierarchy are often well aware that they need to develop their leadership skills. I always find those new to leadership, or those for whom leadership development is a new experience, thirsty for feedback and knowledge on how they may be impacting others. Rarely do I observe resistance among this group to developing personal awareness.

However, as these young leaders are promoted up the organizational hierarchy, something typically changes. This passion for developing self-awareness lessens. Influenced by the organizational acknowledgment of their success as leaders, this drive for personal development decreases. By the time they reach the executive suite, many individuals *assume* they are indeed effective leaders. The earlier desire they had for constant feedback and self-understanding is gone.

While one would hope they are effective leaders, the assumption that they have "arrived" is a dangerous one. The world executives live in is, now more than ever, a changing one. Therefore, they, just like any other leader in the organization, must constantly reflect on who they are and how they need to respond in these new circumstances. The fact that they are at the top of the organizational food chain should not be taken as an assumption of their effectiveness. Just the opposite is true; the immense responsibility they hold demands, I believe, an equally large degree of self-awareness.

Unfortunately, these executives have got it backwards. By not working on their own leadership, they fail to ignite their organization in striving to develop effective leadership. Instead, they send the message that they do not need to work on their leadership, reinforcing the perception that they are perfect. This disengages those who work for them and sends a message of arrogance. It's a classic example of a disconnect between intent and impact—and it's a dangerous one.

Many of today's executives, raised in the era of the heroic leader, did not spend a lot of time in the early stages of their career in deep personal reflection. Rather, they were rewarded by achievement, driven by ambition, likely good at maintaining a public façade, and waging office politics. This is not the profile of someone who commits time and energy to soul-searching. Furthermore, self-reflection may not have been valued and was seen as a waste of time by those in positions of power. In my work with leaders at all levels within organizations, it is typically those who are lower down the hierarchy and the younger generations that are most willing to reflect on who they are. Leaders such as Mike find it both uncomfortable and inappropriate to delve deeply into personal thoughts and feelings. As Mike told me, "If I wanted to do that, I'd go to a shrink. I'm doing okay as a leader, so let's just leave it at that." Yet, while he might have been doing okay, unless Mike can change his understanding of what it takes to be an effective leader, he will hold his organization back from great success.

Even if executives are willing to do the work necessary to become deeply self-aware, there are many pressures pulling them away. Their responsibilities are vast and they take them seriously. There is a constant pull away from their personal needs to those of the organization. This centrifugal force is a powerful one and the majority of well-intentioned executives I know do not spend time on their own development, simply because they see it as a luxury—the needs of the organization must come first.

Others' reluctance and blindness

One of the most effective ways to develop self-awareness is to get feedback from others. Unless one's emotional intelligence is superb, hearing from others about what they see in you is invaluable. Unfortunately for executives, getting honest feedback from direct reports, peers, or even their boss is a very challenging activity.

Direct reports. Receiving forthright and unfiltered feedback from followers is a challenge for many leaders. The dynamics of the leader-follower relationship, combined with traditional mental models and a lack of skill or experience in having honest conversations, typically results in followers being reluctant to provide any information to the leader that may be perceived as critical of the leader's behavior or performance. As a result, processes and instruments such as the 360 assessment have been adopted by organizations as a way to extract this information from followers.

This situation is far worse at the most senior levels within an organization. Those who report to executives are eyeing ever-diminishing career opportunities as they get close to the top of the organizational pyramid. If they were to give forthright and honest feedback to the executive they report to, they could jeopardize the relationship and limit their future career opportunities in the organization. Few people are willing to take this gamble and, as a result, the feedback executives receive from direct reports tends to be overly biased towards the positive. Even feedback received through 360s can fail to offer any substantive criticism. For many direct reports of executives, it is simply not worth taking the risk of criticizing their superior.

It is an unfortunate fact of life that direct reports filter information to their executives. In most cases, it is the last thing that executives want. Certainly, the majority with whom I have worked are anxious to hear what their reports have to say—be it good or bad. When someone does actually give them unfiltered feedback (unfortunately, they often must rely on external parties such as myself to share this information with them) they willingly embrace it.

So the problem does not lie with the tyrannical executive. Rather, it is the executive who is open to feedback and naïvely assumes that because of this, and the good relationship he or she has with direct reports and other colleagues, feedback and open information will be free-flowing. This is rarely the case, though, and the effective executive acknowledges the dynamics that get in the way of free-flowing information and is proactive about seeking both good news and bad. (Techniques for doing this are outlined in the next chapter.)

Peers. Another valuable source of feedback are peers. The individuals whom you work alongside can see things from a different perspective, providing valuable information on the impact you may be having on others. For many executives, this can be done on a collegial basis without the complex dynamics that occur through a reporting relationship.

Unfortunately, the politics frequently present around the executive table results in executive peers often being reluctant to give each other the feedback. The dynamics of an executive team are complex and are discussed in more detail in Chapter Nine and Chapter Ten. Suffice to say that members of an executive team are very conscious of the CEO's authority and are reluctant to be seen as challenging it in any way. They also recognize that one of their team will likely be a successor to the CEO and, therefore, they tend to tread carefully in their relationships with their peers. Further complicating these dynamics are individuals' career clocks, which lead them to consider how much more time they will be working and what they wish to achieve within this ever-closing window. These dynamics tend to result in naturally competitive individuals becoming even more competitive. This, in turn, impacts trust and compromises quality relationships within the team. This situation is hardly the environment for team members to supply quality feedback to each other.

The CEO. An individual's superior is often seen as the person who is responsible for giving feedback to that direct report. Unfortunately, simply because you are someone's boss does not necessarily mean you have a good handle on how this individual is leading others. Filtered information is commonplace.

At the executive level, this situation is even worse. CEOs typically handpick their team and thus can be blind to their shortfalls. I once worked with a CEO who, when rating his team members on their 360 reports, gave every person a perfect score on every behavior. He had selected each one of them to be a member of his team and, therefore, was blind to their deficiencies. In this case, as in many organizations, the CEO's bias was reinforced by filtered information. In his defense, he had asked those who reported to his executive team for their feedback on their superiors. For the reasons discussed above, all he heard from these direct reports were positive comments. Yet, in confidential coaching conversations, these same direct reports told me all about the leadership deficiencies of their supervisors.

The other problem a CEO has in giving honest or relevant feedback to his executive team members is the fact that his interactions with them may be somewhat limited. Executives are busy, and the centrifugal force that pulls them away from their own development to the organization is very strong. CEOs have limited opportunities to see their executives in action, particularly when it comes to how they lead others. More often than not, they may see them performing for the external community rather than leading internally.

Furthermore, the notion that executives at the top must, by definition, be good leaders is often a strongly held belief by the CEO. As one CEO told me when talking about the leadership abilities of his team, "If they haven't learned to lead properly by now, then we have a real problem." It had not occurred to this CEO that every individual, regardless of the position they hold within his organization, must constantly reflect on and develop their leadership. Those who fail to do this hold the organization back from greatness.

Developing self-awareness must not be regarded as an event. It is not something that happens when you start in a leadership position and can be checked off a list. Nor is it something that happens once a year at performance appraisal time or when you go on a leadership development program. Rather, it must be an ongoing process that yields an ever-deepening development of personal understanding. As circumstances and the environment change, you must continually reflect on how you respond to that environment, how you manage yourself, how others react to you, the impact you have on them, and what you might have done differently. The next chapter offers some specific techniques and processes for gaining self-awareness.

Chapter Five Takeaways

1. Developing and nurturing a deep and profound self-awareness is essential for any executive who wishes to create a highly effective organization. It is important that executive self-awareness does not get neglected in preference to organizational issues that are seen as more pressing, more urgent, and, ultimately, more important.

2. There are three elements embraced in the concept of self-awareness: who I am, how I impact others, and how I manage myself.

3. Real awareness means not only understanding your values, default behaviors, and mental models, but also knowing and appreciating how these elements developed and evolved as you grew as a person and a leader.

4. Having a good sense of who you are as a person and a leader is not sufficient if you fail to recognize how you impact others. Executives must be sure to differentiate between intention and impact.

5. Self-management does not mean putting on an act and being someone you are not. Rather, it means developing to the later action logic stage that allows you to have control over those things by which you define yourself.

6. There are many factors that get in the way of executives becoming deeply self-aware. These include the following:
   ○ A decrease in the drive for personal development due to the organizational acknowledgment of their success as leaders.
   ○ A centrifugal force that pulls them away from their personal needs to those of the organization.
   ○ Mental models that suggest to executives it is unnecessary, uncomfortable, and inappropriate to delve deeply into personal thoughts and feelings.

- ○ Direct reports filtering information to their executives because they are unwilling to jeopardize the relationship with their boss and, potentially, limit future career opportunities.
- ○ The dynamics and politics of the team at the top getting in the way of peers offering quality feedback to each other.
- ○ CEOs being blinded by the effectiveness of their direct reports as they handpicked them and receive nothing but filtered information regarding their effectiveness.

CONDUCT A PERSONAL LEADERSHIP AUDIT

I invite you to reflect on this question: Are you prepared to accept that others may see you differently than you see yourself? Prior to conducting a personal leadership audit, it is advisable to take stock of how ready you are to truly learn about how you lead. However, be warned. Unless you possess a real willingness to readily explore, accept, and work with any data that you receive, it is inadvisable to even start the process. A great deal of harm has been done by leaders in organizations who solicit information on their performance, and then either refuse to accept it or choose not to effect self-change.

A number of options are available for conducting a personal assessment of your leadership. At the high level, these can be broken down into *passive* and *active* options. Passive options employ the use of external parties and tools. Those who are being assessed do little in the initial stages except, perhaps, complete a self-assessment. Once the data has been gathered, leaders are then presented with information on such things as their personal preferences or how others view their leadership. At this point, they need to decide what to do with this information. Often there is no obligation to explore it in greater depth, to discuss it with others, or to be accountable for changing behavior. However, without these elements, self-knowledge will increase, but change may not occur.

Active options demand that individuals play a significant role in gathering data about their leadership, which can be extremely effective. The active method requires individuals to solicit information themselves, without the support of third parties or confidential questionnaires. The conversations that must take place while implementing active options build relationships and, consequently, enhance leadership. However, while they may be more effective, such options are difficult to implement, particularly at the executive level. Therefore, while it is ideal to use active options to conduct a personal leadership assessment, in many cases, the organizational culture and individual skill level suggest that a passive option may be a more appropriate selection.

PASSIVE OPTIONS
Using a third party
Many executives choose to use an individual who is external to the organization for feedback on how they are leading. This may be a coach, consultant, or trusted advisor. The selection of this individual is critical. Some things to consider are the following:

- What is the perception of this individual within the organization? While it is important that the assessor has the trust of the executive, the assessor must not be seen by the organization as being overly biased towards this individual or "in the pocket of the executive." The assessor must have the respect and trust of the entire organization.
- What is the assessor's level of knowledge and expertise of leadership? The assessor may be an outstanding business consultant or life coach, but does he or she truly understand executive leadership at the level that is required and have the skill and expertise to probe and fully explore the dynamics of the situation?
- Does the assessor have a depth of experience doing this kind of work in many different organizations or has his or her exposure been limited to only a few? It is difficult to get a comprehensive understanding if one does not have the experience to benchmark the results.
- Does the assessor understand the business and organizational realities that the executive faces, and have the knowledge and credibility to make suggestions for future development that are realistic and manageable?

A number of options are available for the assessor. He or she may choose to conduct confidential interviews with direct reports, peers, and supervisors of the individual. Alternatively (and often in addition to the interviews), he or she may simply shadow the executive to see how the executive is performing as a leader. A report may be prepared, conversations take place, and ideally, a development plan is worked out.

Provided the right assessor is selected, this method of sizing up how the executive is leading is extremely powerful. A great deal of in-depth knowledge can be obtained and specific examples witnessed of both effective and ineffective leadership. The shadowing methodology is particularly useful, provided sufficient time is spent with the executive. I once shadowed a CEO (I'll call him Philip) whom I had known for many years and with whom I had a great relationship. Our relationship was open—we laughed a lot and engaged in many no-holds-barred conversations. This was the Philip I knew, and while I recognized we had a fairly unique relationship, he assured me that the relationship he had with his direct reports was somewhat similar.

However, when I saw him in action, I realized he was sorely mistaken. While there was much joking among the executive team, for the most part, any substantive conversations directed towards Philip were clearly guarded. I caught many nonverbal cues and subtle eye contact between team members as the conversation approached an element of controversy. It was clear to me that the humor was masking nervousness. Philip had no idea what I had observed when I reported back to him later in the day. He and I then determined that I should gather more information by consequently talking to his team members individually, which I did once we had finished our due process in terms of preparation. I was then able to gather more insight about the reasons they were reluctant to say what was truly on their minds; it was a combination of not wanting to challenge Philip, compounded by some complex executive team dynamics. (I'll talk more about this team in Chapters Nine and Ten.) Suffice to say that once Philip had this information (and in his case he was more than willing to accept it), he was able to change the way he interacted with his team, both individually and collectively. The dynamics of the team changed, as did his relationship with each member and, as a result, the organization ultimately became more effective.

Personal preferences assessment tools

A plethora of assessment tools and instruments are available to help leaders understand who they are as a person. Such tools are invaluable in helping leaders understand their biases, preferences, and strengths.

The Myers Briggs Type Indicator (MBTI), developed by Isabel Myers and Katharine Briggs as an application of Carl Jung's theory of psychological types, is one of the most popular assessment tools. Jung's theory is based on opposing ways of gaining energy, gathering or becoming aware of information, deciding or coming to conclusions, and dealing with the world around us. The MBTI seeks to measure preferences and does not measure skills or abilities in any area.

Emotional intelligence (EQ) assessments are also very popular. These assessments provide individuals with insight into their core competencies related to emotional intelligence. Self-awareness, self-regulation, and empathy are the three capacities measured. In particular, the EQ in Action profile provides information regarding how the brain interprets reality during stressful and challenging relationship situations, and offers a guide for ongoing development of the self for high-performance and successful relationships.

The Thomas-Kilmann Conflict Mode Instrument (TKI) is designed to assess an individual's behavior in conflict situations—situations in which the concerns of two people appear to be incompatible. The instrument helps individuals to understand how different conflict-handling modes or styles affect interpersonal and group dynamics.

These are just three assessments—many others are available. Without a doubt, they will increase self-awareness. However, the real value comes when individuals choose to use this self-awareness to become better leaders. The knowledge that one has preferences, while helpful, has value only when one has the ability to self-manage around those preferences. On reviewing various assessments, there may be a tendency to declare, "Oh, I know that about myself." Although that may be true, I would then ask how you intend to self-regulate around these known preferences.

The other value for an executive comes from understanding teams and organizations. I work with one organization whose culture is best described as quiet, reserved, conservative, and attentive to details. All the senior leaders have now completed the MBTI, and, not surprisingly, we find a high number of what we refer to as ISTJs, a personality style that is best described as serious, quiet, practical, orderly, matter-of-fact, logical, realistic, and dependable. This consistency is clearly aligned to the culture and, for senior executives, has prompted some interesting discussions concerning the present and desired organizational culture.

A 360 assessment

Perhaps one of the most commonly used tools to gain information on how others perceive leaders is the 360 feedback instrument. This tool focuses on the extent to which a leader performs certain behaviors, the assumption being that these behaviors, if performed consistently, will result in the individual leading in the way that is most effective for the organization. While some organizations choose to customize these behaviors through a competency development process, others use behaviors commonly believed to be associated with effective leadership. A behavior description questionnaire is completed by the leader and other individuals who are considered to be knowledgeable about the leader's behavior, such as subordinates, peers, and superiors.

Despite its popularity, as Gary Yukl writes in his book *Leadership in Organizations*, these questionnaires are fraught with problems and are susceptible to several types of bias and error.[1] The use of ambiguous items can be interpreted in different ways by different respondents. Inherent in any 360 is an assumption that behaviors have the same literal meaning for all those being assessed, as well as all those who are doing the assessing. Yet, as B. van der Heijden and A. Nijhof point out, genuine shared understanding of the meaning of concepts is very rare. Therefore, the validity of numerical responses can be suspect, something that is of great concern when 360s are used not just for development, but also as a measure of performance.[2]

In addition, most leadership questionnaires have a fixed-response format that requires respondents to think back over several months or years and indicate how often or how much a leader used the behavior described in an item. An accurate judgment is difficult to make, since the respondent may not have noticed the behavior at the time it occurred or they may be unable to remember how many times it occurred over the specified time period.

Response bias is another source of error. For example, some respondents answer each item much the same way despite real differences in the leader's behavior, because the respondent likes (or dislikes) the leader. Furthermore, some respondents attribute desirable behavior to a leader who is perceived to be effective, even though the behavior was not actually observed. This "halo" effect is very powerful, and while one could argue it at least informs the leader about how he or she is generally perceived, it does little to actually enhance self-awareness in the execution of specific behaviors.

Self-assessment is often influenced by a tendency called the leniency effect, which suggests that individuals are motivated by self-enhancement. This leads individuals to emphasize their merits and downplay their faults, with the net result of over-inflated self-assessment ratings. Self-ratings have been found to differ by one-half to one standard deviation from ratings by supervisors or by near colleagues.[3]

As van Hooft, van der Flier, and Minne point out, the raters in 360 feedback systems are selected on having frequent interactions with the ratee.[4] This results in a personalized relationship, likely leading to subjectivity in the ratings. Furthermore, previous research demonstrates that the agreement between the different rater groups (peers, subordinates, supervisor) in 360 feedback ratings is typically low to moderate. Consequently, summing up the ratings of different rater-categories into one global judgment is questionable.[5]

Our comfort with numerical ratings often convinces us that such assessments are objective. However, this assumption is seriously flawed for a number of reasons. As J. Stewart suggests, most people feel comfortable with the idea of a continuum between subjectivity and objectivity.[6] Yet, to have a continuum, which by definition is bipolar, both poles must be possible. But if assessment always occurs in the head and is, therefore, always and inevitably subjective, the objective pole of the continuum cannot exist. Given this lack of an objective pole, an accurate assessment on the continuum between objectivity and subjectivity is impossible. In addition, involving other people in the rating process to ensure fairness and consistency is based on the idea that subjectivity + subjectivity + subjectivity = objectivity. However, if one rater can be unfair and inconsistent, then so can another.[7]

With all of these problems it would be very easy to dismiss the 360 as offering little to the assessment process. However, while it is important that there is not an over-reliance on this instrument, it does, nevertheless, provide some insight regarding leadership effectiveness. Indeed, it can be an eye-opener, particularly the first time it is used.

I have observed, however, on many occasions that subsequent reports tend to be less revealing for people, so it is not the most effective tool for an executive who has, in his or her rise to the top, received many such reports.

All too often, I have witnessed senior leaders review 360 or other personality assessments with little or no impact. They shrug their shoulders, claim it was interesting, and carry on with no change in their behavior. Indeed, it is rare that passive options *on their own* change behavior. For any passive option to have an impact, the data must be explored, made sense of, and acted upon. In fact, passive options are only truly effective when they are regarded as the source of data for conversation and not an end in themselves.

ACTIVE OPTIONS

We know that a critical leadership practice for any leader is to have feedback conversations. At the executive level, this is both more difficult and more important. Passive options, such as those described above, do little to develop this skill and worse, they tend to abdicate individuals from having such conversations. In effect, it's the easy way out. While providing interesting information, passive options do nothing towards developing a leader's skills in gathering feedback—a critical strategy for any executive keen to increase their awareness and leadership effectiveness.

Active options address this problem. They are harder and often more time-consuming than passive options, yet far more effective in developing leadership and an effective, healthy, and sustainable organization.

Have a leadership conversation

One of the most effective ways of understanding how others view you as a leader is to have a forthright conversation with those who see you in action. Such conversations not only can provide valuable data, but can also significantly enhance relationships. It is a powerful and effective tool for anyone interested in growing their leadership.

Unfortunately, such open conversations are often difficult to execute within organizations. The culture may not encourage it or people may not have the skills to ask the right questions or offer unfiltered data in a way that others can hear. The situation is compounded when the person seeking feedback is an executive. Given these challenges, people often assume nothing worthwhile will come out of such conversations. However, if the process is structured correctly, as outlined below, it can work.

First, make sure you select the right individuals from whom to solicit information. Feedback is most valuable when there is a genuine desire on both sides for a meaningful and authentic exchange of perceptions. Thus, consider including your supervisor, mentor, coach, direct reports, peers, and key clients to whom you provide service. Make sure you include those who you believe will give you the most authentic feedback, know you best as a person, have worked closely with you as part of a team, or seem to be very different from you, perhaps in the way he or she thinks or acts. Do not include those who frequently tell you what you want to hear—they will find it hard to give you any critical feedback.

Give thought to what you can do to ensure the conversation is an authentic one and the information you gather is of good quality. Consider

- Sending the questions to your interviewees ahead of time;
- Scheduling the interview away from the office in a comfortable, neutral place; and
- Scheduling enough time for in-depth discussion (an hour or more).

Ask questions that make it easy for the interviewee to speak honestly. For example, do not ask, "What do you think about my leadership?" Such a question will likely result in platitudes. Rather, considering asking questions such as the following:

1. How would you like me to be as a leader?
2. Where am I too comfortable as a leader?
3. What are my blind spots? What do I need to stop avoiding?
4. Where do I shine?
5. In what areas do I need to change priorities?
6. What is the most powerful step I could take to grow as a leader?
7. What do I need to risk to get there?
8. What is my reputation as a leader?
9. What else are you willing to tell me about my leadership that makes you nervous to say out loud?

What matters most in conducting a personal leadership audit through conversations is simply having a dialogue. The questions should prompt such a dialogue. Listen hard, be curious, and know that if the interviewee is simply showering you with compliments, they are likely being guarded in their conversation.

Self-reflection

The ideal way for any individual to conduct a personal leadership assessment is through self-reflection. Emotionally intelligent leaders are aware of who they are as a person and what they stand for. They know and can manage their own emotions and are aware of the emotions of others. They do not rely on others to inform them—rather, they have a highly developed sense of self-awareness that comes through frequent, honest, and rigorous self-reflection.

Self-reflection is a critical practice for any leader. In a study of senior leaders, 63 percent of respondents suggested that self-reflection and self-appraisal were two primary tools for identifying performance areas needing attention, improvement, and action.[8] Respondents cited the importance of regularly taking time to critically review the manner in which they were currently handling situations, tackling problems, and allocating their time. This process was described as a vehicle to "step outside" the situation or issue in question, as a chance to "catch one's breath," and as taking time to "pinpoint personal problem areas." Respondents spoke of the real challenge of taking time for self-reflection and review, but also mentioned the high price of not doing so. Self-reflection is viewed by many at the executive level as a luxury for which there is no time.

Quality self-reflection requires a commitment to one's own growth and development. It is not simply a matter of tweaking behaviors. It requires a decision to spend time thinking rather than doing. In organizations that value output and results above all else, this is no easy task. Strategies for overcoming this pressure and creating more time for reflection are discussed in detail in Chapter Eight.

When using the reflective process to increase self-awareness, some find it useful to create structured processes to guide them. Certainly those new to reflection find this helpful. Later on, simply clearing your mind can produce wonderful results. As a starting point, consider using the questions you may have asked others in feedback conversations and outlined earlier in this chapter. R. Kaplan presented these additional questions in the *Harvard Business Review*:

- How often do I communicate a vision for my business?
- Have I identified and communicated three to five key priorities to achieve that vision?
- If asked, would my employees be able to articulate the vision and priorities?
- How am I spending my time? Does it match my key priorities?
- How are my subordinates spending their time? Does that match the key priorities for the business?
- Do I give people timely and direct feedback that they can act on?
- Do I have five or six junior subordinates who will tell me things I may not want to hear but need to hear?
- Have I, at least in my own mind, picked one or more potential successors?
- Am I coaching them and giving them challenging assignments?
- Am I delegating sufficiently? Have I become a decision-making bottleneck?
- Is the design of my company still aligned with the key success factors for the business?
- If I had to design my business with a clean sheet of paper, how would I design it? How would it differ from the current design?
- Should I create a task force of subordinates to answer these questions and make recommendations to me?
- What types of events create pressure for me?
- How do I behave under pressure?
- What signals am I sending my subordinates? Are these signals helpful, or are they undermining the success of my business?
- Is my leadership style comfortable? Does it reflect who I truly am?
- Do I assert myself sufficiently, or have I become tentative?
- Am I too politically correct?
- Does worry about my next promotion or bonus cause me to pull punches or hesitate to express my views?[9]

Ultimately, what matters are not the questions you ask, but how deeply you reflect. Self-reflection allows you to get in touch with who you are. As K. Cashman reminds us, "If leadership is the act of going beyond what is, it begins by going beyond what is within you. Your inner calm attracts others by communicating a sense of comfort and thoughtful counsel. It translates into executive presence—a confident demeanor that is not easily shaken by external circumstances. Being centered equips you to deal with change, enables you to refresh yourselves and achieve more with less effort, and gives you the mix of energy and calmness you need to achieve better balance."[10]

Regardless of the form it takes, completing a personal leadership assessment is not the end, but rather the beginning. It simply informs you how you are doing in relation to the vision you have for your leadership. It can offer clues as to which action logic frame dominates. Although on its own a leadership assessment is unlikely to do much, it can provide a great foundation to set about changing some aspects of your leadership. The ways to make these changes are explored in the following chapter.

Chapter Six Takeaways

1. Few leaders have such a highly developed emotional intelligence that they do not require some assistance in assessing how they are leading. A personal leadership audit is necessary, regardless of hierarchical level.

2. Conducting a personal leadership audit should only be done if there is a real willingness to readily explore, accept, and act on what is learned.

3. There are passive and active options available for conducting a personal assessment of your leadership. Passive options are those that employ the use of external parties and tools, and require limited commitment on the part of the person being assessed. Active options demand that individuals play a significant role in gathering data about their leadership and, thus, can be extremely effective.

4. Passive options include using a third party, completing a personal preferences assessment, or using a 360 assessment tool. Care must be taken in using 360 assessments, as they are fraught with problems and are susceptible to several types of bias and error.

5. While passive options can offer some insight regarding leadership effectiveness, they are really only truly effective when they are regarded as the source of data for conversation and not an end in themselves.

6. Active options are harder and often more time consuming than passive options, yet far more effective in developing leadership and a profitable, healthy, and sustainable organization.

7. One of the most effective active options is to have a forthright conversation with those who see you in action. Such conversations not only can provide valuable data, but can also significantly enhance relationships.

8. Self-reflection is a critical practice for any leader and the ideal way for any individual to conduct a personal leadership assessment. Quality self-reflection requires a commitment to one's own growth and development. It is not simply a matter of tweaking behaviors; it requires a decision to spend time thinking, rather than doing.

9. When using the reflective process to increase self-awareness, some find it useful to create structures, processes, and defined questions to guide them.

EMBARK ON A LEADERSHIP MAKEOVER

If you have done the work you need to and conducted a thorough personal leadership assessment, you are now faced with a critical decision. What are you going to do about it?

Let's be clear: you must do something. Unless you elected to use a passive assessment option, which was conducted in private, it is likely common knowledge within at least certain parts of your organization that you have gathered information about your leadership. Executive reflection and development are still not normalized within organizations, so when executives engage in any form of leadership audit, word spreads quickly throughout the organization. Do not be naïve and assume that your assessment is only going on behind closed doors.

This organizational knowledge presents a significant opportunity for any executives wanting to dispel the myth of the heroic leader in their organization. By publicly acknowledging that they are deeply committed to developing their leadership, that they are "works in progress," and that they are by no means perfect leaders, they achieve a couple of objectives. First, such "executive humanness" typically is welcomed by many in the organization who have, for many years, viewed executives as out of touch and arrogant. Contrary to what many executives may believe, this willingness to express vulnerability rather than gloss over any imperfection inspires confidence and does not plant seeds of doubt.

Second, such declarations set the stage for a culture of leadership learning to be embedded throughout the organization. The executive who declares that leadership is important but is seen as doing little to develop his or her own leadership capacity does not have the organizational credibility to ask others to work on their leadership. Worse, such strategies promote the perception of executives who are overly confident, egotistical, and disconnected with how others perceive them.

Therefore, I would never advocate doing a personal leadership audit in private. There is much to be gained by sharing with everyone in the organization the fact that you are working on your leadership. You need not share your specific findings, but you can certainly take the evaluation process into the public domain.

WHAT TO CHANGE
To change or not to change

Simply because you have received information from others that they would like you to change in some way does not mean that you have to implement these changes. Rather, it informs you of what they perceive as your strengths and weaknesses. It is up to you to decide whether these changes are ones that you wish to adopt. There are many points to consider:

- If you were to make the suggested changes, would it bring you closer to the vision you have for your own leadership?
- Are the desired changes practical or realistic? For example, oftentimes the request is for executives to be more available and visible to employees. While some changes may be appropriate, it is rare that an executive can spend all the time that is asked of them with employees. Other external pressures demand their time as well.
- Are you willing to do what must be done in order to implement the changes? If not, do not waste your time and energy on a shell game.

Ultimately, you must make the decision about what you are going to do moving forward. However, if you choose not to change in accordance with the feedback received, you have an obligation to close the loop. This means having a conversation with those people who gave you the feedback, explaining why you do not plan to implement the changes they suggested. The fact that you now know how they are thinking can inform the quality of conversation that you have with them.

Don't do the obvious

Having decided what feedback you are going to take to heart, it's now a matter of determining the things you wish to change. For example, you may decide you need to be a better listener, coach others more, give more frequent feedback, or articulate a clearer vision. One thing to understand at this point is that the behavior you pick is not critical. Everything is intertwined—change one thing and others will also change. I often see people agonizing at this point over what they should do. The reality is, at this stage, it matters that you do *something* more than pick the perfect strategy.

It is at this stage that most well-intentioned leaders fail to do what is truly required to change. They select things they wish to change and merrily go about their way changing them.

Unfortunately for them, it's not as simple as that. While they may have picked behaviors that do indeed need to change, they often fail to unearth the root cause for such behaviors and, therefore, any attempts they make to shift their behavior will either not be sustained or, in many cases, simply fail.

Let me share an example. I was once coaching an executive, Christine, who, after doing a thorough personal leadership assessment, came to the conclusion that she needed to be a better listener. True enough, she did. She had a reputation throughout the company as a poor listener and I had also witnessed this on many occasions.

The thing was, I believed Christine actually had good listening skills. When I challenged Christine to consider her listening skills, she conceded that, for example, if her ten-year-old daughter came home from school really upset, she was able to put everything aside, listen really closely to what she had to say, and help her daughter deal with her problem. In other words, when it mattered enough to Christine, she could be a good listener. The issue was not, therefore, that Christine did not know *how* to listen, but rather that she chose (usually subconsciously) *not* to listen. Together, we started exploring the reasons for this behavior and, in short order, we determined that Christine was a strong-willed character who really was not that interested in others' opinions, who rather enjoyed being a heroic leader. Of course, she did not state this publicly, but as we talked, she soon realized that when people approached her to discuss a matter, it often felt like an annoyance to her to be interrupted in her already overbooked schedule, and this annoyance showed. It was only when she began to work on some of her foundational leadership beliefs that Christine was able to enhance the listening skills she already possessed to some degree.

Another executive I worked with, John, really had trouble giving people honest feedback. He would talk in circles to avoid giving anyone the straight goods if it might upset them—classic behavior of someone who is at the Diplomat frame of action logic. In John's case, he did in fact lack the skills required to speak authentically, and some behavioral development work was required in this respect. However, while his newly acquired skills certainly helped him, on their own, they were insufficient. What John needed was help in seeing relationships more objectively. With much nudging and coaching, he gradually started to be straight with people. Along the way, he recognized that he did not need to define himself by these relationships, moving from the Diplomat to the Expert frame. When he understood this dynamic in greater detail, John was able to ensure his behavior shifted and became embedded permanently in his leadership.

So the question to ask is not just what needs to change, but what is driving this behavior in the first place. If it really, really mattered, could you do it? If your answer to this is yes, then why are you not doing it? To what extent is the way you define yourself (your stage of action logic), your beliefs about leadership, and your mental models inherited from the past getting in the way of what you have the ability to do? You may need some skill development, but more often than not (particularly at the executive level) what you likely need is a shift in perspective. And this only comes with support.

MAKING CHANGE HAPPEN

As I pointed out in Chapter Four, progression to later action logic frames is not a quick or simple process. This is the case with any significant behavioral change. However hard it may be, it is possible provided the following pieces are in place:

1. A deep commitment to change. Lip service doesn't cut it.
2. A willingness to reflect deeply and become increasingly self-aware.
3. A committed and relevant support structure.

I have said it before and I will repeat it again: Going through the motions of change does more harm than good. Don't put on a show for your employees. If you are not willing to "do change properly," then do not attempt it. Any efforts to put on a show of commitment to your employees will almost certainly create a disconnect and skepticism that will take years to overcome.

As mentioned in the previous chapter, reflection is critically important. However, for many executives it is a difficult change not because of any unwillingness on their part, but because they are simply too busy. This role overload issue and strategies to address it are outlined in the following chapter.

The third essential item required for change to happen is support.

Senior leaders need support

Don't fool yourself. It is virtually impossible to develop your leadership on your own. Some form of support is essential. For many senior leaders, the notion that they need to develop their leadership and also require support to do so is quite a radical idea—one that often takes them out of their comfort zone. Yet support is required for a number of reasons:

- Leadership at the top can be lonely and isolating. This situation is heightened when a senior leader is endeavoring to change his or her behavior. Conversely, the sense of isolation can be significantly reduced by effectively leveraging the support process.
- Different perspectives and different ways of doing things can be considered through an effective support process. Without this, it is sometimes difficult to see the forest for the trees.
- Senior leaders have very little free time. As discussed previously, they often fail to prioritize their own development and, instead, put the needs of the organization ahead of their own growth. Those leaders with a decent support structure will find it easier to carve out time for their own development.
- While many senior leaders intellectually recognize that the model of heroic leadership is outdated for today's organizations, they still struggle emotionally with the notion they may need to rely on others. The development of an effective support structure can help them once and for all to let go of the idea that they are the all-powerful leader. This becomes particularly significant in instances where they are willing to share with the rest of the organization that they are actively using some form of support in developing their leadership.

Those executives who insist on going it alone are, unfortunately, not only still embedded in the heroic leader paradigm, but are also doomed to fail in their efforts to change.

Support options

A number of support options are available for senior leaders. The selection of the option should be driven by the developmental needs and not vice versa. In other words, you first need to decide in which areas you wish to learn, grow, and transform as a leader, and then select the form of support that will best help you achieve this. As obvious as this seems, oftentimes it happens the other way around. An executive is told that a coach has been hired to mentor him and, together, they work out what must change. Or a senior leader is selected to attend an executive education session and through this session he or she determines their personal developmental needs.

While in some cases this may work, often it misses the mark. Ideally, the leader must be able to identify their developmental needs without the support structure. Indeed, this in itself is a mark of an effective leader. The support structure is then in place to help them act on this knowledge.

In some cases, leaders cannot determine on their own in what areas they need to grow. In these circumstances, I suggest that the support be viewed as two separate phases. Initially, it should be focused on determining developmental needs. Once these have been clarified, however, leaders should then consider selecting an alternative support methodology that is closely aligned to their developmental needs.

Coaching. With the overuse of the word "coach," there is a great deal of misunderstanding regarding coaching. I view it as a spectrum that is defined by the degree of prescriptive advice that the helping professional offers. At one end of the spectrum, we have those who are closer to counselors, therapists, or psychologists. At this end, there is also a plethora of life coaches, grounded in the belief that the answer lies within the individual, who base their practice simply on asking questions. At the other end of the spectrum, there are pure consultants. These are individuals who are seen as experts and hired by organizations and given a clear scope of work. Such consultants base their practice primarily on telling and advocating.

The most effective executive coaches operate in between these two extremes. While they will ask questions, they will also not hesitate to advise. The place on the spectrum in which the skilled coach needs to operate should be determined by the development needs of the leader—as distinct from the talents of the coach.

The coach's role is to take the individual to the place on the spectrum that will best meet their specific needs. And as obvious as this seems, it is not always easy, particularly when coaching those at the top. Many executives appear much more comfortable with a consulting type of relationship, rather than a personal and transformative type of relationship. While the developmental needs may suggest a coaching relationship that is deep and personal, all too often executives find this to be uncomfortable and endeavor to deflect to the "more practical" side, resulting in frustration for all.

Don was just such an executive. Truth be known, he hired me as his coach because he knew he had to model leadership development for the rest of his organization. And while he did have some interest in becoming a better leader, it was not a top priority for him. It soon became clear that he was incredibly uncomfortable talking about the more personal aspects of his leadership. Even though we had some clearly defined goals, at every opportunity he would ask me my opinion as an "organizational expert." It was obvious that Don was deflecting, and only after a very uncomfortable (at least for him) series of conversations was he really able to accept that we needed to move away from the consulting end of the spectrum and more towards (though not all the way) the end where therapists might operate.

Mentoring. Mentoring involves the pairing of two individuals for the specific purpose of developing the skills and capabilities of existing and potential leaders (mentees) through the sharing of knowledge and information by existing leaders (mentors). Unlike coaches, mentors typically have some specific business expertise that will help mentees develop in their career.

Often, senior leaders find themselves in a position of mentoring others rather than being mentored themselves. While there is much to be gained by having numerous mentees within an organization, such relationships should not preclude the mentors from becoming a mentee themselves. I once worked with Greg, a young CEO, who had risen to the top quickly and been thrust into the top position with very little preparation. He was keen to do a good job, was willing to learn, but struggled with no longer being a member of his peer group. Furthermore, he really did not understand how to be the top leader of the organization—the previous CEO had been very distant and was by no means a great role model. I suggested to Greg that he would benefit from finding himself a mentor outside of the organization. Greg knew of and admired someone with whom he had golfed on numerous occasions. The mentor was 20 years his senior, was in a similar but not competitive industry, and was more than happy to take this young CEO under his wing.

A good mentor possesses the skills and information to assist the mentee with their specific development goals and is committed to the mentee's development. Mentors also benefit from the relationship by, for example, gaining cross-functional knowledge and further enhancing their own skills in developing others. Furthermore, at the senior level, mentoring others often fulfills the need to leave some form of legacy among those who are entering the twilight of their career.

Mentoring will only be successful when both the mentor and mentee are comfortable with the goals, processes, and expectations of the mentoring relationship. The experiences of the mentor must align with the objectives of the mentee, both parties must have the time to meet, and there must be a degree of chemistry between the pair.

Although organizational programs exist in which mentors are found for employees, often at the senior level individuals are left on their own to find a mentor whom, more often than not, may be external to the organization. Therefore, consider the following:

- Whom do you know from your "network," whether it be the Board of Trade, Rotary Club, boards of directors, professional or trade organizations, peer groups, sporting groups, children's schools, etc.?
- Who is successful in your field or area of interest?
- Whom do you admire or respect—in your company, industry, or field?
- Who are the people you know who have influence?
- Who thinks you have potential?
- Who has encouraged you?
- Who has helped you in the past and may help again?

Make a list, then

- Research the person's background and find out everything you can.
- Make contact, either directly or through a mutual contact.
- Request help—make a simple request, tell them why you admire them and ask for advice.
- Consider what you can offer in exchange—you'll be surprised.
- Prepare a list of questions, focus on the mentor, ask about their history.
- Meet—and depending on the nature of the relationship—discuss goals and desired outcomes.
- Follow up—keep the first meeting brief, respect their time, and send a thank you. Try some of your mentor's suggestions and share results.
- If the relationship has value, ask to meet on an ongoing basis.

Peer Support. One of the most effective forms of support is that which takes place in a group among peers in a highly functioning team. The most significant behavioral changes I have ever witnessed in the workplace have always occurred when peers have been integral to the change process. It does not matter where the team is in the organizational hierarchy, but rather whether the team is characterized by high degrees of trust, authenticity, and a shared purpose.

Unfortunately, as I will discuss in Chapters Nine and Ten, such traits are rare among executive teams. Indeed, there are many dynamics that occur around the executive table that impede real and genuine support for personal development.

But regardless of whether or not the team of which they are members is highly functioning, individual peers can offer great support to any leader who has developmental ambitions. More importantly, being at the senior level does not preclude this. Peers can adopt many of the roles often assumed by coaches, such as a sounding board, conscience, mirror, role model, etc. Depending on their experience levels, they can also act as a mentor. However, for the relationship to be effective, heroic expectations must be well and truly quenched by those seeking support. The willingness to be vulnerable in front of peers is essential.

Workshops. Within organizations, leadership development workshops often provide the primary form of support for enhancing leadership. The best workshops are those that are customized to the organization, to the group in the room, and to the current environment in which the organization is operating. The greatest value typically does not occur when individuals are taught a particular skill or model, but when participants engage in active and real dialogue about both the issues they face in the workplace and their current development needs. This dialogue is more rich when participants have similar experiences and are from the same organization.

Workshops are important in helping create a common language and culture within the organization. However, on their own they are not enough to change behavior. For an executive, the value comes from engaging with others within the organization. The knowledge gained from such interaction is often invaluable. It is folly, however, to believe that simply attending a workshop will change an executive's behavior. While it will not do any harm, without some other form of support, whether from a coach, mentor, or peer, behavior change is unlikely. The exception to this is if there is a series of workshops occurring at regular intervals, if the focus is on genuine communication, conversation, and feedback, and if participants are held accountable for changing their behavior. In such cases, workshop participants become peers (regardless of their position in the hierarchy) and learn the skills of peer development, which in turn, results in changing behavior, even among senior leaders.

While workshops may not offer the best support methodology for executives, they do, nevertheless, play a critical role in creating a successful organization and are discussed in more detail in Chapter Thirteen.

Executive Education Courses. Executive education courses held at prestigious universities or colleges are popular among senior leaders. And while leaders may benefit from the knowledge gained through such courses as well as the relationships built with fellow "senior" participants, it is rare for individuals to change their behavior in deep and profound ways as a result of their experiences. As a colleague suggested to me, such programs often do more to indicate the future organizational successors and boost egos, rather than actually develop their leadership. They consume both financial and time resources, but in many organizations, these courses are a rite of passage. While for some they may be an appropriate developmental support methodology, I would argue that for most organizations, the time and money required for these courses could today be better spent developing customized programs either for the organization or the individual.

Chapter Seven Takeaways

1. Any senior leader who has participated in a leadership assessment must act on their newly acquired knowledge. By publicly acknowledging a commitment to developing their leadership, they dispel the notion that they are out of touch and arrogant. Furthermore, by acknowledging they are working on their leadership, they set the stage for a culture of leadership learning to be embedded throughout the organization.

2. Ultimately, each leader must decide whether adoption of the recommended changes is realistic, practical, and helpful in achieving the personal and organizational visions.

3. Once a required change is identified, leaders should not simply "try and get better." Instead, they must reflect on what is driving this behavior in the first place. Their stage of action logic, beliefs about leadership, and mental models inherited from the past will all impact their behavior. Although they may need some skill development, more often than not (particularly at the executive level) they likely need a shift in perspective.

4. Successful behavioral change requires a deep commitment to change, a willingness to reflect deeply, and a committed and relevant support structure.

5. Senior leaders, perhaps more than any other within an organization, need support while changing and developing their leadership. This is due to the isolation often felt at the top. Excessive workloads can cause leaders to often lose perspective or fail to prioritize their own development, and the need to experience a paradigm other than that of a heroic leader.

6. Coaches can offer excellent support. The most effective executive coaches must be able to operate in between the two extremes of consultant and personal coach. They must also be familiar with the complexities of the executive role.

7. Senior leaders can also find great support in a mentor and should not restrict themselves to simply being a mentor for others within their organization. Often at the senior level, individuals are left to find a mentor on their own whom, more often than not, may be external to the organization.

8. Individual peers can offer great support to any leader who has developmental ambitions. Peers can act as a sounding board, conscience, mirror, role model, etc. Although executive team dynamics sometimes preclude an effective level of peer support, in cases where the team is highly functioning, peer support can be extremely powerful for both individuals and the organization as a whole.

9. Workshops can offer a form of peer support to participants. However, on their own, they are not enough to change behavior. The exception to this is if there are a series of workshops occurring at regular intervals; the focus is on genuine communication, conversation, and feedback; and participants are held accountable for changing their behavior.

10. Executive education courses often do more to indicate the future organizational successors and boost egos than actually develop their leadership. While for some they may be an appropriate developmental support methodology, for most, the time and money required for such courses could today be best spent developing customized programs either for the organization or the individual.

PUT YOURSELF FIRST

If you're like many of the clients with whom I work, you're probably more on the stressed, tired side than the energized, rested side. Indeed, in today's boundary-less world, the workload and time pressure that leaders experience every day is rapidly becoming a crisis, particularly at the top of the hierarchical pyramid. We struggle to find the answer. Time management has been replaced by work-life balance, yet nothing seems to change. Still we keep working hard, making promises to ourselves that this situation won't continue.

In all my work with senior leaders in organizations, I have yet to meet one single individual who did not want to be an effective leader and part of a successful organization. And while many of the problems, both at a personal and organizational level, are rooted in old models and paradigms, perhaps the most significant problem lies in an executive's inability to manage themselves in a manner that is healthy and sustainable. In shouldering huge organizational responsibilities, the passion for learning is subsumed. Executives spiral down a path of constant work and rarely are able to find time to recharge, refresh, and learn. They are viewed by others in the organization as distant and arrogant, while constantly having to make huge sacrifices for the good of the organization. Therefore, unless carefully managed, such good intentions can easily result in unsuccessful, toxic organizations.

Take Barry, for example. He's the COO of a 4,000-strong resource company—and he's a mess. He tells me that he literally has no free time in his calendar for three months. He works nonstop and considers the weekend a success if he finds the time to attend his son's hockey game—where he spends time checking his BlackBerry. He travels around the world, is continually changing time zones, and readily acknowledges that his own health and well-being has taken a back seat to the needs of the organization.

Barry is by no means a weak leader—quite the opposite in fact. I've known him for some time and he has the potential to be a fabulous leader for the organization. He is humble yet driven, personable and strategic, and he's practical and visionary. He has a reputation in the organization as being a good guy who's always willing to listen.

Unfortunately, Barry's strength has become his weakness. His willingness to be accessible comes with a huge price. In trying to do the right thing, he's ultimately doing the wrong thing. Barry no longer has the energy to lead in the way he needs to. He has a bad case of role overload.

THE PROBLEMS OF ROLE OVERLOAD

Role overload takes shape when individuals believe that the resources available to them are inadequate to deal with the demands of the job. Quite simply, they feel that they have too much to do in the amount of time available. The result is a Catch-22, where individuals experience a high degree of distraction and stress, which in turn compounds the situation.[1]

Role overload is an increasing problem in organizations. In 2001, 56 percent of employed Canadians reported high levels of role overload, an increase of over 14 percent since 1991. A survey of 150 human resources executives indicated that 70 percent of them believed employees in their firms were overburdened with work.[2]

The impact of role overload is a serious and increasing problem in many work environments. For example, in a survey of 270 salespeople in diverse industries,

- 72% of respondents reported that their job demands had prevented them from exercising regularly
- 69% of respondents reported that their job demands caused them to put on weight
- 59% reported that it caused them to become ill
- 49% indicated that it harmed their marriage or a significant relationship
- 37% suggested it contributed to a long-term health condition
- 33% reported it caused them to smoke or drink more alcohol
- 18% indicated that job demands prevented them from finding a significant other[3]

These are not simply unfortunate statistics, but are issues that significantly impact an individual's effectiveness—and ultimately, the company's bottom line. While this study refers to salespeople, I would argue that the situation at the executive level is significantly worse. The demands and associated degree of accountability felt by leaders typically intensifies as one reaches the upper echelon of the hierarchical pyramid. I have yet to come across an executive who has time on his or her hands. Most fail to take all the vacation to which they are entitled.

Clearly, one of the most serious problems with executive role overload is the impact on personal health. In the years since I've known Barry, he has gradually been putting on weight. He knows he must exercise more, but he just can't seem to find the time. His own exercise program continually takes a back seat to the needs of others in the organization. The dangers of his lifestyle are emphasized to him by doctors every time he has annual executive medical, yet the cycle continues. Barry is rapidly becoming a heart attack waiting to happen.

On the organizational front, problems are inevitable when an executive takes on too much and cannot control role overload. For example, in Barry's case, the organization has become dependent and reliant on him. His scope of work is so vast that should the proverbial bus come along, the organization would be extremely vulnerable without him. Through great intentions, Barry has made himself irreplaceable.

This situation is compounded when we consider how others view Barry within the organization. While all are happy to let Barry take on this role, many state, at least privately, that they have no desire to succeed him. These bright and, in many cases, young vice presidents are looking at the toll the job is taking on Barry and making conscious decisions to never assume his role. The organization does not yet know it, but problems with succession are inevitable.

ROLE OVERLOAD CAUSES SUCCESSFUL LEADERS TO FAIL

Despite his best intentions and talents, Barry is actually becoming a worse leader over time. While he got to his present position through high performance, with role overload, those factors that contributed to such performance are at risk.

High performance is known to result from self-regulation resources, such as self-efficacy beliefs and challenging personal goals.[4] Self-efficacy refers to individuals' beliefs that they possess the skills and resources necessary to succeed at a specific task.[5] When individuals become overloaded at work, this self-efficacy becomes compromised as they start to question whether they can in fact succeed. This question impacts self-efficacy, which in turn, has a direct impact on performance.[6] The situation is exacerbated for successful individuals such as Barry and other senior executives. Research suggests that high performers tend to be more affected by the distraction and stress of overload than are lower performers.[7]

There is increasing evidence that when one is experiencing role overload, the brain actually fails to function in a way that it can make smart decisions. This is not just a matter of simply being tired. Rather, a neurological event occurs which results in a compromised decision-making capacity.

E. Hallowell in the *Harvard Business Review*, offers an explanation of the neurology that clearly illustrates the extent to which an individual leader (and by implication an organization) is at risk when an individual is desperately trying to deal with more input than he possibly can.[8] In these circumstances, the part of the brain that governs survival starts to take control. In this mode, the deep, survival areas of the brain direct the executive functioning regions that guide such things as decision-making and planning, the organization and prioritization of information and ideas, and various other leadership tasks. The survival regions primitively interpret the messages of overload and furiously fire signals of fear, anxiety, impatience, irritability, anger, or panic. These alarms force the executive functioning frontal lobes to send messages back to the deep centers saying, "Message received. Trying to work on it but without success," which, in turn, causes the survival centers to send even more powerful messages of distress back up to the frontal lobes. As Hallowell suggests, the whole brain simply gets caught in a neurological Catch-22.

Meanwhile, in response to what's going on in the brain, the rest of the body shifts into crisis mode and changes its baseline physiology from peace and quiet to red alert. In this state, the executive function reverts to simple-minded black-and-white thinking; perspective and shades of gray disappear, intelligence dims. In a futile attempt to do more than is possible, the brain paradoxically reduces its ability to think clearly—something that is a serious problem when dealing with the complexities of leadership.

In its most extreme case, the result is not pretty. When role overload has caused a leader to operate in survival mode, the result is impulsive judgments, as the individual angrily rushes to bring closure to whatever matter is at hand. He or she feels compelled to get the problem under control immediately, to extinguish the perceived danger. Gone are flexibility, creativity, a sense of humor, an ability to deal with the unknown, the big picture, and the goals and values he or she stands for.

At these moments, there is a danger of melting down, throwing a tantrum, or blaming others. However, more common at the executive level is an opposite reaction in which individuals, firmly embedded in their own heroic paradigm, categorically deny or avoid the problems, only to spiral down a path of individual and organizational destruction. It's a classic case of the boiled frog scenario—place a frog in a pot of boiling water and it will jump out; put it in cold water and gradually heat the pot to boiling and the frog will remain until it is boiled.

Many of the problems regarding role overload can be traced back to the dominant action logic frame through which an individual makes sense of the world. Those at the Expert or Achiever stages will have an inherent tendency to overwork. Experts want to do things perfectly in the office and will tend to work at all hours of the day or night to ensure perfection. Achievers define themselves by results and output. If they were to fail to get something done, it would likely destroy their sense of self.

Overload is an adaptive problem

The issue of overload, overwork, and burnout is one that must be taken seriously by organizations. Yet the solution is not easy. The terminology used to address the problem itself reveals the extent to which we have grasped the complexity of the issue. It is commonly referred to as work-life balance. Consider for a moment the irony of this term. It suggests that when we are at work we are not engaged in life. Life is something that happens outside of work and the challenge is to find the right balance between when we are doing one versus when we are doing the other.

Such thinking is simplistic at best. Rather than looking for a balance, I believe we must look for an integration, whereby we live in the moment without guilt or concern that we should be investing energy elsewhere. And it is this integration that is the mark of an effective leader. Leadership itself is full of conflicting priorities; those who are able to adopt a later frame of action logic and are, therefore, more effective leaders are able to integrate these divergent priorities into a coherent and comfortable whole. Thus, the integration of the different elements of life, whether that is work, family, or recreation, is the mark of a well-accomplished leader.

This issue of role overload within today's workplace is complex, deep, and not easily resolved. Those who try to address it through simplistic policies or time management courses assume that it is a technical problem for which the answer is known. Usually, they unsuccessfully engage only in single-loop learning, in which individuals, groups, or organizations modify their actions according to the difference between expected and obtained outcomes.[9] The result might be a brief respite from the daily stresses, but does nothing to inherently resolve the problem on a permanent basis.

At issue is what R. Heifetz and D. Laurie refer to as an adaptive problem—those challenges for which the solution is unknown, unclear, and undiscovered. The resolution of such problems requires that we relinquish some of our deeply held beliefs and learn new skills.[10] We must engage in double-loop learning and question the values, assumptions, and policies that led to the actions in the first place.[11]

The resolution to this problem therefore requires deep reflection and thought, both on a personal and organizational level. Organizational challenges, and the manner in which a culture can be built to prevent role overload, will be addressed later in this book. Just like everything concerning organizational effectiveness, all attempts to address the problem must first start at a personal level.

In the past, role overload has always been viewed as rooted in problems with time management practices. However, as we move beyond the single-loop learning that such beliefs afford, alternative focuses for management must be adopted. As illustrated below, time management must move into energy management, which in turn, must move into self-management.

Figure 8.1   Time→Energy→Self-Management

Enough has been written on time management. While at some level it requires tactics to help maximize efficiency, it also requires making smart choices regarding how one spends one's time. Many are familiar with the time management matrix.[12] The challenge in implementing this logical and rational model is ensuring the filter through which one assesses both importance and urgency is based on personal and organizational leadership visions and not on old paradigms and traditions. Furthermore, it requires considerable self-management skills to move out of the quadrants of deception and waste.

	Urgent	Not Urgent

Important	Quadrant of Necessity
	Crises
	
	• Pressing problems
	• Deadline-driven
	  projects
		Quadrant of Quality
		and Personal
		Leadership
		• Prevention
		• Relationship building
		• Recognizing new
		  opportunities
		• Planning recreation

Not
Important
	Quadrant of Deception
	• Interruptions, some
	  calls
	• Some mail, some
	  reports
	• Some meetings
	• Proximate, pressing
	  matters
	• Popular activities
		Quadrant of Waste
		• Trivia, busy work
		• Some mail
		• Some phone calls
		• Time wasters
		• Pleasant activities

ENERGY MANAGEMENT

An alternative perspective is offered by Jim Loehr and Tony Schwartz in their book *The Power of Full Engagement*. They propose that rather than worrying about completing all the activities in the time they have, leaders should instead consider their workload from the concept of the energy they have to get it done.[13] The theory of energy management is simple, but compelling. Unless we have energy, we cannot possibly lead effectively. Just as intelligence emerges in different domains, the same is true with energy. Our energy comes in the form of physical energy, emotional energy, mental energy, and spiritual energy. Leaders not only need to pay attention to their own energy, but also the energy of those they lead. Indeed, Loehr and Schwartz consider leaders to be the stewards of organizational energy.

The foundation of our energy is our physical state of being. If we are well rested, well fed, fit, and healthy, we will have physical energy—nothing earth-shattering here. But the piece we often miss is that this state is essential for effective leadership. How can we be emotionally intelligent or have mental clarity if we are exhausted? We can't. We know that. Yet despite the fact that having sufficient energy resources are a prerequisite for effective leadership, most executives I know fail to make this a priority. As busy leaders, many fail to find the time to eat properly, to exercise, and to get enough sleep. They jump on planes, travel through time zones, grab a quick snack when they can, and wind down with a few drinks at the end of the crazy day. As in Barry's case, their physical well-being seems to take a back seat to the job of leading.

No one can lead effectively if they adopt practices such as these. Effective leadership starts with taking care of yourself—by committing to eat right, getting enough rest, and exercising regularly. If leaders do this, they create the possibility that they can lead effectively. Without it, all their best intentions will likely fail to reach fruition.

To ensure you have physical energy you should

- Eat five or six low-calorie meals a day
- Drink lots of water
- Get seven to eight hours of sleep per day
- Go to bed early and wake up early
- Take a recovery break every 90 to 120 minutes (which means no more four-hour meetings—your employees will love you for this!)

Another energy domain is that of emotional energy. This is that feeling of being up—being positive. When leaders have emotional energy, they can be emotionally intelligent, portray a sense of confidence, and inspire others. Physical energy is a precondition to attaining emotional energy. With sufficient physical energy we are able to commit to seeing things as positive, looking at the world through a "cup-half-full" lens—the very foundation of emotional energy. To ensure you have emotional energy remember these tips:

- Pay attention to accessing your positive emotions. Negative emotions are costly and energy inefficient. To be an effective leader you must be able to access positive emotions in stressful times.
- The keys to accessing positive emotions are self-confidence and self-control.

Mental energy is the energy we need to focus our attention, to concentrate, and to organize our lives. In this world of distractions and overstimulation, it requires mental stamina or energy to stay on task—and to implement Covey's time management matrix. Mental energy comes from visualization, clarity of talk, self-talk, etc. To access your mental energy,

- Ensure you maintain realistic optimism
- Pay attention to mental preparation, visualization, positive self-talk, effective time management

- Remember that physical exercise stimulates cognitive capacity
- Continually refresh and review your vision for personal leadership. It will give the clarity you need to maintain mental energy.

Finally, but in some ways most importantly, there is spiritual energy. Spiritual energy provides the force for action in all dimensions of our lives. It is derived from a connection to deeply held values and a purpose beyond our self-interest. Although for some this is associated with religion, for many it is simply being connected to a higher purpose, above and beyond one's self-interest. It is deeply honoring one's values, which drive us to do what we believe to be right. For example, if we have a deep belief in the value of family, we will move mountains to do what is right for our children, to protect them, and to take care of ourselves so we can be there for them. Amazing things are possible once we move beyond self-interest. So consider your higher purpose: what do you hold dear? Ask yourself if you are honoring your purpose and values in your daily actions. And if not, why not? Have you perhaps lost your way a bit in all this craziness?

We need energy in the physical, emotional, mental, and spiritual domains. But we cannot, and indeed should not, endeavor to maintain high levels of energy at all times. Such linearity wears us down and, ultimately, drains and depletes us of our energy. Instead, we need to adopt an oscillatory energy policy, which means having periods of intense energy usage followed by periods of energy renewal. During periods of high energy use, we are alive, vibrant, pushing the limits, etc., but we can't remain at this peak forever—we need to come down. So at regular intervals, we need to consciously enter a phase of energy renewal by doing whatever it is that refuels and recharges our depleted energy reservoirs—exercising, relaxing with friends, reading a good book. This does not include watching TV or working on the computer—these activities have been shown to drain energy rather than rejuvenate it.

Accepting that leadership means paying attention to energy management requires a paradigm shift. *Instead of managing time, we must manage energy.* We need to seek stress, not avoid it, but this requires us to view downtime as productive and not wasted time. We must view life as a series of sprints, rather than a marathon. This new paradigm suggests that we should use purpose, rather than rewards to fuel energy, and incorporate rituals, rather than self-discipline into our life.

Regardless of whether one adopts time management or energy management strategies, ultimately, the only way to address the issue of role overload is through effective self-management. It requires setting firm boundaries and making what might seem to be tough decisions, which in turn, requires having a deep understanding of self.

Thus, it is crucial, when reviewing how to bring things back to a manageable level, to understand who you are as a person and how you define yourself. Then it requires adopting the development strategies discussed earlier.

The development of your own leadership capacity is the first stage in creating a great organization. While the journey will never be complete, those who have demonstrated a willingness to develop themselves as a leader, and are working on their development on an ongoing basis, are now in a position to consider what is happening with the top team, a subject that is explored in depth in the following chapters.

Chapter Eight Takeaways

1. The workload and time pressure that leaders experience every day is rapidly becoming a crisis, particularly at the top of the hierarchical pyramid. The problem is rooted in executives' inability to manage themselves in a way that is healthy and sustainable.

2. Role overload takes shape when individuals believe that the resources available to them are inadequate to deal with the demands of the job. Quite simply, they feel that they have too much to do in the amount of time available. The result is a Catch-22—individuals experience a high degree of distraction and stress, which in turn compounds the situation.

3. Role overload is very prevalent at the executive level. The demands and associated degree of accountability felt by leaders typically intensifies as one reaches the upper echelon of the hierarchical pyramid.

4. Many problems occur when executives experience role overload. The executive's health and capacity is likely to suffer, the organization becomes vulnerable due to an overdependence on them, and future successors lose interest in assuming the role together with the associated stress.

5. When one is experiencing role overload, the brain actually fails to function in a way that it can make smart decisions. A neurological event occurs, which results in a compromised decision-making capacity. Gone are flexibility, creativity, a sense of

humor, an ability to deal with the unknown, the big picture, and the goals and values for which the leader stands. Therefore, role overload results in ineffective leadership, something that is often denied at the executive level.

6. The issue of role overload within today's workplace is a complex, adaptive problem and not easily resolved. It requires more than simplistic policies or time management courses. Rather than striving for work-life balance, we must look for an integration of all aspects of life. Those who are able to adopt a later frame of action logic and are more effective leaders are able to integrate these divergent priorities into a coherent and comfortable whole, thereby avoiding role overload.

7. Unless we have energy, we cannot possibly lead effectively. Just as intelligence emerges in different domains, the same holds true with energy. Our energy comes in the form of physical energy, emotional energy, mental energy, and spiritual energy. Leaders not only need to pay attention to their own energy, but also the energy of those they lead.

8. We cannot, and indeed should not, endeavor to maintain high levels of energy at all times. Instead, we need to adopt an oscillatory energy policy, which means having periods of intense energy usage followed by periods of energy renewal. During periods of high energy use, we are alive, vibrant, pushing the limits, etc. At regular intervals we need to consciously enter a phase of energy renewal by doing whatever it is that refuels and recharges our depleted energy reservoirs.

9. Accepting that leadership means paying attention to energy management requires a paradigm shift. Instead of managing time, we must manage energy. We need to seek stress, not avoid it, but this requires us to view downtime as productive and not as wasted time. We must view life as a series of sprints, rather than a marathon.

PART THREE

UNDERSTAND WHAT COULD BE AMISS WITH YOUR TOP TEAM

As discussed earlier, the increase in the complexity of organizational life and the associated decline of the heroic leader demand that individual leaders behave differently than they might have in the past. However, the development of an effective organization does not stop with individual behavior. These changes away from a mechanistic organization and the heroic leadership style are profound and have a ripple effect that impacts every aspect of organizational life, something that is not often fully appreciated by those at the top.

We know that no executive can transform an organization for which they are responsible unless they themselves are an effective and highly developed leader. Therefore, organizational transformation starts with doing individual and personal work. But that, on its own, is not enough. While it is a prerequisite, other elements are essential. Indeed, if you think you can transform an organization by transforming yourself, you are still embedded in the heroic model. You must now pay attention to those around you. And the place to start is with the executive team.

Teams are essential to any organization. As Peter Senge suggested in his famous work *The Fifth Discipline*, "Team learning is vital because teams, not individuals, are the fundamental learning units in modern organizations. This is where 'the rubber meets the road.' Unless teams can learn, the organization cannot learn."[1] What is often forgotten is that this applies not only to departmental or cross-functional teams, but also to the executive team. The move away from the heroic model has highlighted this more than ever.

In the past, the CEO ran the organization while the executive team informed and supported him (and yes, it was typically a male). In such cases, the executive team largely assumed either an information sharing or advising role for the CEO. Ultimately, the CEO made the decisions and acted relatively autocratically. This meant that there was no pressing need for the executive team to be a highly collaborative body. They primarily acted as heads of their respective silos, leaving integration to happen at the CEO level.

While such a model might have been effective in the past (and there is much to suggest that it actually was not), there is no doubt that the complexities of today's environment call for a different model. With the CEO shedding the heroic model, the role of the executive team must also change. Increasingly, teams are required to coordinate the implementation of strategic initiatives and make enterprise-level decisions.

If the top team is to collectively run the enterprise and assume the role that the CEO had unilaterally held in the past, the team must be an aligned and cohesive unit. Without cohesion, ineffective and faulty decision-making is bound to ensue. Therefore, a highly functioning, collaborative executive team is essential if organizations are to be competitive in the world today. They must be able to respond to a wide variety of situations and have flexibility and fluidity—something that we only see in highly developed teams.

Others support this notion. As D. Nadler and J. Spencer point out: "The complexities and demands associated with running an enterprise in today's environment require more resources than one person alone can typically bring to the task. As a consequence, executive teams are emerging as a major fixture of corporate governance."[2] Burruss et al. concur: "[Executive] teams are not only a feasible means of providing organizational leadership but . . . they are also increasingly necessary as the demands of top roles outdistance the capacities of any single person."[3]

Consequently, the development of an effective organization in today's world demands the development of an effective executive team whose members are able to move beyond silo thinking and assume collective leadership of the enterprise. Increasingly, research advocates the importance of shared leadership[4] and provides "clear support for the conclusion that the top team, rather than the top person, has the greatest effects on organizational functioning."[5]

It is clear that the extent to which C-suite executives can work collaboratively with their fellow executives directly impacts the bottom line of an organization. Teamwork at the top visibly demonstrates to all employees the expected organizational standards for communication and collaboration. When an executive team is firing on all cylinders, it is able to generate creative ideas and multiple alternatives, and utilize the members' diverse experience to solve difficult and complex problems.

A highly functioning executive team is better able to cope with the turbulence and complexity in the external environment. Edmondson, Roberto, and Watkins state, "Teamwork [at the top] allows the CEO to engage in a participative group process through which diverse members wrestle together with difficult issues to make decisions and build commitment to implementing them, giving rise to strategic leadership effectiveness."[6] Furthermore, as Burruss et al. suggest, "A team approach to executive leadership can provide the flexibility to transcend the traditional style mentality that pervades many organizations and to effectively manage the important but often ambiguous white spaces that live between those silos."[7] The net result is strategic leadership effectiveness and organizational success.

Unfortunately, the reverse is also true. Executive teams consisting of high-performing individuals who put the success of their own divisions ahead of the collective organizational well-being do a tremendous, and often unrecognized, amount of harm. Such behavior sends a clear message to the organization that, despite what may be articulated, what matters most is keeping one's own house in order. A culture of silos and individualism pervades the organization. While individual executives in this group may be respected, collectively, they tend to be viewed with disdain. As a result, employees will tend to blame "them" (as they are typically referred to) for a host of things that are not going well within the organization.

Several in-depth case studies document how dysfunctional group dynamics can lead to errors in judgment and flawed decisions. I.L. Janis's famous work on groupthink attributed certain foreign policy fiascoes to the pressures for conformity that arise within cohesive senior groups,[8] and J. Ross and B. Staw conducted case studies examining how groups of senior executives escalate commitment to failing courses of action.[9]

Executive teams often fail to realize the influence they have within an organization. Not long ago I was discussing this fact with a manager who was two levels below the executive of a large global corporation. For him, the influence of the executive group (both positive and negative) was clear: "People take their lead from the executive team in terms of how they should act to be perceived as successful at [this company] and either conform accordingly, disengage and are not very effective or satisfied, or leave to find a work environment more suited to their values. As such, the executive has the ability to influence culture here in a big way, by modeling the behavior they want to see corporate-wide."

In this same organization, the results of the survey I conducted with managers up to three levels below the executive confirms the importance of the executive (or top management team) leadership. One hundred percent of managers agreed with the statement "I believe that effective top management team leadership is needed for organizations to succeed in today's business environment."

HOW EXECUTIVE TEAMS ARE PERFORMING

Traditional thinking would suggest that the most effective teams are those at the top. Given the influence they have, one would like to think so. Unfortunately, for the most part, their performance seems to be mediocre at best.

Consider the work of Burruss et al.[10] Using a criteria that took into account 1) whether the performance of the team met or exceeded the standards of the people both inside and outside the organization who were most affected by the team's work; 2) how well members work together now to enhance—rather than undermine—their capability to work together in the future; and 3) whether the group experience, on balance, contributed positively to the learning and personal development of individual team members, this group assessed the effectiveness of more than 120 senior leadership teams. As illustrated below, less than one-quarter of the teams were outstanding, a little more than one-third were mediocre, and well over one-third were quite poor. This is hardly a great endorsement of widespread senior leadership team effectiveness.

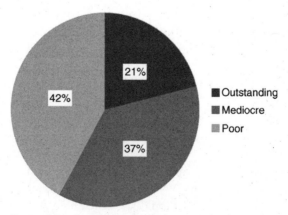

Figure 9.1   Performance of Senior Leadership Team

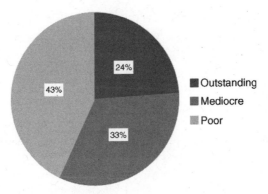

Figure 9.2   Quality of Team and Individual Development

Edmondson, Roberto, and Watkins provide a compelling sum-
mary of research and anecdotal evidence confirming that executive
teams often fail to achieve their potential.[11] While some studies
found that many senior teams do not engage in real teamwork,
others have reported that executive teams can find it difficult to
resolve conflict,[12] build commitment,[13] or reach closure in a timely
fashion.[14]

Research conducted jointly by the executive search firm Heidrick
& Struggles and the University of Southern California's Center for
Effective Organizations surveyed 60 top HR executives from Fortune 500 companies. Only a disturbing 6 percent reported that "the
executives in our C-suite are a well-integrated team."[15]

Many senior teams appear to be unaware that they are perhaps
not as effective as they could, or indeed should, be. In early 2008,
The Refinery Leadership Partners Inc. commissioned Ipsos Reid to
survey 151 C-suite executives across Canada and the United States
about leadership performance and development practices. The results suggest that executive offices across North America are full of
senior leaders who are extremely confident in their own leadership
ability—so confident, in fact, that they may have a distorted view of
their effectiveness. Asked to rate their personal performance as leaders,
74 percent of executives surveyed said they are doing somewhat or
much better than other executives in their industry. An astounding
86 percent of respondents believed they collaborate somewhat better
or much better than other executives do. The majority of respondents
(79 percent) believed they are somewhat, or much more, aware than
their competitors of the issues and challenges facing employees, and
72 percent said that their fellow executive team members are somewhat or much more aware.

This data suggests that executives themselves are unaware of the extent of the problem. Indeed, in all my work with executive teams it is rare that I have come across a group that has a well-developed sense of how effective they are as a team. The insularity of executive teams and a lack of good examples tend to lull them into thinking all is well.

An executive team I have been working with for a number of years has productive relationships with their fellow team members. They enjoy each other's company and have, over the last few years, come a long way in how they relate to each other. Compared with where they were, they have reason to be proud. However, I would not call them a high-performing team by any account. Their conversation is pleasant, but rarely controversial. Outside of the team and in the privacy of coaching conversations, I hear views expressed that are never shared in the team forum. Deference to the CEO is still ever-present and, on more than one occasion, I have witnessed groupthink.

When I ask this team to reflect on its performance, they tell me that they think they are great. They support their argument by saying, "Compared to what we see in other organizations, we're really good." True enough, but I question the standard that they compare themselves to. Executive team excellence is a rare phenomenon and being "better than dysfunctional" is hardly the definition of excellence. These teams lack role models for excellence, which makes it difficult for groups to set realistic, yet high, standards for their team. Put simply, they don't know what executive team excellence looks like and, as a result, they tend to equate a lack of conflict with great team performance. They fail to go outside of their own group to seek real feedback on how they are viewed by others within the organization and fall victim to a degree of complacency around the executive table regarding their own team behavior.

All in all, this paints a disturbing picture of what is happening—or not happening—at the top, regarding executive team effectiveness. As a manager in the organization surveyed on the effectiveness of the team at the top told us: "Leadership among the executive team varies greatly. Conflicts between some of them have a significant impact. These conflicts prevent the development of a strong sense of team throughout [the organization] which prevents us from being able to achieve great things. However, if all members of the executive team showed leadership by consistently putting the company's interests ahead of their own, consistently choosing the company's values, disciplining themselves to focus on the big picture instead of the details, and telling the CEO and board the same things they tell their staff, you would see a significant positive change at the company."

EXECUTIVE TEAM DEMOGRAPHICS

I am often asked what role demographics plays in executive team effectiveness. Can organizational effectiveness be achieved by ensuring the correct demographic makeup of the executive team? In fact, a school of thought exists in which it is believed that the demographic characteristics of the executive team influence organizational strategic choices and outcomes. Researchers have attempted to correlate variables such as age, tenure, education, and functional background to organizational outcomes such as sales growth, innovation, and executive turnover.

Although studies have found relationships between demographic variables and outcomes, the data have produced conflicting results. For example, similarity in tenure has been found by some to be associated with higher organizational performance and growth.[16] However, others have found that tenure heterogeneity is negatively associated with firm performance.[17] Therefore, few, if any, conclusions have been determined from this research. The problem lies in the fact that while the top team's demographics may stay relatively constant, the problems and challenges they are faced with do not. Executive teams are faced with tasks that are complex, variable, and unstructured. The team composition generally remains stable while the situation may not. With each challenge an executive team is faced with, team members likely have differing interests and information. How these differences are handled plays a significant role in determining the ultimate effectiveness of the executive team.

Gender mix on the top team

The one area in which the research has been unequivocal is in the area of gender diversity. Given the traditionally male makeup of the executive team, studies have focused on the impact the inclusion of women in the executive team has on organizational effectiveness. The data clearly indicate that gender diversity at the top boosts the bottom line. For example, in a study of 101 large corporations, McKinsey found that companies with three or more women in a senior management function scored higher than companies with no women at the top on nine criteria of organizational excellence, including key factors such as leadership, accountability, and innovation. Likewise, Pepperdine University found that the 25 Fortune 500 firms with the best record of promoting women to high positions were between 18 percent and 69 percent more profitable than the median Fortune 500 firms in their industries.

The reason for this is clear. Studies at Cornell and Stanford have shown that adding women to the top team changes the team dynamics and "stirs up the pot" in positive ways. This in turn encourages debate and innovation. The London Business School has suggested that in instances where innovation is key, organizations should construct teams with an equal number of men and women in order to maximize the diversity of the talent pool.

While gender diversity will positively impact organizational performance, it is not the only solution. Indeed, there are many barriers that impede executive team effectiveness. Few executive teams with whom I have worked are aware of how the dynamics at the top can impact team performance, thereby failing to take them into account, resulting in the predominance of mediocre executive teams that are common throughout organizations today.

These dynamics are discussed in detail in the next chapter, while Chapter Eleven describes strategies to overcome these dynamics and gain a significant competitive advantage through executive team performance.

Chapter Nine Takeaways

1. In the past, the CEO ran the organization, while the executive team informed and supported him. However, the complexities of today's environment now call for a different model. Increasingly, highly functional executive teams are required to coordinate the implementation of strategic initiatives and make enterprise-level decisions, tasks that, in the past, were performed solely by the CEO.

2. The development of an effective organization in today's world demands the development of an effective executive team whose members are able to move beyond silo thinking and assume collective leadership of the enterprise. Therefore, a highly functioning, collaborative executive team is essential if organizations are to be competitive in today's world. The extent to which C-suite executives can work collaboratively with their fellow executives directly impacts the bottom line of an organization.

3. Executive teams consisting of high-performing individuals who put the success of their own divisions ahead of the collective organizational well-being do a tremendous, and often unrecognized, amount of harm. Such behavior sends a clear message to the organization that despite what may be articulated, what

matters most is keeping one's own house in order. A culture of silos and individualism pervades the organization.

4. Traditional thinking would suggest that the most effective teams are those at the top. Unfortunately, for the most part, their performance seems to be mediocre at best. Research suggests that many executive teams often fail to achieve their potential, do not engage in real teamwork, and find it difficult to resolve conflict, build commitment, or reach closure in a timely fashion.

5. Although studies have found relationships between demographic variables such as tenure, age, education, etc. of the executive team and team outcomes, the research has produced conflicting results. The one exception to this is gender. Research clearly indicates that gender diversity at the top boosts the bottom line.

RECOGNIZE HOW EXECUTIVE TEAM DYNAMICS PROMOTES MEDIOCRITY

Few executives pay much attention to the dynamics that await them as they join the top team. Many assume that the team will function on autopilot with such bright and talented people among the executive membership. However, such naïveté can seriously impact team effectiveness. Indeed, any executive that fails to pay attention to executive team dynamics is likely to alienate themselves from the workforce. The poor team performance described in the previous chapter is inevitable; the world of "them" is further exacerbated and organizational greatness becomes an elusive dream.

BARRIERS TO TOP TEAM EFFECTIVENESS

While it would be easy to offer simplistic explanations for poor executive team performance, a closer examination reveals that many of the problems can be found in some deep-rooted, systemic problems—problems that are faced only by the team at the top. As D. Nadler points out, senior teams are different, and embedded in these differences are a number of factors that make the development of a high-performing executive team very challenging.[1]

Organization versus silo of responsibility

Executives have two domains of responsibility—their own "silo" and the organization as a whole. They live at the intersection of these two places and need to integrate the responsibilities associated with each.

Executives must look down and across the organization. It is only when looking across the organization that the executive team comes into play. While team members may understand this intellectually, it is often a struggle to put the organization's needs ahead of their individual department or division. After all, it is what they have always done. They were promoted to the executive team as a reward for successfully running their group. As I will explain in the next chapter, insufficient work is done on clarifying the purpose of the executive team and, therefore, individual executives assume they are sitting around the table simply to represent the interests of their own group.

In addition, most executives are not rewarded for exceptional senior team performance. Rewards focus on the short term and on successes within their own silos. Providing they at least remain collegial with their peers, they (or at least the CEO) see little incentive to invest in team development.

There is no simple blueprint for when an executive needs to focus on the organization rather than focusing on their own silo. Furthermore, while at times the executive group does need to be a highly effective team, in other instances there is no value in collaborating. These circumstances will be discussed in more detail in the next chapter. However, executives have little training in determining when collaboration is required and when it is not. Instead, they use the times when interdependence is not required to gain comfort that

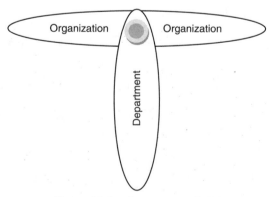

Figure 10.1   Organizational "T"

the executive team can simply remain as a working group and need not become a highly functioning team.

External versus internal

One of the primary roles of an executive team is to manage the external environment. This is an area that places considerable and unique demands on the executive team. More than any other, the team at the top must pay attention to the individuals who are external to the organization. However, nurturing relationships with investors, shareholders, and board members often takes precedence over spending time with employees or with each other.

Years ago, I was asked to work with an executive group that was a long way from being a highly functioning team. During the course of my first meeting with them I was astounded to learn that they never met as a group. When I questioned them about this, it became clear that they viewed their primary role to be the management of the external environment. When time permitted, they met with their employees within their own silo. Meeting together as an executive team was relegated to a much lower priority, and given the pressures of time, it never took place.

This team suffered from the pressures of a centrifugal force that was pulling them away from each other. Despite good intentions, the combination of external demands and geographic limitations (most of this group had extensive world travel schedules) created circumstances that made the development of an executive team virtually impossible.

Divergent information

As a result of being more focused on their own groups or their own external environments, team members often arrive at an executive meeting with quite divergent information. For example, a mining company I worked with had a problem with production at one of its remote mine sites. In this case, the COO clearly had considerably more information than his fellow team members. It set up an interesting dynamic in that team members had taken for granted some assumptions and competing mental models. The COO misinterpreted some of the comments from the team as criticism and he also failed to fully disclose all the information he had. None of this was due to bad intent, but because he failed to recognize the relevance of it.

The failure to fully disclose or fully appreciate information can seriously impact the decision-making process that a top team must engage in. The net result is likely to be a decrease in the quality of the outcome.

Divergent interests

A dominant focus on departmental silos or the external environment can also result in the executive team having different interests. This is much more likely to take place when the purpose of the team has not been clearly defined. And depending on how differing interests are handled, this can lead to what Lax and Sebenius define as "value-creating" and "value-claiming" behaviors.[2] Value-creating behavior, clearly the healthiest option, consists of finding ways to advance similar interests in a way that benefits the organization as a whole. However, when interests are not completely aligned, individuals may be motivated to capture or "claim" as much value as they can. In these cases, individuals may focus on making themselves "look good" at the expense of the collective good.

Value-claiming behavior is extremely problematic at the executive level. It can result in a decrease in the generation of new options; individuals can undermine efforts to advance shared goals; and teams may lack commitment in implementing decisions and be less motivated to work together in the future, as this behavior tends to lead to winners and losers.

A focus on individual departments and the external environment, combined with a mechanistic way of thinking can, therefore, result in a misalignment of team members' knowledge and interests. While this is the case in any team, it is more extreme in an executive team and can be a recipe for executive team dysfunction, regardless of the demographic composition of the team.

Power centralization

Within an executive team, the CEO is not only the leader of the team, but also the leader of the organization. Regardless of whether or not one has moved away from the heroic model, the CEO holds the ultimate power within the team. The CEO can do things no other leader can in terms of shaping the agenda, setting the rules, declaring issues off limits, and making decisions. Given this, no matter whether or not the CEO demands it, in the case of the executive team there is often a degree of social distance between the CEO and members of the team.

Compounding this is the rarely spoken of topic of CEO succession. This plays into the team dynamics quite significantly. In any executive team it is possible that one of the team will succeed the CEO. At the very least, it is on everyone's mind. When this happens, one person wins while some, if not all, of the team lose. The anticipation of this event can become a source of conflict and competition on the team, even if it is not overtly expressed.

This rarely acknowledged and frequently disregarded dynamic has a significant impact on executive team effectiveness. The power that resides with the CEO, whether it be real or just perceived, can cause individual team members to be somewhat guarded in putting forth their views. Not wanting to seem incompetent or vulnerable, few are willing to venture outside of their comfort zone and offer radical or incomplete opinions. Therefore, power centralization with the CEO causes a withholding of information, which exacerbates the inherent dysfunction that exists from team members having divergent information.

Furthermore, executive team members are rarely willing to challenge peers in the public forum, as most are anxious to be seen as team players. I recently coached an individual who was invited to be a guest at a senior operations team meeting. At one point, a colleague sitting next to my coachee whispered his disapproval of what Joe, another VP, was presenting. This individual could clearly see problems with Joe's approach, but was unwilling to openly challenge him. When the person I was coaching questioned the reasons for the silence, his colleague stated, "It's not my job to make him look bad in front of his boss. If what he was saying impacted my department, you bet I would have said something, but otherwise it's not up to me to comment."

Such self-censoring is, unfortunately, all too common in executive teams. As a result, the team fails to learn and grow. Honest dialogue goes underground and is replaced by game playing, in which safe questioning takes the place of genuine challenging. While it can happen in varying degrees, the presence of any form of such politicking can only serve to inhibit trust, quality relationships, and, ultimately, effectiveness on the team.

The irony is that more than in any other group within the organization it is the executive team that must have the ability to engage in real and candid conversation if the complex problems facing an organization on a regular basis are to be addressed. Indeed, it is the complexity of the work requirements that often defines the uniqueness of the executive team. As D. Nadler points out, managing internal operations, external relationships, leadership, and strategic decision-making creates more intricate tasks than those facing other teams.[3]

THE CONTINUUM OF AUTHENTICITY

Regardless of their level in the organization, we know that the most effective teams are those that are able to speak openly, honestly, and with integrity. However, such openness can only help the team (and by extension the organization) when it is done with the best interests of the team in mind. The purpose of the communication combined

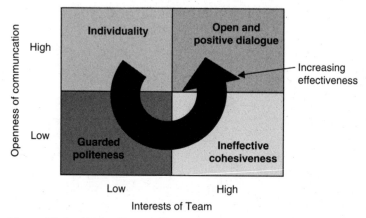

Figure 10.2   Senior Team Effectiveness (Openness of Communication versus Interests of Team)

with its degree of openness will determine whether the communication helps or hinders the group. This can best be represented by Figure 10.2.

Individuality

At the executive level, authenticity itself is no guarantee of team effectiveness. When openness is combined with a focus on a personal rather than an organizational agenda, it can significantly impact the effectiveness of the team. In the worst cases, team members can be openly hostile towards each other. This typically happens when there is no clear purpose for the team and there is little, if any, power centralization. I witnessed this in a group where a young up-and-coming vice president had been transferred from the head office. He openly stated that he viewed his current role simply as a stepping-stone to further his career. His number one focus was making his department look good and he had no interest in working with the executive team—except in instances where it would directly benefit his own group. He clearly exhibited an Opportunist stage of action logic.

He would show up at executive meetings openly hostile, particularly towards one other vice president (whom he regarded as potential competition). The situation was exacerbated by the fact that the CEO was weak, was not well respected, and detested any form of conflict (a Diplomat stage of action logic). His reaction to the hostility was to ask that the two VPs "work it out." The CEO was not prepared to intervene or deal with it in any way. Not surprisingly, the situation was not resolved until the aggressive VP was transferred after a couple of years. The conflict did irreparable harm to the organization, from which it is still suffering today.

When I questioned the CEO about this, his response was interesting (although I did not get anywhere in persuading him he could not ignore this conflict). He believed that the team was actually moving towards high effectiveness, as he believed the conflict was evidence that they had entered the storming phase. What he failed to realize was that the intent of the conflict was not to further the team effectiveness, but to further individual agendas.

Those executives who have risen to the top team of an organization are typically high-powered individuals who have distinguished themselves through individual achievement, rather than through working with teams. While they would have had to develop good working relationships with others in the organization, most attained the executive role by personally being front and center, as distinct from gaining notoriety through building a highly successful team.

With this background, it is not surprising that there is an inherent bias to continue to build their own silo or department, rather than compromise their own group's accomplishments for the common good. While organizational success is important, many members of the executive team view personal success as critical.

In addition, the idea that they may need to learn how to be an effective member of an executive team is tantamount to acknowledging they may be flawed in some way. On more than one occasion I've witnessed executives recoil at the notion that, perhaps, some development may be required in the area of executive team behavior. They see themselves as successful individuals—something that is reinforced by the special meaning that is inherent in executive team membership. As the ultimate team in the organization, membership brings with it a special status and organizational recognition. It's the organizational acknowledgment that great success has been achieved—something that hardly promotes a passionate desire to learn and grow.

Guarded politeness

One of the most common types of communication we see among executive team members is what I call the "guarded politeness" form. In this case, the dynamics of power centralization tend to dominate. Team members are polite and jovial with each other, yet they filter their communication to some degree. At one level, they appear harmonious. Yet at another, they are grossly ineffective.

Executive teams get stuck in "guarded politeness," as they tend to be very conflict averse.

We know the only way that a group of people can develop into a high-performing team is if they are willing to go through a period of conflict or "storming." Regardless of which model of team development one adopts, all models include a phase in which team members are willing to allow differences and disagreements to surface.

Yet this is no easy task for a member of the executive team. Not only do the power dynamics tend to inhibit the individual executive, but the fact that he or she has limited exit options also causes some to be very risk and conflict averse in this regard.

When an individual is a member of a team elsewhere in the organization, there are typically other options available to them if, for whatever reason, things don't work out within their own team— perhaps a move to another department or another region. However, an executive team member does not have this luxury. If their actions cause them to be rejected by a team (or even worse, the CEO), their only option is to exit the team and leave the organization.

This means the stakes are high. Given these limited exit options, most executives instead prefer to play it safe and not rock the boat unduly. It is a rare executive that is willing to challenge his or her peers or the CEO. More often than not, he or she would not take this high-risk strategy, but choose instead to remain on an amicable, yet ineffective, level with team members.

The situation is compounded by the fact that the executive team does not work in a vacuum. They are observed and talked about, and their behavior is frequently analyzed by many people within the organization. Small and inconsequential actions can easily become major events through which others in the organization infer much. This increased visibility will tend to keep the team in a conflict-free, yet ineffective, equilibrium.

The net result is a team in which individuals are reluctant to be honest and choose instead to avoid conflict at any cost. This is the "polite and guarded" team. And it is one that gives rise to executive team "elephants," things that are known but never discussed around the executive table. There are typically four of these "elephants": 1) the distribution of power between team and CEO; 2) succession issues; 3) relationships among team members; and 4) the failure of team members. With no clear boundaries for argument, dissent, or conflict, most executives prefer to turn a blind eye to these touchy subjects.

Ineffective cohesiveness

The behaviors associated with guarded politeness will, after a while, become normalized within the executive team. And it is at this point that the group is cohesive, yet ineffective. While they are more effective than when they are in the guarded politeness phase, communication is rarely more open. Yet their cohesiveness makes them blind to this fact and, worse, makes them very susceptible to groupthink.

Groupthink, a phenomenon first described by I.L. Janis, takes place when individual members are reluctant to put forth contradictory opinions for fear that such opinions may ostracize them from the group. As Janis described it, groupthink is a "mode of thinking that people engage in when they are deeply involved in a cohesive group, when the members' strivings for unanimity override their motivation to realistically appraise alternative courses of action."[4]

Janis maintained that any group can be susceptible to groupthink when they are highly cohesive, isolated from contradictory opinions, and led by a directive leader. The results can be disastrous for an organization, as the group experiences the suppression of dissent, polarization of attitude, and poor decision quality.

R.S. Baron has modified Janis's groupthink model and, instead, proposes a ubiquity model.[5] He contends that groupthink is far more widespread than first thought and is most likely to occur when the group has a strong sense of social identification, individuals have low self-efficacy, and salient norms overvalue shared information.

The implications of both the groupthink and ubiquitous models have profound implications for executive teams. The makeup and dynamics of executive teams suggest that they will be more susceptible to groupthink than most other teams within an organization.

An executive team has a strong sense of identification. They are the top team and are commonly referred to as such within organizations. Membership has its privileges and this "special treatment," whether it be the use of the corporate jet, extraordinary bonuses, or public recognition within the community, further emphasizes the unique and special nature of this team. Within the organization, they are referred to as a very distinct and exclusive group. The executive offices of one group with whom I work are all on the sixth floor. Within the organization, the executive team is known as "the sixth floor." Such labeling only serves to reinforce the sense of executive team identification.

It also serves to strengthen the sense of group cohesiveness. The group feels united, not because they are a high-performing team, but because others view them as different. In other words, the external view unites the team as distinct from internal processes.

At first blush, one would not expect members of an executive team to have low self-efficacy. After all, most appear as confident and capable individuals. But such appearances can be deceptive. As explained in Chapter Eight, excessive demands and overwork can cause individuals to question whether they can be successful. They begin to doubt themselves and may experience something that is surprisingly common at the senior leader level—"imposter syndrome." Those who experience this syndrome start to question whether they actually deserve the success they have achieved. Feelings of being a fraud start to creep into their psyche. Such individuals experience high levels of shame as they set high standards for themselves, yet, often due to things outside of their control, they do not always live up to their own standards. The net result is an increasing cycle of self-doubt and lowered self-efficacy.

Strong salient norms are often a result of an executive team becoming comfortable in the guarded politeness phase. As explained earlier, the power dynamics of executive teams result in a reluctance to offer conflicting views. Norms of guarded politeness start to become established. The team identity strengthens, and the norms become stronger. After a while, such norms become so entrenched that the preconditions for groupthink are established. In this case, executive team members have a greater concern for maintaining harmonious relations with fellow group members than exploring dissenting views. Furthermore, time urgency means groups will tend to favor shared information, rather than differing information. The source of differing rather than shared information becomes further limited by the isolation of the executive group. The common practices of managing up and filtering information mean that the executives fail to gain alternative and differing perspectives from others within the organization, further accentuating the groupthink phenomena.

Open and positive dialogue

As with any group, a team can only call itself effective if the dialogue is open and positive. An executive team is no exception in this regard. The problem is that teams who are either experiencing guarded politeness or have moved into ineffective cohesiveness often manage to convince themselves that all is well. After all, why shouldn't they? They enjoy each other's company, there is a high level of comfort with each other, and they feel supported by each other. Unfortunately, and somewhat naïvely, they equate their lack of conflict with high performance. Their focus is on what they are not, rather than on what they could be.

As outlined in the previous chapter, although the quality of executive teamwork can have a direct impact on organizational performance, a highly functional executive team is a rare phenomenon. This fact, unappreciated by many, should be a serious concern for all. The following chapter will describe in detail the steps that must be taken to ensure exemplary team performance.

Chapter Ten Takeaways

1. Senior teams are different, and embedded in these differences are a number of factors that make the development of a high-performing executive team very challenging. Few executives pay careful attention to the dynamics that await them as they join the top team. More often than not, these dynamics result in poor team performance and ineffective organizations.

2. There are many systemic barriers to executive team effectiveness. These include a bias towards individual departments rather than organizational needs, as well as insufficient time being spent on the internal workings of the organization due to external demands.

3. A focus on individual departments and the external environment, combined with a mechanistic way of thinking, can result in a misalignment of team members' knowledge and interests. While this is the case in any team, it is more extreme in an executive team and can be a recipe for executive team dysfunction.

4. Regardless of whether or not one has moved away from the heroic model, the CEO holds the ultimate power within the team. This rarely acknowledged and frequently disregarded dynamic has a significant impact on executive team effectiveness. The power that resides with the CEO, whether it be real or just perceived, can cause individual team members to be somewhat guarded in putting forth their views. Furthermore, executive team members are rarely willing to challenge peers in the public forum, as most are anxious to be seen as team players.

5. At the executive level, authenticity itself is no guarantee of team effectiveness. When openness is combined with a focus on a personal rather than an organizational agenda, it can significantly impact the effectiveness of the team. In the worst cases, team members can be openly hostile towards each other. When this occurs, the executive team is defined by individuality.

6. One of the most common forms of communication we see among executive team members is the "guarded politeness" form. In this case, the dynamics of power centralization tend to dominate. Team members are polite and jovial with each other, yet filter their communication to some degree. At one level, they appear harmonious. Yet at another, they are grossly

ineffective. Executive teams get stuck in guarded politeness, as they tend to be very conflict-averse. Individuals are reluctant to be honest and choose instead to avoid conflict at any cost. This gives rise to executive team "elephants"—things that are known but never discussed around the executive table.

7. The behaviors associated with guarded politeness will, after a while, become normalized within the executive team. It is at this point that the group is cohesive, yet ineffective. While they are more effective than when they are in the previous guarded politeness phase, communication in the ineffective cohesiveness phase is rarely more open. Yet their cohesiveness makes them blind to this fact and, worse, makes them very susceptible to groupthink.

8. As with any group, a team can only call itself effective if the dialogue is open and positive. An executive team is no exception in this regard. The problem is that teams that are either experiencing guarded politeness or have moved into ineffective cohesiveness often manage to convince themselves that all is well. They equate their lack of conflict with high performance. Only when dialogue is fully open and in the best interests of the team can they call themselves effective.

GET THE TOP TEAM WORKING

The starting point for developing a highly functioning executive team is to recognize that things are different at the top, requiring a different attention and focus. The development of an effective executive team rarely happens by chance, but rather it is a result of paying attention and addressing the dynamics inherent in any executive team. The steps to exemplary executive team performance are neither difficult nor complex. They do, however, require time, energy, and commitment. And this is only possible when executive team development is made a priority.

Executive teams that want to gain a competitive advantage need to focus on three areas—right purpose, right people, and right process. When all of these are in place, the dynamics that impede team performance can be overcome. The impact on the team and, consequently, organizational performance can be profound. However, until the team has a good understanding of how it is currently performing and, can, as Jim Collins reminds us, "confront the brutal facts," mediocrity will prevail.

STEP ONE: ASSESS THE TEAM'S PERFORMANCE

There are a number of ways to assess a team's performance. Not unlike the process that is required to assess individual performance, team members can reflect on, and look for, symptoms of dysfunction or success; employ a variety of assessment tools; or utilize a third party to help them conduct an accurate and honest assessment.

The audit: look for the clues

What are the clues that a team is, in fact, embedded in a zone of mediocrity? Given the lack of decent examples, what becomes important when looking for evidence of open and authentic, team-based dialogue? There are a few indicators that suggest the group, while not being dysfunctional, has yet to achieve real high performance:

- The CEO is rarely, if ever, challenged within the group.
- There has never been a period of "storming" or conflict as the team has strived to improve. Be careful not to confuse this with open, yet hostile, individual dialogue.
- The group is unwilling to admit they struggle with being a high-performing team. Ironically, the team that can publicly acknowledge that they have much work to do in order to become more effective is much more likely to be at a level of high performance than the team that is confident all is well.
- Individuals who go out on a limb and offer contrary opinions that are not quickly embraced by the remainder of the group tend to either (a) back down quickly, or (b) be tolerated simply because they are seen as different and quirky by the group.
- Individuals rarely, if ever, admit they are struggling, have made mistakes, or need help. Vulnerability and its associated emotions make others feel uncomfortable and results in either platitudes or changing of the subject.
- Individual reports are predominantly positive with few, if any, reports that might reflect poorly on individual performance.
- An outsider, viewing interaction within the group, is clearly able to tell which individuals have the most power or authority. Perhaps it is where everyone sits (for example, is the CEO sitting at the head of a table?) or by how others defer to certain individuals with the most authority.
- Individuals rarely offer criticism or constructive feedback to others (including the CEO) in the group forum. Such information, if shared at all, is more commonly taken behind closed doors.

Assessments

A number of team assessments exist that can offer some insight into the level at which a group is performing. Participants are asked for their views on such things as communication, conflict, and trust. All too often I find these tools to be of little use at the executive table. They are too simplistic and fail to take into account the complexities and dynamics of the team at the top. They may work for inexperienced teams, but often they are, with good reason, dismissed by those at the top.

One assessment that has been developed exclusively for the executive team is the TMT assessment developed by my colleagues Scott Borland and Ross Porter of Cygnus Management Consultants (www.cygnus-inc.com). This assessment examines the extent to which the group can adapt to situations in which there may be a divergence of interests and information, assessing the extent to which there is a sense of physiological safety within the team, and reviews how authority is handled. It also offers specific feedback for the CEO or leader of the team about his or her leadership style.

Of all the assessments I have seen geared to testing teamwork at the top, this one is the best. However, it is completed by those on the team who, as discussed earlier, tend to lack a frame of reference for being realistic about their team performance. As a result, they often have a bias and may complete it with an unrealistic sense of optimism about their team. Without some third-party assessment, it is hard to validate the findings.

Third-party review

The most accurate way to assess how a team is performing is to utilize a third party who is independent and competent. Knowledgeable individuals, experienced in working with executive teams and not fearful of confronting those who authorize their invoices, can conduct a comprehensive diagnostic and a subsequent analysis of senior leadership behaviors and their impact throughout the organization. Given that executives are often unaware of the impact they have on others, a thorough diagnostic requires soliciting information from both the executive team members and employees throughout the organization. The range of options is vast and could include the following:

- One-on-one interviews with all executive team members to explore executive leaders' perceptions of their own performance and that of their team members, their perception of current business opportunities and challenges, and their present and anticipated personal leadership challenges.
- A range of assessments:
  - The TMT assessment described above.
  - A 360-type assessment using high-leverage, executive leadership behaviors (executive leadership best practices) as a basis.
  - Individual and executive team EQ assessments. Individual EQ assessments, when combined as a group report, can

shed light on the executive team's patterns of behavior and how they may impact employees in the organization during stressful times.

- A quantitative and qualitative online survey for employees, focused on the extent to which they see executive team members leading in ways that inspire individual performance.
- Focus groups and interviews with a range of selected employees. These discussions will allow data and information unique to the organization to be collected for analysis.

The information gathered should inform the executive team of the following:

- Areas of executive leadership excellence.
- Executive leadership behaviors that negatively impact organizational performance.
- A detailed analysis concerning how both individual and collective executive leadership behavior contrasts to executives in other organizations.
- Specific and detailed recommendations for enhancing organizational performance through the development of defined leadership behaviors, both at the executive and employee levels.
- A proposed methodology for developing these behaviors.
- Other recommendations and suggestions for improving organizational performance over and above executive leadership behavior.

Every time I have conducted such a diagnosis, the executives have been both fascinated and grateful for the data they have received. Yet it is astounding how many are unwilling to put their own leadership under the microscope and choose instead to carry on down the path of ignorance and wishful thinking.

STEP TWO: GET THE RIGHT PEOPLE ON THE TEAM

As discussed earlier, executives often find themselves on the top team as a result of outstanding individual achievement. However, at the very top of an organization, while individual achievement is important, team collaboration is essential. While the nature of this collaboration will, to some extent, be dictated by the agreed-upon purpose, individual team members must behave in ways that support the team, while at the same time leading their own group.

Such behavior is most commonly found in those who have attained at least an Individualist and, ideally, a Strategist stage of action logic.

These individuals are able to integrate contradictory perspectives and define themselves not by what they have achieved within their immediate area of responsibility, but by the achievement of more significant strategic objectives. However, it is the behavior of the Achiever that most often gets rewarded through promotion to the executive team.

It is important to recognize that the skills required for effective team membership are different than those required to successfully manage a functional department. While some may be able to adapt, not all will. As Burruss et al. suggest, "Function, title, and past experience or expertise are not adequate tickets for admission. Rather, it is essential that those who serve on the executive team have outstanding collaborative skills, the ability to think strategically, empathy and integrity, and skills and experience relevant for the future."[1]

Individuals must be confident enough to challenge traditional paradigms and mental models. They must be able to overcome the challenges of power centralization and not unilaterally defer to the very person who appointed them to this prestigious group—the CEO.

It is the rare executive team that has openly, and without reservation, discussed what skill sets are required of those on the senior team. All too often, assumptions are made that functional heads are required—regardless of whether or not they have the collaborative and strategic skills required to lead the enterprise. While some might argue that this is a job for the CEO, I believe that there is much to be gained by clearly defining the behaviors expected of executive team membership. Such a discussion can clearly set behavioral expectations for all, but also be used in succession and talent discussions. It can help remind the team members of the reasons they are on the team—something of which they are not always clear.

STEP THREE: DEFINING A COMPELLING PURPOSE

Not long ago, I was working with an executive team. They were all there—the CEO, the COO, and a mass of senior VPs. Conversation was jovial and they clearly enjoyed each other's company. I then asked them what their executive team's purpose was. A stunned silence ensued and they looked at me as though I was crazy. It was a question they had never really considered. They were a team simply because they were the heads of their respective departments.

This group of executives had no idea why they came together as a so-called team. In fact, when I polled them individually, it soon became apparent that there was a great deal of confusion about why they were gathered around the executive table. Some thought they were there simply to share information about what was happening in their department, while others believed their role was to make critical strategic decisions. Still others thought their role was to bring to the CEO any concerns they had about the organization's ability to meet plans. The net result of this confusion was an ineffective team. The team met regularly, talked about much, but achieved nothing. While they enjoyed each other's company, increasingly, many saw the meetings as getting in the way of their real jobs, tolerating them only because the CEO had mandated them.

Burruss et al. outlined four possible types of executive teams:

- Those that exchange information only,
- Those that advise the CEO,
- Those that coordinate the implementation of strategic initiatives, and
- Those that make enterprise-level decisions.

Clarifying the type of team that is required is the first stage of defining a clear and compelling purpose around which the team can unite. Without such a purpose, confusion and frustration will typically ensue. A purpose that is consequential, challenging, and clear can unite the team.[2] On a personal level, it guides executives as they deal with the ambiguity of leading in the "T"—i.e., leading their own department versus the organization.

Different circumstances call for different types of teams. In my experience, the purpose of the team coming together is not the same in every instance. In some cases, it may be to exchange information, while at another time, a strategic decision may be required. There is no right or wrong. However, what does matter is that every person sitting around the table is clear on what they are doing there and what role they are expected to play. Yet, the desired purpose often does not surface, assumptions are made, and frustrations and ineffectiveness ensue. Such circumstances lead to resentment about time being wasted and often to team members wishing they could get on with their "real" job.

STEP FOUR: CREATE A SENSE OF PSYCHOLOGICAL SAFETY

The dynamics of executive teams are such that creating the conditions of psychological safety is indeed a challenge. However, not unlike the development of teams elsewhere in an organization, with sufficient focus and energy it can be done. But with executive teams, the pressures of the business often take precedence over such "luxuries" as team development experiences. As a result, while the executive professes their desire to be a team, in reality, they contribute little, if any, progress towards this elusive goal.

The irony is that perhaps one of the most challenging teams to be a part of is the executive team. Furthermore, it is also likely the highest profile and most influential. Yet most executive teams are unwilling to dedicate the time and energy that is required to become an effective team, placing a low priority on such efforts. But the few that do can gain a significant competitive advantage.

Let me give an example. Team A and Team B, both the senior teams of an organization, hired me to help them become more effective teams. While neither was highly dysfunctional, they were both less than stellar on the team scale—perhaps a five out of ten.

Team A felt pressured by the demands on their time. Finding time in their calendars was a real struggle. In the space of a two-year period, they managed to commit to a total of five days to work on their team skills—six half-day sessions and two full days. Sessions took place approximately four times a year, with most of these being on-site and full of delays and interruptions. This senior team wanted to develop but was simply unable to set realistic boundaries on other demands.

Contrast this with Team B. The president was clear that a commitment was necessary if the members were to fully develop as a team. Together, he and I worked out the schedule for team sessions. He then informed the team ahead of time and demanded that they set aside the time. The group committed to some intense work and met for two or three days every three months, for an 18-month period. Not surprisingly, the change in team effectiveness was dramatic. Not only were we able to address the team dynamics that got in the way of creating a psychologically safe environment, we were able to develop skills that remain with this group today.

How have the changes made by these two teams impacted their respective organizations? In the case of Team A, while I witnessed changes in openness around the executive table, such changes were imperceptible to others in the organization. This group continued to be seen as distant and out of touch, and when faced with a series of production crises, the organization was slow to respond and slow to recover. Employees clearly had little confidence in their executives to respond to the crises in a rapid and meaningful way. Eventually, things did turn around and production returned to normal, but this took a couple of years. I would argue that had the executive team invested in themselves along the same lines as Team B, the executive team would have listened to the signals earlier (the head of production was reluctant to share possible problems with his team members), they would have been able to engage in an open debate without finger pointing, and they would have garnered confidence from employees through decisions that were clearly aligned, relevant, and realistic. Ultimately, the situation could have been dealt with quickly and efficiently.

The organization led by Team B also faced a crisis—in this case due to a collapse of the local economy. But the team was able to respond quickly and effectively. The executive team was able to explore options, garner the ideas and support of many others in the organization, and change strategy swiftly. The confidence that the rest of the organization had in the executive team was critical in getting everyone on board quickly with the new direction. The net result was that this organization not only survived a significant economic downturn, but also actually increased its market share. The entire executive team saw very clearly that the team development work it had done beforehand was instrumental in an ability to respond to the crisis.

Executive team development can happen in much the same way as the development of teams at other levels in the organization. What is required is no different—an external facilitator knowledgeable of, and not intimated by, executive teams, a private environment that promotes openness and real dialogue, time, and commitment. What is not necessary is luxurious surroundings and a sense of exclusiveness. Privacy is required not to hide from the rest of the organization what is happening, but simply to ensure that the individual members of the executive team can drop their guard and be real and vulnerable without judgment from others. It is for this reason an external facilitator is essential. Internal facilitators, though they frequently look with glee at working with the executive team in this arena, cannot accomplish what an external facilitator can, and more often than not, they actually impede team progress.

The facilitator must push the individual executives to be completely open with each other and, in so doing, help them create the conditions for psychological safety. The results can be dramatic. I remember working with an executive team that was polite, but extremely guarded. After a considerable amount of work, the members were able to fully participate in an exercise in which everyone openly recounted what each other's reputation was. It was done in the spirit of learning and it was powerful. The president learned he was seen as weak and indecisive; the head of HR learned he was seen as ruthless and viewed as the person who was doing the president's dirty work; the VP of marketing learned that she was seen as distant—and so it went on. As a result of this exercise, the team learned that it could provide valuable data to each other in a way that was helpful and useful. A sense of psychological safety had been created, while at the same time, individuals had gathered useful information on how their actions and behaviors were perceived by others.

STEP FIVE: HAVE THE RIGHT PROCESS

A group in which there is a sense of psychological safety should be able to openly discuss how they best work together. Again, there is no one right way. More to the point, it is determined by both the defined purpose of the group and the extent to which there are divergent interests and information among the group. The most appropriate process depends on the extent to which there is divergence in information and interests. Decisions must be made on how best to structure debate and reach a decision, given the varying degrees of interests and information. A group that has a sense of psychological safety can make these process decisions without being bound by egos, outdated mental models, or self-interest.

When the team has similar information, a more collaborative process can work. In these cases, the leader (or another individual if the group deems this more appropriate) should act as mediator and facilitator, allowing people to speak freely. If possible, the groups should strive for consensus.

Conversely, if members of the group have differences in interests or information, a leader may need to be much more involved in the decision-making process. In these instances, a structured process is likely required, such as utilizing various structures like sub-groups, assigning roles, and asking team members to explain and defend alternatives. A structured debate should take place in order for private information and interests to surface.

WHO'S RESPONSIBLE? DEVELOPING THE TEAM WHEN YOU'RE NOT THE CEO

Much of the literature on executive teams points to the role of the CEO. Without a doubt, the CEO does play a critical role in developing his or her team. What if you're not the CEO, but simply a member of the senior team? Is it your place to do anything? And what could you do if your views are not embraced by the CEO?

I believe the notion that we must abdicate the development of the executive team to the CEO is another example of returning to the era of the heroic leader. Let's not be naïve or idealistic and assume the CEO is aware that the team may be less than effective or that the members know what to do about it. Senior team members who are reluctant to raise the issue of executive team effectiveness and abdicate their leadership are falling prey to the power centralization dynamic. While organizational power makes it easier for the CEO to implement change at the top, other team members must not shirk their responsibilities.

What can be done depends on the circumstances—there is no blueprint. However, I suggest you consider some (or all) of the following strategies:

- Start by getting yourself some support. An executive coach who understands executive team dynamics can be really helpful.
- Align yourself with other executives who also recognize that the team could be more effective.
- Educate yourself and others on executive team dynamics.
- Bring in outside experts to talk to the CEO—on more than one occasion. CEOs have listened to me, but dismissed an identical message from their direct reports.
- Identify data points to confirm your views. Try to get agreement on doing an assessment on the team.
- Provoke the CEO into soliciting the views of others.
- Use whatever data you already have from such things as employee surveys.

As a senior leader, you have a responsibility to ensure that you are an effective leader and the top team is an effective team. Effective teams and leaders lay the foundation for creating a great organization. They are not "nice to haves" that you will fit in when time allows. Rather, they are the critical elements without which all other organizational efforts will be ineffective.

Chapter Eleven Takeaways

1. Executive teams that want to gain a competitive advantage need to focus on three areas—right purpose, right people, and right process. When all of these are in place, the dynamics that impede team performance can be overcome. The impact on the team and, consequently, organizational performance, can be profound.

2. There are a number of ways to assess a team's performance. Not unlike the process that is required to assess individual performance, team members can reflect on, and look for, symptoms of dysfunction or success, employ a variety of assessment tools, or utilize a third party to help them conduct an accurate and honest assessment.

3. The skills required for effective team membership are different from those required to successfully manage a functional

department. At the very top of an organization, while individual achievement is important, team collaboration is essential. However, executives often find themselves on the top team as a result of outstanding individual achievement. There is much to be gained by clearly defining the behaviors expected of executive team membership and ensuring those on the top team have the required collaborative and team skills.

4. All executive teams must have a clear and compelling purpose around which they can unite. The purpose must be consequential, challenging, and unambiguous. It may be to only exchange information, to advise the CEO, to coordinate the implementation of strategic initiatives, or to make enterprise-level decisions.

5. Executive team development can happen with an external facilitator who is knowledgeable about, and not intimidated by, executive teams; a private environment that promotes openness and real dialogue; time; and commitment. With a skilled facilitator, conditions of psychological safety can be created and the dynamics of executive teams overcome. Unfortunately, most executive teams are unwilling to dedicate the time and energy that is required to become an effective team and place a low priority on such efforts. Yet the few that do can gain a significant competitive advantage.

6. A group in which there is a sense of psychological safety should be able to openly discuss how they best work together and have a well-defined process. This is determined by both the defined purpose of the group and the extent to which there are divergent interests and information among the group. Decisions must be made on how best to structure debate and reach a decision, given the varying degrees of interests and information. A group that has a sense of psychological safety can make these process decisions without being bound by egos, outdated mental models, or self-interests.

7. The development of the executive team need not be abdicated to the CEO. Senior team members who are reluctant to raise the issue of executive team effectiveness and abdicate their leadership are falling prey to the dynamics that result from the centralization of power with the office of the CEO. While organizational power makes it easier for the CEO to implement change at the top, other team members must not shirk their responsibilities.

GET THE BOARD ON BOARD

No discussion of the executive can be complete without paying attention to what is happening at the board level. The board is an integral part of the organizational system and, therefore, it must also act in ways that reflect the changing landscape and shifting paradigms. Unless the board and the senior executive team are closely aligned, problems are inevitable. Most executives wouldn't conceive of their direct reports working on something of which they had no knowledge, but they would, I hope, listen with openness and interests if these individuals presented a compelling business case for paying attention to a new venture. The situation between executives and directors is no different.

For the most part, boards are made up of individuals who currently hold (or have previously held) senior leadership positions within organizations—former or current CEOs, senior experts in financial and legal domains. These individuals are not dissimilar to those who lead the organization for which they are a director. Therefore, they likely have the same views, the same paradigms, and the same experiences. The chances are high that they operate primarily in the mechanistic model. Indeed, there is much evidence to suggest this is the case. Furthermore, many of the pitfalls that face the senior management team are also evident at the board level, including having a distorted sense of their own effectiveness, having an area of focus that overly represents the mechanistic model, and paying little attention to the human side of the organization. The net result is a board that simply perpetuates organizational ineffectiveness.

I know of some executives who are aware that their board is operating primarily in the mechanistic model, but they choose to turn a blind eye, believing it is not their place to challenge directors. Such an attitude is reminiscent of the heroic era and is, I believe, not in the best interest of the organization. Senior executives who take the initiative in this regard, and actively engage the board in discussions of engagement and culture, are acting in the best interests of the organization and the shareholders.

AWARENESS OF EFFECTIVENESS

In earlier chapters, I maintained that senior executives are, for the most part, unaware of how they are perceived by others and are both overconfident in their abilities and out of touch with how their leadership performance compares to that of their peers. This, in itself, should be of concern to boards, but even more disturbing is seeing a similar picture taking place at the board level.

A study of board effectiveness conducted by Heidrick & Struggles in conjunction with the Center for Effective Organizations at the University of Southern California's Marshall School of Business found that 95 percent of directors rate their boards as either effective or very effective overall. The study incorporated responses from 768 directors, of whom nearly 75 percent were outside directors at about 660 of the 2,000 largest publicly traded companies in the United States. However, that same study suggests that CEOs tell a different story: "In our extensive work with boards, CEOs in informal conversations almost universally confide that they have at most one or two very effective directors who provide wise counsel, offer advice on key issues, and contribute both formally and informally to the direction of the company. A fortunate few CEOs say they have as many as three or four such directors. Roughly, then, only about 10–20 percent of directors are seen by CEOs as effective. Further, say CEOs, their top management team often regards working with the board as a de-motivating experience."[1]

Consequently, we have an unaware senior executive team being guided by an equally unaware board. This is hardly a picture that inspires confidence in our organizations.

Board expertise

As with other issues, the composition of the board bears a remarkable similarity to the issues regarding the composition of an executive team. However, when it comes to the mix of skills and expertise, boards unfortunately tend to lag behind the teams they are overseeing.

When I first started working with senior executive teams, it was not unusual to see the HR function absent from the table. I remember one large global organization had relegated its senior person in charge of human resources to a director—a full level below that of a vice president and three levels removed from the CEO. Ironically, this organization publicly stated it valued people, yet its culture was very much driven by the CEO, who was a wheeling and dealing, salesman.

But times have changed, and the value of having someone representing the HR function as an active and equal member of the executive team is now, for the most part, recognized by those at the top.

The same cannot be said for boards. Research presented at the 2008 annual conference of the National Association of Corporate Directors, revealed that less than 2 percent of all director seats are filled with executives with an HR background. Julie Daum, the head of Spencer Stuart's corporate practice, estimates that the percentage of HR executives on S&P 500 boards is "minuscule."[2]

The lack of HR representation is reflective of the focus and emphasis boards tend to place on the people component of the business. The idea of having a board that lacked in auditing, finance, or legal expertise is unimaginable. Not so, when it comes to expertise in people, culture, and leadership.

IS THE BOARD PAYING ATTENTION TO WHAT MATTERS?

The lack of focus on the people of the organization means that the information received by boards is incomplete at best, and a misrepresentation at worst. Yet directors appear to be unaware of what they are missing. The overwhelming majority (95 percent) of directors say they are satisfied that they receive sufficient information to do their jobs.[3] This is true enough if they see their job solely as paying attention to short-term corporate performance. However, nothing could be further from the truth if they were paying attention to the people side of the organization.

As discussed in the first chapter, we know that corporate performance is directly connected to employee engagement levels. As the 2007 Towers Perrin study showed, firms with the greatest percentage of engaged employees reported average annual operating income increases of 19 percent, and earnings-per-share increases of 28 percent.

Meanwhile, those with the lowest percentage of engaged employees reported declines of 33 percent in operating income, and 11 percent in earnings per share.[4] Furthermore, in 2004, Hewitt showed that employee engagement at double-digit-growth companies exceeds employee engagement at single-digit-growth companies by an average of more than 20 percent.[5] The 2007 Towers Perrin study also identifies senior leadership behavior as one of the five primary drivers of employee engagement (along with company reputation, commitment to corporate social responsibility, and sufficient opportunities for learning and development). With an alarming 38 percent of employees reporting that they feel partly to fully disengaged at work, it is time all boards paid attention to leadership at the top, company culture, and people management.

Although directors believe they receive sufficient company information in most areas, there is no doubt that board training, information on people management, and company culture lag behind. Only 33 percent of directors say they monitor company culture to a great or very great extent, and only 32 percent closely monitor human capital.[6] When they do pay attention to the people side of the business, it is typically limited to discussions concerning executive compensation or CEO succession.

Directors would do better to focus more on the people practices that could engage the workforce, with its associated impact on organizational performance. The numbers are clear. But, as with many of today's executives, a mechanistic mindset causes directors to focus more on the harder side of business than the soft.

BOARD ORGANIZATION

As discussed earlier, a senior team works most effectively when it puts the needs of the organization ahead of the needs of the members' own departments and when the members can overcome the tendency to solely represent the interests of their functional department. Yet, board organization frequently demands a return to the silo and functional head role. As J. Lorsch and R. Clark point out, boards are "overemphasizing committee work instead of harnessing the intellectual power of the whole board to deal with complex matters. Instead of working collaboratively with management, they're creating or perpetuating dysfunctional relationships that cast directors as corporate police who enforce rules and trace managers' missteps, rather than as guides who help managers choose the right path."[7] Once again, a mechanistic mindset dominates.

WHAT TO DO
Value the human side of the business

It is time that boards paid attention to leadership, engagement, and culture within organizations. It has been clearly shown that these things impact the bottom line and thus, if directors really wish to act wisely on behalf of shareholders, they would be negligent in their duties if they ignored these critical elements of organizational performance.

The research clearly suggests that both senior executives and directors may lack self-awareness. As a result, directors are likely unaware that the information that is reaching them regarding leadership may be somewhat distorted. Given this, boards must act on the assumption that their executives do not have an accurate sense of how they and others in the organization are performing as leaders.

Just as those below the executive level have a tendency to filter information to their superiors, the same is sometimes true of those at the senior executive level, when giving information concerning the people side of the business to the board. While recent fiascos have ensured that the hard numbers are accurate and honest, the same cannot always be said when addressing such issues as engagement, quality of leadership, or organizational culture. A director who relies solely on a senior executive's interpretation of events is being naïve and irresponsible.

It is thereby essential that the board gather information from other sources in order to gain an accurate picture of what is happening within the organization, whether it is organizational-wide, within the executive team, or regarding individual executive leadership effectiveness.

Focus on organizational engagement

Given the connection between employee engagement and the bottom line, directors should insist on some form of organization-wide assessment of employee engagement. This may take the form of an engagement survey, employee satisfaction survey, focus groups, or regularly talking to those at the front line about how they see the business. There is a myriad of options and it is not critical which ones are selected. What matters is that directors have a way to hear, firsthand, how things are within the organization. Those that rely solely on the CEO or on executive reports may not be getting the full picture. I know of one CEO who readily confesses, to anyone who asks, that he is always the last one to know what is going on within the organization. Yet it is this same CEO who files reports with the board on such things as employee engagement. Something is clearly wrong with this process.

Knowing what is happening with employee engagement is only part of the solution. Board members must insist that it be given a priority, both challenging and supporting the senior management team to ensure it is a competitive advantage. Metrics should be included in the bonus structure of executives and, if appropriate, committees and subgroups set up to place this issue on an equal footing with other board responsibilities.

Pay attention to the executive team dynamics

Board members would be wise to understand the dynamics present in any executive team (as described in Chapter Ten) and look for any telltale symptoms of whether these dynamics may be impeding senior team effectiveness. There are a number of ways to do this. One of the simplest is to become curious and observant of the interpersonal dynamics of the executive team. As R. Brunswick and G. Hayes suggest, board members should be on the lookout for signs as to whether a CEO intimidates the senior team to the point that no one will dare tell him or her bad news.[8] Is there a healthy exchange of views and ideas? Has a rivalry between two members of the senior team gone beyond the point of healthy competition to the point that it is hurting the quality of senior management's decision-making? Directors should also conduct their own exit interviews when senior executives or high-potential employees leave the organization.

Aside from these informal observations, directors should consider conducting a thorough assessment of the executive team effectiveness. Don't assume that because there is no conflict, it is a highly effective team. As described in Chapter Ten, the team may be guardedly polite or ineffectively cohesive. Directors must recognize the dangers to the organization of being at any of the other three stages (individuality, guarded politeness, and ineffective cohesiveness), insisting that the executive team does what it takes to be at the highly effective stage.

Focus on executive leadership behavior

The cornerstone of effective leadership is self-awareness, yet research presents a picture of executives out of touch with their own abilities. Given this, directors should be adamant that all executives conduct a thorough diagnosis of their leadership performance. Once all agree on the strengths and weaknesses of the individual executives, the board must then insist that executive leadership development take place. Finally, executives' leadership behavior must be tracked and rewarded, like all other executive performance measures.

Assessing performance

Given that it can be challenging for executives to get a true sense of how they are leading, it is important for board members to insist that executives embark on a thorough and complete assessment. In addition, board members should be closely involved in the design of such an assessment, and be conscious that others within the organization might have experienced a side of the executive not seen by the board. (The manner in which executives can assess their leadership performance is described in detail in Chapter Six.)

Alternatively, directors can assess executives themselves. This would require directors questioning the top layer of management about their own perception of their performance and their efforts to develop the next management level. The assessment should then expand elsewhere, exploring mid-level managers' views of senior leadership and direction, as well as discussions with those lower down the organization's hierarchy.

While it is advantageous for directors to interact with employees at every level of the organization, such an approach may be limited in its effectiveness. With politics rampant at the top of organizations, it may be difficult for directors to gain an accurate assessment of executive leadership performance. Employees have a tendency to filter information given to top management. Directors would likely evoke similar, if not more pronounced, behavior. Consequently, directors who want to conduct a true assessment on the executive's leadership effectiveness may consider utilizing a competent third party who has credibility among both the senior executives and directors. However, be aware that boards who retain external consultants to conduct individual or team executive assessments need to ensure that such individuals report directly to the board, not indirectly through either the CEO or the head of HR.

Insist on executive leadership development

Once both executives and directors are clear on how executives are performing as leaders, an executive leadership development plan can be created. Leadership development, which is discussed in more detail in the following chapter, is not a one-time event. The very qualities and skills that allowed executives to get to the top yesterday could be hurting their performance today. If directors want executive leadership to remain relevant and effective, they must insist that senior leaders continually develop their skills and practices.

A board needs to emphasize two key things when it comes to executive leadership development. First, it must demand that executives make time for it. We know that executives face a host of conflicting priorities and they are busier now than they ever have been. Once executives understand that their leadership behavior directly impacts employee engagement—that their leadership behavior is an executive priority—they will be more inclined to make time for development. The behavior of the board is critical here; directors must insist that executive leadership development not be relegated to the side of their desk.

Second, the board must ensure that executives are spending their time effectively. Many executives have a preference for acquiring information when it comes to leadership development. They read about it and attend seminars or conferences. While I would never discourage these activities, we also know that acquiring knowledge, on its own, does little if anything to change leadership behavior. Leadership development is about driving positive behavioral changes; reading a book or article can support development by providing fodder for dialogue and inquiry, but it is unlikely to change behavior.

It is, I believe, the board's responsibility to ensure that not only does executive leadership development take place, but that it is done in the most cost-effective and time-efficient way possible. Activities should be selected that will address the needs identified through the assessment process, as well as allowing for realistic integration into an executive's busy schedule. Some executive leadership development options are described in Chapter Seven.

I advocate a customized and integrated approach to executive leadership development, with a focus on high-ROI activities such as coaching and intense senior leadership team development. It's been my experience that when senior leaders are visibly engaged in their own leadership development, employee engagement and commitment to learning are considerably higher than when senior leadership development is not apparent. We see a marked change in employee engagement, morale, and commitment when executives talk openly about the personal development activities going on behind closed doors.

Given this, boards should be leery of executive development activities that do more to stroke the ego than change behavior. While executives might enjoy participating in high-priced executive programs at business schools, the return on such programs is questionable. Rather, directors should insist activities are done on-site whenever possible and are discussed with employees when appropriate.

Organize for effective leadership

Boards may articulate the need for strong, effective leadership and people practices, but they often do little to back such declarations with action. To do so, they must integrate their desire for high employee engagement (or whatever other metric is deemed appropriate) into many aspects of board responsibilities.

This means, as noted earlier, ensuring there is expertise in the board in this arena. Accountants and lawyers may not have the necessary expertise in people practices. Organizational development experts, whether experienced senior level consultants or internal practitioners, are a valuable asset to any board.

The board must then be structured to reflect this area of focus. Executive development and employee engagement should be integrated with succession conversations. Some companies have figured this out. For example, GE, Chevron, International Paper, and the former AlliedSignal, have board committees that address management development and successions issues.[9]

Finally, executives should be assessed and rewarded not just on short-term financial performance, but also on such things as employee engagement. Relevant metrics should be implemented. These should be tracked and reported on with the same diligence as other metrics, such as financials and safety.

In today's business environment, leadership development is just as important as any other executive responsibilities. Boards must be more aggressive and insist that executives actively develop those vital skills that keep their employees engaged and their company competitive. It may require a significant investment of resources by the organization—and a great deal of courage from its executives—but the returns will be worth it. Within the current state of leadership at the top, it's certain that organizations and individuals that seize the opportunity to increase their executive leadership capacity will gain a competitive edge over those that don't. And boards have an obligation to shareholders to insist that this occurs.

Chapter Twelve Takeaways

1. The board is an integral part of the organizational system and, therefore, it too must act in ways that reflect the changing landscape and shifting paradigms. Many of the pitfalls that face the senior management team are also evident at the board level, including having a distorted sense of their own effectiveness, having an area of focus that overly represents the mechanistic model and paying little attention to the human side of the organization. The net result is a board that simply perpetuates organizational ineffectiveness.

2. Boards often lack specific expertise in HR. This lack of HR representation is reflective of the lack of focus and emphasis boards tend to place on the people side of the business. The idea of having a board that lacks in auditing, finance, or law expertise is unimaginable. But this is not so when it comes to expertise in people, culture, and leadership. Directors would do better to focus more on the people practices that could engage the workforce, with the associated impact on organizational performance. With many of today's executives, a mechanistic

mindset causes directors to focus more on the harder side of business than the soft.

3. It is essential that the board gather information from other sources in order to gain an accurate picture of what is happening within the organization—whether it is organization-wide, within the executive team, or regarding individual executive leadership effectiveness.

4. Given the connection between employee engagement and the bottom line, directors should insist on some form of organization-wide assessment of employee engagement. Board members must insist that this be given a priority. Metrics should be included in the bonus structure of executives and, if appropriate, committees and subgroups set up to place this issue on an equal footing with other board responsibilities.

5. Directors should consider conducting a thorough assessment of the executive team effectiveness. They should not assume that because there is no conflict the executives are a highly effective team. Directors must insist that the executive team does what it takes to be highly effective.

6. Directors should be adamant that all executives conduct a thorough diagnosis of their leadership performance. Once there is agreement on the strengths and weaknesses of the individual executives, the board should insist that executive leadership development take place.

7. Boards should be leery of executive development activities that do more to stroke the ego than change behavior. While executives might enjoy participating in high-priced executive programs at business schools, the return on such programs is questionable. Rather, directors should insist activities are done on-site whenever possible, and they are discussed with employees when appropriate. There is a marked change in employee engagement, morale, and commitment when executives talk openly about the personal development activities going on behind closed doors.

8. Executives should be assessed and rewarded not just on short-term financial performance, but rather on such things as employee engagement. Relevant metrics should be implemented. These should be tracked and reported on with the same diligence as other metrics, such as financials and safety.

PART FOUR

DEVELOP EVERYONE'S LEADERSHIP

To create a great organization, those at the top must be great leaders—both individually and collectively. As I've stated many times, this is essential. But great leaders at the executive level are not enough. Those who believe the success of an organization lies simply in the performance of a few individuals at the top of the hierarchy are still living in the era of the heroic leader.

Organizations can only be great if every single individual who works for that organization behaves in ways that facilitate greatness. While effectiveness at the top is a prerequisite, ultimately, executives must do what it takes to ensure everyone within the organization is behaving in ways that maximize organizational effectiveness. Simply put, great organizations require great behavior by everyone.

So how can you make sure that thousands of employees behave in ways that make the company great? Clearly, direct supervision is not an option. Ultimately, all employees must behave in an effective manner, regardless of whether someone is "watching over them." Furthermore, it's not something that happens simply by making impressive pronouncements about the kind of organization you want or by sending a memo around suggesting how people should behave. Effort is required to create a culture that defines, nurtures, and supports what is required.

ORGANIZATIONAL CULTURE

Culture is another of those words (along with leadership) that gets bandied around a lot in organizations, often without a common understanding of what it refers to. Just like leadership, there are many and various definitions of culture. Executives who want to create a great organization will inevitably need to pay attention to, and likely change, organizational culture. A review of some of the more relevant definitions can inform these executives about what needs to change and how this might happen.

For example, T. E. Deal and A. A. Kennedy in their book *Corporate Cultures* draw on the *Webster's New Collegiate Dictionary* definition: "The integrated patterns of human behavior that includes thought, speech, action, and artifacts, and depends on man's capacity for learning and transmitting knowledge to succeeding generations."[1] Conversely, J. P. Kotter and J. L. Heskett reprise the *American Heritage Dictionary* definition: "The totality of socially transmitted behavior patterns, arts, beliefs, institutions, and all other products of human work and thought characteristic of a community or population."[2] E. H. Schein, in *Organizational Culture and Leadership*, defines the culture of a group as "a pattern of shared basic assumptions that the group learned as it solved its problems of external adaptation and internal integration, that has worked well enough to be considered valid, and, therefore, to be taught to new members as the correct way to perceive, think, and feel in relation to those problems."[3]

The list of definitions is long; those listed above open a brief window into the main concepts regarding organizational culture. And while the definitions vary in some respects, they do share some common themes. Culture can be best thought of as a collection of patterns, beliefs, and behaviors that are created and transmitted. As B. Barger suggests, words and concepts such as feeling, thinking, acting, perceiving, and reacting collectively appear to connect all the definitions that have evolved over time.[4]

Given this, it is clear that changing employees' behavior so that they consistently act in ways that create a great organization will require changing culture. At first blush, this may seem a daunting task. Senior leaders who do not understand how to change culture, and with it employees' behavior, risk implementing yet another failed change initiative.

Highly effective cultural change can be successfully implemented, but only by thoughtful and committed efforts. Those who say it evolves over time or who attempt to change it by fads, fix-its, or magic bullets are, I believe, abdicating their leadership responsibilities and failing to grasp what can be gained by changing the culture. Their lack of knowledge or comfort with the process is causing them to turn a blind eye to the possibilities.

Cultural change can happen through the mechanism of leadership development. Leadership development, carried out properly, can transform organizations, change culture, and ensure that everyone in the organization behaves in ways that creates a great organization. It need not take a long time, but it does require a big commitment.

This commitment demands that executives be knowledgeable and supportive of the process through which culture transforms and behaviors change. For many executives, leadership development falls under the jurisdiction of those in HR. And when leadership development is really more focused on skills development rather than behavioral and cultural transformation, HR is where it should live. In these cases, leadership development is better labeled as leadership training—I'll describe what I mean by this later in this chapter. But be aware that leadership training won't bring about cultural change and it sure as heck won't create a great organization.

As described earlier, executives at the top have both organizational and departmental responsibilities. Strategies or initiatives that impact the organization as a whole must also be owned by the executive as a whole. While a specific executive may coordinate or spearhead those things that fall within their area of expertise, other executives must be active, knowledgeable, and proactive in their implementation. Consider the role of the executive team in the budgeting process. While the CFO clearly plays a critical role, it is a process that involves all executives and managers. Leadership development is no different.

Any executive who wishes to create a great organization must therefore be knowledgeable of the process of organizational transformation through leadership development. Those who assume this is simply the responsibility of HR are failing to recognize both the importance and the strategic nature of leadership development.

Despite the fact that it can transform an organization, most executives I work with are not that familiar with the world of leadership development. Many have not participated in a state-of-the-art program themselves and often have some outdated concepts about what makes for a good development experience. Others have simply assumed it is the role of the HR department to deal with a concept they find soft and nebulous. However, if, as I am arguing, executives cannot abdicate the responsibility for leadership development to others, then it is necessary for them to understand such things as the difference between development and training, and what makes for a good leadership development program.

AN EXECUTIVE'S GUIDE TO LEADERSHIP DEVELOPMENT

Leadership development can transform organizations and make them great. Leadership training cannot. What is the difference? And what makes a good program? How can an organization maximize impact?

These are all questions that are critical for any executive who wishes to transform their organization. Any executive, regardless of their line responsibilities, must be knowledgeable of the process—in the same way that executives must be knowledgeable of the budgeting process. You don't need to be an expert—that is up to external or internal consultants. You do have to know enough to support a good investment and put the brakes on a bad one. What follows is a high-level overview, which will guide you in the process of developing everyone's leadership in the most cost- and time-effective manner.

Who should be developed?

As discussed earlier, leadership is not positional. It happens outside of the formal organizational hierarchy and can occur throughout the organization. Indeed, the most effective organizations are those in which everyone sees themselves as a leader—regardless of the title on their business card.

Yet, despite this, when organizations invest in leadership development they typically restrict participation only to those who are in a management or supervisory position. In addition, there is typically a greater investment in those towards the upper end of the hierarchy than those who are merely supervisors. Implicit in this decision is the assumption that those at the top can develop the leadership of those at the bottom.

This is a recipe for failure. Worse, it flies in the face of the frequently articulated belief that everyone is expected to lead. It's a classic case of a misalignment between words and action.

If everyone is expected to lead, then everyone must be developed as a leader. It is not just for those in managerial or supervisory roles. Great organizations develop the leadership of all employees, regardless of role. The differences in responsibilities may determine what leadership development actually looks like, but not exclude it. Any form of development for the front line must clearly be affordable and scalable, but those working on the front line should be given the same opportunities to develop their leadership as those who have positional leadership responsibilities.

Few executives I know fully appreciate this. Despite what they say about leadership not being positional, their actions tell a different story. However, those who appreciate the importance of investing in the development of leadership among all employees and are willing to look at creative options to ensure this can happen effectively will undoubtedly lead their organization to greatness.

Development versus training

Simply put, leadership training is more about knowledge acquisition and skill development than behavioral change. It is education versus transformation. It is individualistic versus collective. It is superficial exploration versus deep. It is short term versus long term. Leadership training has its place, but make no mistake about it—if you want to create a great organization you need more than leadership training.

Many are unaware of the difference between training and development and use the terms interchangeably. The danger of this is that the intervention and the desired outcomes do not align. Behavioral change is required, yet a two-day skills training course is implemented.

The following chart identifies some of the key differences between leadership training and development:

	Leadership Training	Leadership Development
Purpose	To provide knowledge and develop skills that will be applicable in specific circumstances.	To change day-to-day behavior, regardless of situation.
Degree of personal learning	On the surface and focused on knowledge acquisition. No inclusion of sense of personal inquiry.	Deep. Touches core values. Involves development of whole person.
Content	Standardized—same for all. Content and outcomes are closely linked.	Customized to individuals and group. Content viewed as a means to the outcome, not the outcome itself. All content is focused on application of competencies in order to achieve organizational vision.

(*Continued*)

Integration of relevant and current organizational issues	Minimal integration.	Significant integration. Content adapted to ensure relevance to individuals' day-to-day work, to resolve immediate and pressing issues facing participants.
Facilitator skill level	Basic skills required. Able to engage group in following pre-defined content.	High level of skill. Able to adapt agenda to meet needs of group. Must have in-depth knowledge of the way leaders develop.
Role of facilitator	Shares knowledge, provides exercises to develop skills.	Creates experiences in which participants learn from each other. Integrates new knowledge and provides tools as appropriate.
Role of ambiguity	Viewed as poor facilitation, disorganization.	Viewed as key learning experience, deliberately designed as part of program. Realistic, pressured situations in which to learn, fail, and try again are key developmental opportunities.
Role of workshops	Central to the experience. Value of course often determined by value gained from workshop.	Part of a larger experience. Workshop not viewed as an end in itself, but as a way to continue the learning journey and to enhance group relationships.
How learning happens	Learning happens by taking people away from work.	Learning happens by providing people opportunities to learn from their work.

Measurement and assessment	Skill or knowledge acquisition demonstrated in workshop. Often measured by post-workshop assessment by participants.	Measures linked to organizational strategies as well as observable behavior change on the part of the participant. Much of the measurement is not based on participants' views, but by what is noticed by those around them and by organizational results.
Outcomes	Skill development and new knowledge. Assumption is participants will apply new skills and knowledge—the application of this is left to the participants. Success is defined as high level of skill within pre-existing criteria—excellence within box.	Application of competencies in the workplace in order to achieve the organizational strategies and vision. Ability to impact organizational direction and growth, to challenge what is, to think outside the box.

A FEW CRITICAL DESIGN FEATURES

There are a number of practices that can make the difference between leadership development that changes culture, and leadership development that does nothing more than make people feel good. Any leadership development program that will have an organization-wide impact needs to have the following features.

Customization

Forget off-the-shelf programs. They will not change the culture. What you need are programs that are customized on three levels.

First, they must be customized to the organization. They must take into account the organizational reality, the present culture, and the desired future culture. In other words, they must be relevant. One size does not fit all when it comes to leadership development.

Secondly, they must be customized to the group that is learning together. The most effective learning happens in groups or communities.

(I'll discuss this in more detail in Chapter Sixteen.) However, programs that assume that each group in an organization faces identical challenges and views organizational life from similar perspectives misses the point. Every group I have ever worked with has been unique. While some similarities, defined by the present culture, are always there, the issues that are front and center vary. Programs must acknowledge and be customized to these issues.

Finally, the program must be customized to the individual. Leadership is an intensely personal affair and, therefore, accommodations must be made for each individual to learn in different ways at different rates. Just as groups have their own issues, so do individuals. A quality program must be able to accommodate individual differences, whether it is through coaching or other less expensive options.

Flexible and dynamic
A program that does not change, evolve, and grow will rapidly become out of date. Leadership development involves an endless cycle of learning. Through the process itself, knowledge is acquired and culture starts to shift. This information must then be fed back into the program, the implementation of which produces more information. Thus, the most effective programs are those in which organizational learning is continually being implemented, along with developments in the field of leadership. Consistency must lie in the messaging, while design and delivery can evolve.

Variety of different developmental experiences
The best leadership development involves a wide variety of different developmental experiences that take place over an extended period of time and provide ample opportunity to change behavior in the workplace. They may be workshops, team meetings, coaching, mentoring, on-the-job exercises, readings, case studies, and webinars, etc. There is no right or wrong. What matters is that the right balance of face-to-face time within the learning cohort versus on-the-job application is achieved. Events such as workshops build relationships and increase knowledge, but it is back at the job that real change happens.

Self-reflection
As explained in Chapter Four, those who hold later action logic frames will be better equipped to effectively master the challenges of leading in today's turbulent environment. Leadership development must, therefore, help participants explore different frames with a view to moving to a later stage of action logic. This is only possible

if periods of quality self-reflection are integrated into the leadership development experience.

Cohort model

Do not expect individuals to learn or change on their own. The most effective learning happens within a group of between eight and 20 people. A group of fewer members does not create enough diversity or safety. Above 20 attendees, individuals can disengage from the group. In the right size of group effectively facilitated, relationships develop, networks are built, and trust is gained. The creation of a safe environment in which people can take risks, try different behaviors, and create the kind of culture that will, in turn, create a great organization is critical.

Rapid rollout

Changing culture means getting people to change their behavior and, as quickly as possible, making the new behavior the accepted norm. This is simply not possible if there is too great a time between new cohorts starting leadership development. One client I worked with understood this, jumped in with both feet, and committed to starting a new cohort every month. Within three years, this organization went from being fragmented and at risk of having a strike, to being voted one of the top organizations to work for in Canada. Without a rapid rollout, such success would have been impossible to achieve.

HOW IT WORKS: A CASE STUDY

The challenge

In June 2005, I implemented a comprehensive leadership development initiative with an international client, which had a specific goal to increase its market share by 11 percent to 40 percent, an unprecedented number considering the industry and the firm's competitors. To support this goal, the company also wanted to become one of the best employers in the region. The CEO felt strongly, and I agreed, that leadership development would help the organization achieve both targets.

The solution

The executive team was highly committed to both the process and their own development (both individually and as a team). Everyone agreed to make time in their hectic schedules for facilitated two-day workshops every two or three months. In these workshops, I worked with participants to understand who they were as leaders and how others in the organization experienced their leadership. I gave them plenty of skills and tools to lead others and their organization effect-ively. By practicing the skills of leadership with each other, they built their own relationships, learned to become vulnerable with each other, and started communicating effectively and honestly.

Two months later, I followed a similar process with the next group of managers in the hierarchy and onward down through the organization. In short order, everyone in the organization was involved in some form of leadership development. While those towards the upper end of the hierarchy continued to have focused workshops, other employees had development delivered by the managers (and supported by some of my colleagues).

At the same time, my colleagues and I worked with the HR department to integrate leadership throughout their systems. This was an important step and one that often gets forgotten in organ-izations. It is essential to have systems and structures that support the desired leadership behavior. Leadership must be integrated into such things as performance management, talent management, re-wards, and recognition, etc. Specifically in this case, we helped them define leadership competencies, revise performance plans based on those definitions, and link their talent management system to their leadership goals.

As with most intensive leadership development initiatives, this work set off a chain reaction of deep and lasting change. Using the skills acquired in the workshops and through individual coaching, managers across the organization began to speak openly. As the qual-ity of conversations increased, underlying conflicts that had been hindering change—and thus growth—surfaced. The executives could finally see what had been getting in the way of the vision. They put aside personal agendas, developed a more effective decision-making process, and began to act.

As they gained confidence in their capabilities, the executive team spent less time ensuring the president was aware of their accomplish-ments and more time leading. As the president gained confidence in his team, he was better able to focus on strengthening critical relation-ships with the parent company. Seeing that the executive team had become more effective, the parent company gave this client greater autonomy in running the business.

Meanwhile, the same changes were happening with managers at other levels. Self-awareness was increasing, authentic conversations were happening, and issues were being resolved. Managers realized that if they spent more time creating a motivating environment, they could spend far less time worrying about people issues. Productivity increased as empowered employees began to put that extra bit of effort into projects they understood and believed in. New ideas were voiced and enthusiastically pursued.

As a result of the leadership development work done across the organization, this client has experienced a significant shift in how it does business, and that added up to bottom-line returns:

- The company increased market share from 29 percent to 35 percent, in a local industry that generates an estimated $3.5 billion a year in sales.
- They increased employee engagement by 18 percent.
- While economic downturn in the client's sector resulted in a 15 percent drop in sales in the market as a whole, this client experienced only a 2 percent drop in overall sales, with some brands actually increasing by 6 percent.

These days, there are mounting challenges in this client's operating region. The market is down and the economy is stumbling. In their region, sales have dropped by 15 percent. Yet with this client, sales have declined only 2 percent and in some brands, sales have increased by 6 percent. Why the difference? Leadership development. While other organizations are in retreat, panicking, and embracing a heads-down silo approach, this client is instead treating this as an adaptive challenge that they must work through together. Leveraging the relationships the organization forged through leadership development, people are collaborating like never before. They are risking more, supporting each other, and creating an environment that is innovative and confident. Their latest engagement survey indicated that they have 95 percent engagement. With these levels of engagement, a drop in market sales is simply a blip on the horizon and not a crisis.

Developing the leadership of all employees is no easy task, yet it is an essential one for executives. However, today's executive must understand that it likely will require a paradigm shift, much in the same way as the paradigm shift regarding effective leadership and effective senior leadership teams is required. As experts at the Centre of Creative Leadership suggest, "Increasingly, leadership is defined not as what the leader does, but rather as a process that engenders and is a result of relationships—relationships that focus on the interactions of both leaders and collaborators instead of focusing on only the competencies of the leaders. Leadership development practices based on this paradigm are more difficult to design and implement than those that have been popular for the last several decades in which the objective was to train leaders to be good managers."[5]

Chapter Thirteen Takeaways

1. Organizations can only be great if every single individual who works for that organization behaves in ways that facilitate greatness. While effectiveness at the top is a prerequisite, ultimately, executives must do what it takes to ensure everyone within their organization is behaving in ways that maximize organizational effectiveness, creating a great organization. This requires creating a culture that defines, nurtures, and supports what is required.

2. Cultural change can happen through the mechanism of leadership development. Leadership development, when carried out properly, can transform organizations, change culture, and ensure that everyone in the organization behaves in ways that create a great organization. It need not take a long time, but it does require a big commitment.

3. Any executive who wishes to create a great organization must be knowledgeable of the process of organizational transformation through leadership development. All executives must understand the difference between development and training, and what makes for a good leadership development program. Those that assume this is simply the responsibility of HR are failing to recognize both the importance and the strategic nature of leadership development.

4. If everyone is expected to lead, then everyone must be developed as a leader. Leadership development is not just for those in managerial or supervisory roles. Great organizations develop the leadership of all employees, regardless of roles or responsibilities. The differences in roles and responsibilities may determine what leadership development actually looks like, but it does not exclude it.

5. Leadership training is focused on knowledge acquisition and skill development. Leadership development is focused on behavioral change. Leadership training has its place, but it will not transform organizations. Those who want to create great organizations must instead invest in leadership development.

6. The best leadership development program is based on a cohort model customized to the organization, the cohort, and the individual; is flexible and dynamic; offers a variety of different developmental experiences; includes time for quality self-reflection; and is rolled out rapidly across the entire organization.

GET OTHER EXECUTIVES ON BOARD (OR OUT OF THE WAY)*

To create great organizations, ideally, all executives individually should be great leaders and the executive team should be a highly effective team, aligned with the greater goals. That's the ideal, but let's be honest—for many, it is simply wishful thinking. In reality, some executives will get on board with a new way of leading, while others may continue to lead using methods that have always served them well in the past. But is organizational greatness possible without 100 percent buy-in at the top, particularly if the focus is to develop everyone's leadership throughout the organization?

We have known for some time now that in order for leadership development to succeed and transform cultures and behavior, executive support is key. But what does that really mean? Does it include all of the executive team or just a select few? And what does support look like? Approval, involvement, or something else?

The issue of executive support for leadership development intervention is a complex one. Unfortunately, all too often those responsible for leadership development speak in generalizations ("We don't have executive support for this"), without due consideration of the variables that must be taken into account when assessing the degree

---

*This chapter is based on an article, model, and associated description developed and written in collaboration with Mark Frein of The Refinery Leadership Partners, Inc., at a time when I was the co-principal of The Refinery. The model is therefore the intellectual property of The Refinery. Used by permission.

of executive support. And support can come in varying degrees. The question that any executive wishing to create a great organization through the leadership development of others needs to ask is: Does sufficient support exist within the various executives to warrant the implementation of a leadership development intervention?

When considering executive support, three variables are in play:

1. The degree of influence of each executive member;
2. The purpose of the leadership development initiative; and
3. The nature of the support given.

The kind of support required is dependent on the influence the executive has in the organization and the extent to which the leadership development intervention is a strategic change initiative. Simply put, the greater the influence and the more strategic the intervention, the more active and dynamic the degree of support required.

EXECUTIVE ORGANIZATIONAL INFLUENCE

Let us first look at the variables that exist within the executive ranks. The one word "executive" is used to describe several individuals, each of whom has differing degrees of influence within the organization, which ultimately determines the extent to which support for leadership development is required.

Organizational influence is driven by a number of factors and stems from power. The more that individuals control resources, form important alliances, and possess admired qualities, the more their co-workers defer to their ideas and directives.[1] The structural determinants of influence, such as the authority bestowed upon an individual by virtue of the position he or she holds within the organization, formalize the power aspect. A CEO has more authority and, thus, influence than other members of the executive team. Likewise, a senior vice president will have more authority and influence than a vice president. Organizational influence stemming from authority carries great weight in traditional, hierarchical organizations, but less so in flat organizations, where power is distributed more evenly.

Above and beyond power, influence can stem from the use of effective influence tactics such as ingratiation, threats, the use of reason and logic, and coalition building.[2] In addition, research suggests that influence stems from personal characteristics and, specifically, the fit between the person and his or her organization. Extraverts tend to have more influence in a team-oriented organization, whereas conscientious introverts attain more influence in an organization in which individuals work alone on technical tasks.[3]

This suggests that the formal authority of various executives is not sufficient to determine their degree of influence within the organization. Even if two individuals have the same level of power, they may differ in their levels of influence, if one uses more effective influence tactics than the other does or has a personality that is better matched with the culture of the organization. For example, a CEO may have the greatest organizational authority, yet a COO in charge of the organization's operations may wield the most influence. Organizational influence may be present around the executive table, but it is often the up-and-coming young leaders seen as future successors who will have the most influence within the organization. Those around the executive table may have a lesser influence, particularly if they are heading for retirement.

The degree of organizational influence an executive holds determines the type of support required for a leadership development initiative. While the nature of the leadership development intervention is also a factor, it is safe to assume that more overt support is needed from those with significant organizational influence. Conversely, less support is required from those with less organizational influence.

PURPOSE OF THE LEADERSHIP DEVELOPMENT INTERVENTION

Leadership development undertakings vary in their purpose. When the organizational culture needs to be changed and the focus is on creating a great organization, leadership development is strategic in nature. Such initiatives tend to be full-scale, organization-wide interventions focused on behavioral change and are best regarded as organizational change initiatives. Conversely, leadership training focused more on education and knowledge acquisition is unlikely to change the very essence of the organization and, therefore, can be considered more tactical in nature.

Leadership development that can, in any way, be considered strategic or transformational requires significant executive support. In this regard, it is no different from other strategic undertakings such as an acquisition, new marketing initiative, launch of a new product, etc. It would be difficult to envision these strategic initiatives taking place without full executive support. Leadership development focused on organizational transformation should be no different.

THE DIFFERENT TYPES OF EXECUTIVE SUPPORT

The final factor to be considered is the different forms of support that an executive can offer. All too often, such support is viewed as an absolute; you either have it or you do not. In reality, executive support can come in many shapes and sizes, from being active participants in the learning or organizational sponsors, to simply permitting the program to take place and not sabotaging it.

When faced with a leadership intervention, an executive may adopt a continuum of attitudes. At one end of the spectrum, he or she may actively oppose it. At the other end, the executive may be willing to support, sponsor, and be actively involved in it. In between these two extremes, the executive may adopt a number of different attitudes such as indifference, acceptance, or ownership.

When an executive is resistant and expresses active opposition, he or she has concluded that a learning initiative is unnecessary, either culturally or from an expense point of view. While they may not openly verbalize their opposition, they may passive-aggressively sabotage the program by preventing their people from participating, criticizing or discouraging new behaviors and ideas promoted in the program, or withholding funds in some way. The key strategy with these negative executives is to get buy-in from them on at least some element that they will support. If this simply cannot be done, then move them to a place where they can do no harm. Of course, whether or not this will be possible will be determined by the degree of influence the executive has and the strategic nature of the leadership development intervention.

One of the most common attitudes embraced at the executive level is disinterest or indifference. It typically occurs when a senior executive embraces an old paradigm, believing that the accountability for people and organizational development does not lie within his or her scope of responsibilities, and consequently abdicates everything to HR, the organizational development group, or external consultants. Such abdication also will occur in instances where senior executives are secretly uncomfortable with their lack of knowledge in the arena of leadership development and organizational change. While those in the HR function may relish the freedom and responsibility given to them when executives are indifferent, the chance of any initiative gaining traction within the organization is slim at best. The initiative will likely be viewed as "only" an HR program and seen as irrelevant to strategy. Furthermore, it is likely that participants—especially senior managers—will conclude that the executives don't care about development given their absence. This typically makes it hard for anyone to take development seriously, in ways that make it effective. It is certainly possible to do "training" without any executive interest, but it is foolhardy to believe that initiatives "supported" by a disinterested executive will have any major organizational consequences—unless that executive has very limited influence within the organization.

The first level of positive support is interest and acceptance. In this case, executives understand the possible benefits of the intervention and, therefore, are likely to support the initiative in one or more ways. For example, they may be present for the launch and closure, they might ensure their people are freed up sufficiently to spend time on their learning, and they may support any changes in behavior they see. While clearly such behaviors are more effective than those exhibited by a resistant or indifferent executive, all too often, executives convince themselves that simply accepting and being interested in the program qualifies as sufficient support.

In these cases, executives are underestimating the impact of their actions. Interest with neither involvement nor accountability is a long way from what is required to create meaningful organizational change. Participants will "read" meaning into the lack of "skin in the game" from the executive and conclude that this is not a strategic imperative. Equally, a lack of accountability around the initiative can mean that it is not tied to specific organizational strategies.

When executives become involved, they step inside the initiative, not only as a supporter, but also as an active participant. In this case, an executive will shed his or her hierarchical hat and participate in the learning alongside other organizational employees. This is a significant step that demonstrates to all employees that learning is important and that the leadership development intervention is valued by the organization. While managing executive participation requires careful planning to keep traditional hierarchical patterns out of the environment, the payoff can be powerful.

More effective than simple participation, the next level of support is one in which an executive takes accountability for the impact and success of the intervention. By taking accountability for learning strategies, an executive publicly acknowledges the intervention as a tool for organizational change. This executive frequently and publicly pays close attention to the program and, in so doing, sends a loud message to participants that it is an important initiative. While they may attend launches and graduation just like the interested executive, their tone is different and the questions they ask portray a greater passion and commitment. They are focused on outcomes, impact, and results, continually staying in touch with how the program is unfolding. Regardless of the role they have in the organization, accountable executives ensure the initiative is integrated into other parts of the organizational system, not relying solely on those in HR.

The rarest kind of support is the one that can lead to the most significant organizational impact—when the executive is invested in the initiative emotionally, personally, and organizationally. The invested executive combines the very best of the involved and accountable executive. By assuming accountability for learning strategies, executives see the learning as a tool for organizational change. By being an active participant and investing in their own development, executives publicly acknowledge they have a responsibility in the organizational transformation and it is not simply up to others to implement the strategic change.

Executives are more likely to become "invested" in the leadership development initiative when organizational development or HR professionals involve them in strategic organizational and people development. These "experts" must demand that executives make such initiatives part of strategic planning *and* invest time and commitment into their own personal development. This level of support can create amazing results and is exactly what is required for a high-impact organizational change intervention.

To recap, we have three variables:

1. The degree of influence of each executive member;
2. The degree of strategic importance of a leadership development initiative; and
3. The different types of the support given.

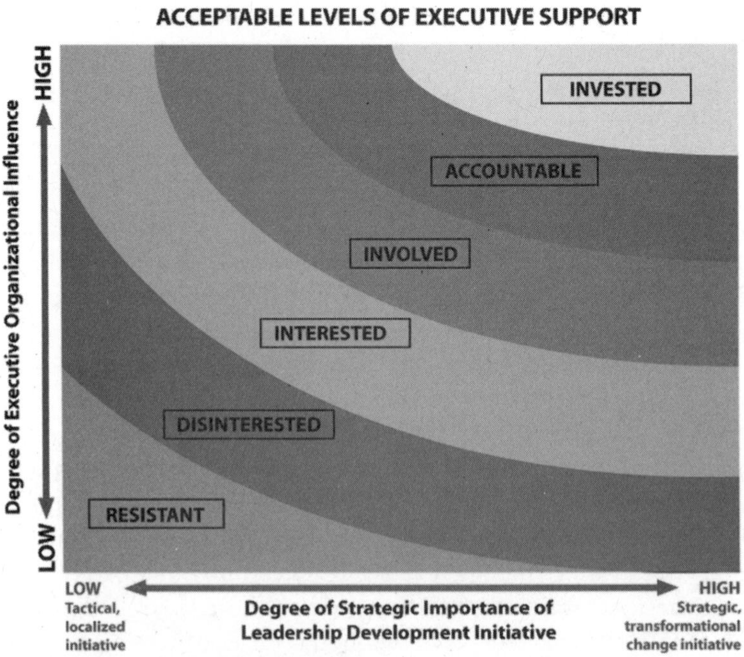

ACCEPTABLE LEVELS OF EXECUTIVE SUPPORT

Figure 14.1   Acceptable Levels of Executive Support

Figure 14.1 demonstrates how these variables interact and can be used to assess if sufficient executive support is present. By determining the strategic importance of the leadership development initiative as well as the degree of organizational influence, the required level of support for each executive can be determined.

By focusing on individual executives rather than executives as a whole, this model can shed light on what needs to be done in cases where some executives are not exhibiting sufficient support. This individualized approach can prove to be invaluable for those who are committed to implementing the initiative—whether they are other executives, internal organization development or HR practitioners, or external consultants.

HOW IT WORKS—A REAL-LIFE EXAMPLE

Company Y was a small organization consisting of just 250 employees. It had gone through a series of changes in ownership from being a small, family-owned business to being owned by a large, multinational organization based in the United States. Employees yearned for the earlier days when there was little bureaucracy, when everyone knew each other, and things were less frenzied. The parent company was increasingly becoming frustrated by what it perceived as a lack of efficiency at Company Y. The executive recognized that something must change, so the president charged the VP of HR with implementing a leadership development intervention. This intervention needed to fundamentally change the culture and, therefore, it was seen as a significant strategic intervention—or rating 10 out of 10 on the transformational scale.

The executive consisted of six members:

- Michael, the president, was a well-liked and highly respected individual. Although he was viewed by many employees as a "weak" leader, the culture was such that the CEO had considerable organizational influence within the organization. He was thoroughly supportive of leadership development and saw it as a way for him to improve his own personal leadership skills.
- Harry, the VP of HR, was not well respected. He was seen as heartless and arrogant, and the guy that did Michael's "dirty work." He was, however, committed to the organization and believed that leadership development was essential to keep the parent company off their backs. It did not occur to him that he might need to develop his own skills.

- Patrick, the VP of customer service, was somewhat aloof. While the employees in the service department liked him a lot (once they got to know him), he had a reputation of being quite difficult to work for. He did not see any harm in leadership development and thought it might be a good idea for others. He viewed it primarily as an HR initiative.
- Diane, the VP of sales, was well regarded but, having worked in the organization for just one year, was seen as having little influence among employees. She was very positive about the implementation of a leadership development initiative and hoped that it would give her an opportunity to develop her own skills and establish more credibility within the organization.
- Natasha, the VP of marketing, was popular among most employees. Widely regarded as Michael's successor, Natasha had considerable influence. She believed that this was a critical strategic intervention for the organization. She also recognized that she had much to learn in terms of her own leadership.
- Ian, the CFO, was due to retire in a couple of years. Although he had been with the company since the early days, he was generally regarded as living in the past and had very little influence in the organization. He regarded leadership development as "fluff" and forcefully expressed this to the executive group.

Given these executive profiles, was there sufficient support for the initiative to proceed? By looking at the diagram we can determine the answer to this question.

Person	Degree of required support	Degree of actual support	Sufficient support?
Michael, CEO	Invested	Involved	No
Harry, VP HR	Involved	Accountable	Yes
Patrick, VP service	Involved	Disinterested	No
Diane, VP sales	Interested	Involved	Yes
Natasha, VP marketing	Invested	Invested	Yes
Ian, CFO	Disinterested	Resistant	No

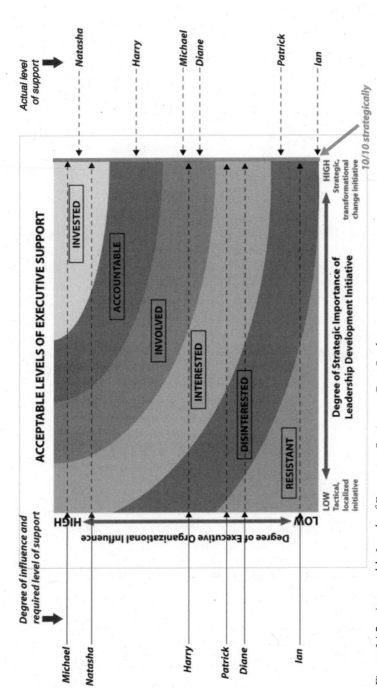

Figure 14.2   Acceptable Levels of Executive Support—Case Study

This analysis shows that there was sufficient support from half of the executive. Given the strategic importance of this initiative, it was essential that three executives increase their level of support. Michael needed to become invested, Patrick had to be involved, and Ian had to move from resistant to at least disinterested.

The critical executive was Michael. While it was positive that he was prepared to be a participant in the program, he needed to take on a bigger leadership role and view this as a strategic intervention. To do this, I sat down with Michael and identified some specific, measurable outcomes to assess progress and success in much the same way as was done with other strategic initiatives. The concept of using leadership development to transform organizations was new to Michael—up until this point he had simply assumed the objective was primarily skill development. However, through several conversations with me and other internal stakeholders, he gained clarity over the purpose of the initiative and soon became invested in its success.

For the initiative to succeed, Patrick needed to move beyond just interest to involvement, while Ian had to move from resistant to disinterest. Given their degrees of influence in the organization, there was no need for a higher level of support at this stage.

Following an executive team meeting in which Natasha spoke passionately about the role of the executive in supporting this initiative, Patrick started to change his level of support. From his initial understanding, he began to recognize how this could help him as well as his team. In short order, he told Michael he was willing to be a participant.

Ian presented a different challenge and one that had to be dealt with head-on. This job fell to Michael who, having become invested in the initiative, was unprepared to tolerate any executive potentially sabotaging the program. Michael met with Ian, laid out the objectives of the initiative, and told him in no uncertain terms that, while he did not have to be a full supporter of it, he must, at the very least, avoid interfering in or impeding it in any way. While Michael would have preferred that Ian be more supportive, he recognized that it would take time they did not have to get Ian to move to a positive level of support. Given Ian's level of influence within the organization, neither Michael nor I considered this to be a "show stopper." Michael hoped that once things got moving, the momentum of a supportive executive team engaged in their learning would have a positive influence on Ian.

The necessary executive levels of support were soon attained. However, this did not happen without time and effort. A series of one-on-one conversations and team discussions were the keys to success. Had this not happened, I can confidently say that the leadership development intervention would not have transformed the organization in the same way.

For organizations to move down the path to greatness by developing leadership across the organization, it is essential that there is an alignment of the degree of executive support and the objectives of the leadership development initiative. It is a step that, unfortunately, is not always thought through. Any executive involved at any level with a leadership development intervention would be well-advised to assess and address their own requirements, as well as those of their peers.

Chapter Fourteen Takeaways

1. For leadership development to succeed and transform cultures and behavior, executive support is key. This support can come in varying degrees. The kind of support required is dependent on the influence the executive has in the organization and the extent to which the leadership development intervention is a strategic change initiative. Simply put, the greater the influence and the more strategic the intervention, the more active and dynamic support is required.

2. The more impact the intervention will have on the organization, the more support is required. Leadership development that can be considered strategic or transformational in any way requires significant executive support. In this regard, it is no different from other strategic undertakings such as an acquisition, new marketing initiative, launch of a new product, etc.

3. When faced with a leadership intervention, an executive may adopt a continuum of attitudes. At one end of the spectrum he or she may actively oppose it. At the other end, the executive may be willing to support, sponsor, and be actively involved in it. In between these two extremes, the executive may adopt a number of different attitudes such as indifference, acceptance, or ownership.

4. When an executive is resistant and expresses active opposition, he or she concludes that a learning initiative is unnecessary, either culturally or from an expense point of view. While they may not openly verbalize their opposition, they may passive-aggressively sabotage the program by preventing their people from participating, criticizing, or discouraging new behaviors and ideas promoted in the program or by withholding funds in some way.

5. One of the most common attitudes embraced at the executive level is that of disinterest and indifference. It typically occurs when a senior executive embraces an old paradigm and believes that the accountability for people and organizational development does not lie within his or her scope of responsibilities and, instead, abdicates everything to HR, the organizational development group, or external consultants. Initiatives framed against a disinterested executive will have no major organizational consequences, unless that executive has very limited influence within the organization.

6. The first level of positive support is interest and acceptance. In this case, executives see the possible benefits of the intervention and, therefore, are likely to support the initiative in one or more ways. While such behaviors are more effective than those exhibited by a resistant or indifferent executive, all too often executives convince themselves that simply accepting and being interested in the program qualifies as sufficient support.

7. When executives become involved, they step inside the initiative not only as a supporter, but also as an active participant. In this case, an executive will shed his or her hierarchical hat and participate in the learning alongside other organizational employees. This action demonstrates to all employees that learning is important and the leadership development intervention is valued by the organization.

8. When executives take accountability for learning strategies, they, in effect, publicly acknowledge the intervention as a tool for organizational change. This executive frequently and publicly pays close attention to the program and, by doing so, sends a loud message to participants that it is an important initiative.

9. The rarest kind of support is the one that can lead to the most significant organizational impact—when the executive is invested in the initiative emotionally, personally, and organizationally. By being an active participant, as well as by paying strategic attention to the intervention, executives publicly acknowledge they have a responsibility in the organizational transformation and it is not simply up to others to implement the strategic change. Executives are more likely to become "invested" in the leadership development initiative when Organizational Development/Human Resources professionals involve them in strategic organizational and people development.

10. For organizations to move down the path to greatness by de-
    veloping the leadership of everyone, it is essential that there
    be a match between the degree of executive support and
    the objectives of the leadership development initiative. Any
    executive involved at any level with a leadership development
    intervention would be well-advised to assess and address
    their own requirements, as well as those of their peers.

FIGURE OUT COMMUNICATION

It seems as though every organization has communication problems. If anything goes wrong, more often than not, the blame is directed at inefficient and ineffective communication. Poor communication can rapidly result in an organization collapsing into dysfunction. Conversely, effective communication can bind an organization together, influence and cement behavioral changes throughout the organization, and redefine a new and effective culture.

Given this, any executive interested in creating a great organization should pay careful attention to communication. But this is not an easy task and is one that is considerably more complex than simply creating a professional and well-run communications department. While such departments play an important role, communication is not something that can be abdicated. Rather, it is a critical strategy that every executive must consider to be of equal importance to the other aspects of their job. The move away from the heroic leader has significantly raised the importance of effective executive communication. Unfortunately, this fact is not fully appreciated by all who reside at the top of organizations, as evidenced by some disturbing research.

In surveying over 80,000 employees worldwide in 2007, Towers Perrin found that just 38 percent of employees believe that senior management communicates openly and honestly. While 44 percent of employees believe that senior management tries to be visible and accessible, only 40 percent believe that senior management effectively communicates the reasons for key business decisions.[1]

The authors of this report offer some explanation for these poor scores: "Part of the problem is that many top executives began their careers in specific technical disciplines, such as finance, engineering, or the law. They bring primarily rational/analytical skills to their roles, when what are increasingly needed today . . . are 'right brain' abilities such as empathy, communication skills, and the ability to synthesize ideas and perspectives."[2]

In an earlier survey of 25,000 employees representing 17 U.S.-based companies conducted in 2005 by Towers Perrin as part of its Communication Effectiveness Consortium, it was found that less than half (45 percent) of these employees say senior leadership both talks and listens, creating an environment of two-way communication. Furthermore, employees who said their senior leaders demonstrated a sincere interest in their employees' well-being rated communication effectiveness in their company 12 points higher than those who did not. Of note, however, is that, as in other studies Towers Perrin has conducted, less than half of all respondents—in this case 42 percent—actually feel their senior leadership demonstrates sincere interest in them.[3]

WHAT IS IT AND WHY DOES IT MATTER?

But what is effective communication? Part of the reason communication problems so frequently seem to occur is that the definition of communication itself is so wide reaching. Towers Perrin used its survey data to determine a definition from the employee perspective. While senior leaders may have a different viewpoint, employees define effective communication as

- Open and honest exchanges of information;
- Clear, easy-to-understand materials;
- Timely distributions;
- Trusted sources;
- Two-way feedback systems;
- Clear demonstrations of senior leaderships' interest in employees;
- Continual improvements in communication; and
- Consistent messaging across sources.

What is clear from reviewing this list is that there is a critical element embedded in communication—it is two-way. In other words, it is not simply one person informing another. Rather, it is an interactive dialogue in which information is exchanged, explored, and made sense of.

In my experience, most executives understand the importance of communication. However, rather than seeing it as an interactive exchange, they view their role primarily as articulating some form of inspirational future to the employees within an organization. They see themselves as the holder of the vision and, therefore, confidently talk about it at every opportunity. However, while this is certainly an important role, it represents only a fraction of what employees are looking for from their executives when it comes to communication.

Again we see how the model of heroic leadership continues to drive executive behavior. If we assume that those at the top are all-powerful and all-knowing individuals, then, naturally, what matters most is that these leaders focus on sharing that knowledge with others within the organization. There will be little to be gained by soliciting input from those lower down the hierarchy.

But when we embrace a more collaborative and adaptive model, we must change the manner in which communication occurs. In this model, the views and opinions of everyone throughout the organization must be solicited and valued, *particularly by those at the top*. The notion that senior leaders can articulate a vision for the future without fully comprehending the reality of those whom they are leading is folly at best.

Yet clearly this is happening. The report card on executive leadership leaves much to be desired. Any senior leader wishing to create a great organization must recognize and appreciate what effective executive communication looks like in today's organizations. It is "less lecture" and "more dialogue," less telling and more listening, less closed-mindedness and more questioning, and less assuming and more curiosity.

Such communication can only take place if senior leaders make it a priority and have the personal interest, skill level, and knowledge to make it happen. To do this, I believe executives must focus on three things regarding communication—attitude, awareness, and methodology.

You'll note that communication skills are not on this list. Some might find this strange, since such skills are emphasized in virtually every leadership program. This emphasis suggests that people do not know how to communicate and need to be taught how if we expect them to be effective leaders. I beg to differ. As humans, communication is crucial to our development and our survival. I have yet to meet anyone who lacks the skills to communicate. When the situation matters enough, people can be wonderful communicators. Consider, for example, how people communicate outside of their work environment to friends and family. I am not suggesting that we all communicate perfectly all the time. However, in situations that are believed to be important or critical, we are, generally, able to communicate well. For example, I have no doubt that someone who has been told they are a terrible listener can, in fact, be a fabulous listener when their child turns to them for help.

I do believe we overemphasize communication skill development and downplay the importance of attitude and awareness. And nowhere is this more important than in the domain of the senior executives. Surely those at the top understand communication is important and have the skills to communicate. Yet as discussed earlier, there appears to be a problem with senior leadership communication. I believe this is not a skill problem, but more a problem with attitude, awareness, and a lack of understanding of the various communication methodologies.

ATTITUDE

A certain mythology surrounds the executive floor. Regardless of how senior leaders view themselves, others in the organization often feel intimidated by those at the top. They see senior executives as larger than life and often can't see past the position to the person. These are hardly helpful perceptions when it comes to creating effective communication.

It's important to understand that these limitations exist not necessarily because of anything the senior leader has done. Rather, it is because of paradigms and mental models that exist within the organization. I don't mean to be snide here, but I have yet to meet an executive who is not a human being—yet this fact is not widely appreciated throughout the organization. For example, I worked closely with an individual who, for a number of years, was a general manager. He's down to earth and very approachable. A short time ago, he was promoted to the position of vice president. He recounted to me that he was astounded how people no longer seemed as relaxed around him. As he put it, it was as though he had turned into a different person. Yet he had done nothing other than change his title and scope of responsibilities. It was the preconceived ideas of the employees that changed things.

Given these limitations, it is essential that those in potentially intimidating positions behave in ways that send a very clear message that they are human, real, and approachable. They need to have a great communication attitude. An executive must be capable of not only addressing shareholders and the board, but also of having some very real dialogue with the front-line workers. This means showing up as a person and not a position.

The adoption of an effective communication attitude goes hand in hand with the adoption of a collaborative, non-heroic leadership model. When those at the top are truly interested in what those at the bottom have to say, everything else falls into place. But when those at the top pay lip service to the contribution of others, disconnects are reinforced and the organization collapses into dysfunction and misalignment.

Emotional intelligence can drive an effective communication attitude. Those leaders who have a good sense of self, as well as understand and are empathetic towards others, will have the flexibility to be able to relate to their employees, whatever their level. And it is this flexibility that is key. At times, employees are looking for inspiring and energizing visions. Yet at other times, they just simply want to be heard and know that those who are making critical, strategic decisions at the top understand the reality of those at the bottom. Executives must know when to talk and when to listen. They must have the attitude to overcome all the systemic communication barriers that are embedded in an organization.

Senior executives must also ensure there is a clear alignment between the messages communicated and the actions they take. When words are espoused yet actions send a different message, organizational distrust develops and, in short order, a "communication problem" emerges. For example, I recall working with one organization whose president frequently articulated how much he valued work-life balance. But this same individual demanded that employees work ridiculous hours and sacrifice holidays and family time. Clearly, despite what he said, work demands were first and foremost.

AWARENESS

We all know that leadership requires good communication skills. After all, it is through communication that leaders lead. What is not always appreciated is that those at the top must have the skills to address a diverse audience and to overcome the communication barriers that are inherent in that position. In other words, average is simply not good enough.

As stated previously, I believe most executives have the skills to communicate. But that doesn't mean they do it. Even if they have a great communication attitude, they need to have a finely tuned awareness of how communication changes when one is in the executive domain. They need to understand the systemic and cultural barriers and act proactively to overcome them.

Communication is the transmission of meaning from one person to another or to many people, whether verbally or nonverbally. A simple representation is given here:

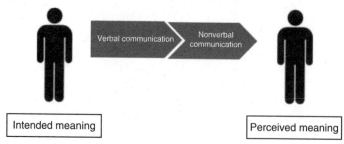

Figure 15.1   Communication Model (1)

In reality, there are two other factors that complicate what at first glance appears to be a simple process. Each person, the sender and receiver, is actually in their own reality. This reality can very easily create a wall around the person—and a barrier to communication. This is better represented as follows:

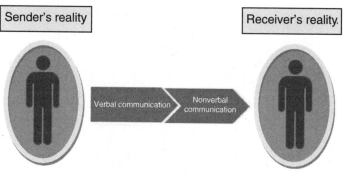

Figure 15.2   Communication Model (2)

Different action logic frameworks mean that each individual has his or her own world formed by their own experiences, perceptions, ideas, etc. They will perceive, experience, and interpret things differently. The same event will always be perceived a little differently by each person. Therefore, reality is not an absolute.

This likely isn't new information, but what deserves special consideration is how these realities become deeply embedded when either the sender or the receiver is a member of the senior executive. As suggested earlier, paradigms and assumptions abound about the senior group. Such mental models inherent in any senior team increase the likelihood that the different realities will be vastly dissimilar. In effect, the standard communication process becomes even more challenging when it involves dialogue between "us" and "them." Information is shared through what I call a "senior executive filter." Those at the top must have a full and realistic awareness of this filter and how it impacts communication if they are to communicate effectively.

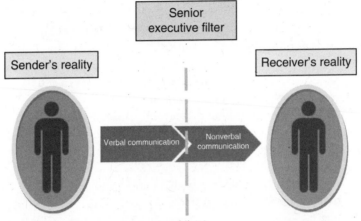

Figure 15.3   Communication Model (3)

The impact of the filter will vary according to the culture of the organization and the communication attitude of the executive. An open, non-hierarchical organization combined with a collaborative executive will lessen the impact of the filter. Conversely, traditional organizations led by heroic leaders will significantly increase the filter effect. But even in the best-case scenario, the senior executive filter will likely compromise the quality of communication.

The filter is driven to a large extent by self-censorship by all parties. Employees are often reluctant to give executives the straight goods, preferring instead to withhold any information that may reflect poorly on their own performance. On the flip side, executives, knowing that they must instill confidence in the future, are often reluctant to share the realities of the organization's challenges with employees. In effect, the executive filter causes a withholding of information and a reluctance to share bad news with others.

Executives who are not aware of the impact of the filter or, worse, who blindly accept it, are inviting communication problems. The organization will be built upon a fabrication of incomplete information. Those at the top will lack the critical information on which to base their strategic decisions. Those at the bottom will feel disconnected from those at the top. The net result is organizational ineffectiveness.

There is no excuse for poor communication within an organization. However, executives must recognize, understand the impact of, and work to overcome the executive filter. This awareness is critical if they are to create a great organization.

Unfortunately, many executives simply accept it as a fact of life. A CEO with whom I work frequently tells me that he is the last to know what's going on in his organization. As I have told him on numerous occasions, this is simply not good enough. In another organization, the vice president of HR has never once visited one part of the operation that consists primarily of hourly maintenance workers. She's told me she feels uncomfortable and out of place in this environment and no one talks to her anyway. She has accepted this as a given and has not once entertained the notion that it is unacceptable.

An executive who wishes to create effective communication must make the effort to do so. While awareness of the filter is the first step, several strategies can be used to overcome communication barriers:

- Ask questions in such a way that people will tell you their truth. A question such as "How's it going?" will likely yield platitudes. Conversely, "Tell me one thing that frustrates you at work" will likely yield a more honest response.
- Listen more than you talk. Communication is two-way—one-way information sharing will be significantly influenced by the filter.
- Show your human side. Talk about your feelings, your family, and your concerns. Do as Jim Collins in *Good to Great* suggests—confront the brutal facts while having an unwavering confidence in the future.[4]
- Do not allow the communications department to be your messenger. Write your own speeches and talk in your own language.

The impact of the executive filter does not require you to communicate differently. Rather, it demands that you communicate exceptionally well. In interactions where there is no filter, mediocre communication might suffice, although it is not recommended. This is certainly not the case when an executive filter is present—this awareness is key to effective executive communication.

METHODOLOGY

Assuming executives have the right communication attitude and are aware of the impact of the executive filter, the challenge then becomes how best to connect with, and communicate to, employees. It is no easy task, particularly for those executives whose organization is far-flung. How can a dozen or so key individuals meet the communication needs of thousands of employees?

Traditionally we have believed that people want to "press the flesh." Employees want to see and connect with their executives in person. And while walking around, visiting sites, or conducting "town hall meetings" or "fireside chats" are all excellent things to do, in large organizations, it simply is not possible to do it enough. When executives and employees see each other on just one occasion every year, communication will not flourish or improve. These face-to-face interactions happen too infrequently to ensure a free flow of information.

Other executives rely on such things as quarterly newsletters or video broadcasts. While these techniques do no harm (provided that the "real" executive talks and is not one who presents as cold and distant), they are unlikely to improve communication to the extent required by a great organization. Furthermore, given that communication is a two-way flow of information, a CEO talking at the rest of the organization would hardly be classified as effective communication.

The challenge becomes how to engage in a relevant two-way dialogue with thousands of people. Recent changes in communication technology have opened the door to possibilities. Social networking sites and such tools as blogs and Facebook promise to transform executive-employee relationships—provided they are done right.

Social networking can create communities that, in many ways, resemble face-to-face communities. While the mechanism and its universal availability, accessibility, and independence from geographic and, perhaps, economic constraints are different, online communities, like the more traditional community, create a forum to communicate. Yet the community itself will only thrive if there is effective communication.[5]

With any social network (as with any community), there is one thing that is essential if it is to survive and flourish—conversation. As M. Meyer suggests, "In order for social media to work, conversations have to ensue, abound, and be maintained. Not only that, there has to be a purpose to those conversations."[6]

Social media allow an executive to converse with many employees in a way that simply is not possible through traditional means. But the key is the notion of conversation. Social media should be used to create two-way communication in which those at the top can share some of their selves, be real, be human, and be connected. It is a methodology that can be leveraged to engage employees in a manner that has not happened in the past. But, as with everything, it can only work if it is done right.

Social media, when used effectively, can provide a forum for individuals to share views, be heard, send messages, and receive feedback. It can provide an opportunity for connection and that elusive thing called communication. Today, large organizations can connect all of their employees or members with Facebook. Some are finding an added advantage of using an internal, secure version of Facebook. This has helped organizations to dramatically increase their internal networking and collaboration.[7]

Likewise, organizations are starting to realize how Twitter can be used to increase organizational effectiveness. Twitter is a micro-blogging service that allows friends, family, and co-workers to communicate and stay connected through the exchange of short, quick answers using no more than 140 characters per message. Young people often use Twitter for answering the question "What are you doing?" However, as D. Burrus suggests, "Business users could change that question to: What problem are you trying to solve?"[8] Several companies have used this as a fast way to solve problems and you may also find that you could solve problems faster by using Twitter.

While an increasing number of organizations have started using social networking sites as a form of internal communication, many are, unfortunately, doing it in a way that does little to increase the quality of communication within the organization. Posts, while purportedly coming from an executive, are often clearly written by someone in the communications department and used simply to present the company line. Comments are screened and the whole thing has an aura of company propaganda. In such cases, it likely harms employee engagement more than it helps.

But there is hope. As a case in point, I recently heard of one organization that appears to be getting it right. It has an executive blog and, since instituting it (and supporting it with various employee meetings and newsletters), its employees' perception of senior management has risen by 20 percent. The key is not just to have a blog, but doing it right. What does that mean? There are four essential practices:

1. The executives must write the posts themselves. This is critical, but also hard. Those at the top frequently rely on communications specialists to write their messages, but that's not what employees want. They want to hear the real voice of the real executive. Communication is not a job that can be outsourced at all times. The organization I referred to above admits this has been a struggle, but it is also a critical success factor. The role of the communications department is to insist it be done and also to check that nothing the executive has written will get the organization in trouble—a kind of communication safety net. But that is all the communications department does.

2. All comments to the blog must be approved by someone within the organization. Often, this is a job for the communications department. However, unless the comment is directed towards an individual or in some way contravenes the company values, it should be approved. People will soon stop responding if negative comments are screened out. If you value authentic communication, then all critiques must be published provided they are written in a respectful manner.

3. Any comment that is not suitable for publication is forwarded (in confidence, without any indication of the author) to the senior executives. The communications department responds to the author and explains why the comment was not made public.

4. All members of the senior executive are expected to write a posting for the blog at regular intervals. By not restricting the blog to one individual, the executives have an opportunity to present a common front. In organizations where senior executives are seen more as functional heads than as a highly performing team, the structure of the blog can go a long way towards developing more favorable perceptions of the quality of teamwork at the top.

These rules of thumb can be applied to all social networking sites. Unfortunately, all too often, the fear of what might happen holds the organization back from creating a social networking site. Images of disgruntled employees bad-mouthing the top team come to mind.

However, such a strategy is equivalent to not asking employees how they're doing for fear they may serve up some bad news. It is shortsighted and those who are nervous about truly opening up the communication lines would be well advised to reflect on their organizational responsibilities. They should also know that the conversation they are fearful of is already happening in the organization—it is just underground. By bringing it to the surface, concerns and problems can be addressed and the organization can move forward.

As things stand at the present time, senior executives are out of step with the communication needs of their employees. While communications departments can help, ultimately, it is the senior executives themselves who must change. Those at the top need to have a different attitude towards communication, a different awareness of the barriers that are inherently present (regardless of how great their intentions are), and they need to learn and leverage different communication methodologies. Only through strategies such as these can organizations move towards greatness.

Chapter Fifteen Takeaways

1. Ineffective communication can rapidly result in an organization collapsing into dysfunction. Conversely, effective communication can bind an organization together, influence and cement behavioral changes throughout the organization, and redefine a new and effective culture.

2. The move away from the heroic leader has significantly raised the importance of effective executive communication. Given this, any executive interested in creating a great organization should pay careful heed to communication. This is considerably more complex than simply creating a professional and well-run communications department, as executive communication cannot be abdicated. Research suggests that executives are not meeting the communication needs of their employees.

3. Communication is an interactive dialogue in which information is exchanged, explored, and made sense of. Employees define effective communication as open and honest exchanges of information, clear, easy-to-understand materials, timely distributions, trusted sources, two-way feedback systems, clear demonstrations of senior leaders' interest in employees, continual improvements in communication, and consistent messaging across sources.

4. Executives must adopt an effective communication attitude. This goes hand in hand with the adoption of a collaborative, non-heroic leadership model. When those at the top are truly interested in what those at the bottom have to say, everything else falls into place. An executive must be capable not only of addressing shareholders and the board, but also of having some very real dialogue with the front-line workers. It is showing up as a person and not a position.

5. Paradigms, assumptions, and mental models abound about the senior group, which, in turn, increase the likelihood that the different realities will be vastly different. Information is shared through a "senior executive filter." Those at the top must have a full and realistic awareness of this filter and how it impacts communication, if they are to communicate effectively. Executives who are not aware of the impact of the filter or, worse, accept it are inviting communication problems.

6. Executives are faced with the challenging task of engaging in relevant two-way dialogues with thousands of people. It is no easy task, but recent changes in communication technology have opened the door to many opportunities. Social networking sites such as Facebook and Twitter and the use of blogs promise to transform executive-employee relationships—provided they are done right.

CREATE COMMUNITIES

The transformation of an organization from a mechanistic, silo organization to one that can nimbly and effectively adapt to today's environment requires many things from executives. It demands that they adjust their own leadership behavior, the executive team starts acting like a real team, every individual in the organization is developed as a leader, and communication is adapted to meet the demands of the new organization.

But this, in itself, is not enough. These tactics lay the foundation for change, but will not galvanize change without some deliberate action to facilitate and support individuals to work outside of traditional boundaries. When this occurs, the rigidity of a hierarchical organization is replaced by an organization in which people look not to the top for answers, but to each other. This requires that "communities" be established across the organization in which people can learn and solve problems together. And this requires creating and implementing structures.

A structure is a process that, when implemented, supports and drives behavior. For instance, meetings are perhaps one of the most common structures within organizations. The frequency with which groups meet and the manner in which meetings are conducted are key factors in determining how individuals in the group interact with each other. I once worked with an executive team (at least they called themselves a team) that never once met on its own. Rather, the members met as part of a larger management group. This structure influenced the way they communicated and behaved with each other and the rest of the organization. It was only when they started to meet as an intact team that their behavior changed to become more collaborative.

In today's environment, effective organizations require structures that can span organizational boundaries and facilitate the development of a learning culture. As G. Furlong and L. Johnson suggest, "What is required is a learning structure that allows for the questioning of the organizational paradigm relative to the business environment."[1]

The structures that are relevant in today's organizations and that allow traditional boundaries to be spanned can take several forms and are known by a variety of names. Networks, interest groups, and communities of practice are all based on the idea that people throughout the organization who might not traditionally interact with each other have ongoing relationships, collectively share information, and solve problems.

Leadership development that takes place on a cohort basis (as the very best leadership development should) inherently develops communities. Yet, all too often, the focus of such leadership development is individual behavior change. While this is certainly an important aspect, it is the relationship-building aspect of leadership development that can create an adaptive organization able to bridge silos and respond quickly and effectively to today's challenges. Unfortunately, this fact is rarely appreciated or leveraged enough by those at the top, resulting in lost opportunities to create a great organization. Any executive who wishes to create a great organization would be well-advised to develop a broad network of communities.

COMMUNITIES IN THE ORGANIZATIONAL CONTEXT

What are the defining features of a community, regardless of the context? We look for such things as a unified body of individuals, common interests, joint ownership, or participation. Individuals who are members of communities interact and talk to each other. They have an identity and a sense of belonging.

It is in this context that I use the word "community." I believe it is important to recognize the need for individuals and organizations to connect with each other across boundaries. While the notion of a "community of practice" that serves primarily as an information-sharing forum has gained steam in many organizations, other connections are also critical. I regard communities as networks combined with a purpose, and it is in this context that we explore organizational communities.

Organizational communities build relationships and develop trust in a way that more traditional organizational groups cannot. L. E. Lesser and J. Storck suggest that communities foster "connections among practitioners who may or may not be co-located, relationships that build a sense of trust and mutual obligation, and a common language and context that can be shared by community members."[2]

Communities differ from work teams. Storck and Hill identify the following differences:

1. Team relationships are established when the organization assigns people to be team members. Community relationships are formed around practice.
2. Similarly, authority relationships within the team are organizationally determined. Authority relationships in a community of practice emerge through interaction around expertise.
3. Teams have goals, which are often established by people not on the team. Communities are only responsible to their members.
4. Teams rely on work and reporting processes that are organizationally defined. Communities develop their own processes.[3]

Teams are primarily organizationally driven, established by those with more authority in the organization and who are accountable for organizational results. In effect, they are the formal structure for individuals to interact with each other. Teams can be named, represented on an organizational chart, and included in such things as strategic plans.

Communities are different. While they may initially come together as a result of some form of organizational intervention, the boundaries are less rigid and the processes less formal. Membership is not determined by hierarchy or position, but by common interest instead.

While the formal structure of teams makes them evident to all, the same cannot be said of communities. Indeed, some of the most powerful communities are "underground" communities. Often referred to as "skunkworks," these groups typically assume a high degree of autonomy and establish norms in which they feel unhampered by bureaucracy or management oversight. The net result is often innovation or rapidly changing culture.

Teams exist through organizational formality, regardless of their level of effectiveness. The same cannot be said for communities. A community with no common sense of purpose, few quality relationships, and poor communication will simply not survive. When the effort to sustain them outweighs the individual benefit, they simply cease to exist. The organic nature of their evolution allows for a timely death when required.

HOW CAN COMMUNITIES OF PRACTICE IMPACT ORGANIZATIONS?

Members of communities interact, talk to each other, learn together, and solve problems together. In so doing, they foster organizational trust, help the organization learn, and can transform an organizational culture. It is through communities that the focus can be dispersed from those at the top of the organization to the entire organization. Adaptive organizations are created through the fostering of organizational communities. Organizations without flourishing communities will remain firmly embedded in the mechanistic paradigm.

Through communities, connections and networks are developed among employees who may, or may not, work in the same area. Relationships are built that create a sense of trust and mutual obligation. A common language and context are shared by community members that can span silos and the boundaries caused by geographical constraints. Knowledge can be shared across traditional structural boundaries and silos. This, in turn, can create an organization that can learn and discover new ways of doing things.

Unstructured problems can be solved more readily as communities typically engage people with different perspectives and different areas of expertise. Ultimately, this can foster an environment in which business performance is positively impacted. Lesser and Storck identify four ways in which communities can create value:

- Decreasing the learning curve of new employees.
- Responding more rapidly to customer needs and inquiries.
- Reducing rework and preventing "reinvention of the wheel."
- Spawning new ideas for products and services.[4]

CREATING EFFECTIVE COMMUNITIES— AN EXECUTIVE'S CHALLENGE

Unlike structured organizational teams, communities can be very informal. While at times they may be created by an organizational edict, often they simply evolve organically. This scenario presents challenges to any executive who wishes to promote communities within his or her organization. A hierarchical, power-based mandate will simply not work.

The answer lies in the development of structures. Structure can provide the opportunity for communities to be formed. It is, therefore, essential that structures be created in which communities can evolve, thrive, and flourish. It is in this domain where executive responsibility clearly lies.

What kind of structures can be used to launch communities? Many options are available.

A leadership development program can create communities. A cohort model that engages employees from different areas of the organization connects people, gives them a sense of identity, and builds relationships, which, in turn, lead to the creation of community. Some form of action-challenge program that requires employees to tackle a significant problem within their regular workplace environment can cement the community. It is for this reason that leadership development designed to transform organizations should only happen in such a way that long-lasting communities can be established. One-off or external programs do not contribute in this regard.

The formation of a group to share a new process or knowledge can also lead to the creation of a community. More than just "lunch and learns," groups can be created to explore ways in which new technologies might be implemented, new knowledge shared, or new innovations developed. In such cases, the group may well grow beyond its original mandate and, providing that the process and the manner in which it worked together is beneficial for all, may become a sustainable community.

Any cross-functional group that gathers together to address a challenge facing the organization can rapidly evolve into a community. I have facilitated innumerable staff meetings that start with a cry of "they should" and conclude with "we will." Their collective commitment to address an issue can be the catalyst to ongoing relationships and developing trust. In effect, such a group acts in a similar manner to a leadership development cohort involved in some kind of action challenge.

Organizational sponsorship in some form of community work can also create internal communities. Employees may gather from various sectors of the organization and, with a common purpose, work together to meet some community needs. In doing so, they themselves form a community that they subsequently choose to sustain within the organization.

These are just four examples of structures that can lead to communities. Some commonalities are evident:

- They all require a willingness to allow people to meet. While such meetings are sometimes regarded as "non-productive" time, it is rare that a real community can be initiated without an investment of time.

- They typically take someone in an authority position to initiate and authorize the implementation of the initial structure. Once launched they can take on a life of their own.
- Members of the future community need to have a shared experience together. Such an experience creates a sense of identity and belonging—one of the critical features of a community.
- The structure must accommodate people beyond traditional organizational boundaries. This means the agenda is not driven by those in charge, and participants are not restricted to a narrow department or division.

Once the community has been formed, the challenge then lies in permitting sufficient freedom that it can be sustained. It is at this point that I frequently see executives fail to commit. Not understanding the importance of community, they neglect to give employees sufficient time to allow the community to flourish. Budget cuts and time restrictions mean relationships and trust cannot flourish. It becomes too hard for individuals to make it work and the communities die.

Executives who support and nurture communities need to ensure they do the following.

Provide and allow for opportunities in which members of the community can connect

Once the community is established and relationships have been built, face-to-face time becomes less critical. The community can be sustained to some extent through other connections—social networking sites, conference calls, e-mail communication, etc. However, on their own there are not enough and there likely needs to be some face-to-face time if the community is to thrive. Senior leaders have a role to play in supporting such opportunities. Face-to-face time may happen through meetings, training sessions, planning sessions, or knowledge fairs.

Senior leaders also need to ensure that communities are provided with the technologies that can facilitate collaboration. As obvious as this appears, it is not always the case. I once worked with a group of front-line supervisors who, during a leadership development program, developed a very strong sense of community. However, when they returned to the workplace they were unable to sustain this connection, as only some of them had access to a computer. Not surprisingly, the community languished.

Allow time and space for relationship building among individuals

As Lesser and Storck point out, "While making connections is an important part of the community building process, the willingness of individuals to share knowledge requires additional time and effort. Employees need the opportunity to interact with each other so that they can evaluate the trustworthiness of others and gauge a sense of mutual obligation."[5] Relationships are enhanced by working together to solve a problem or implement an initiative. When "real time" projects are worked on together, the community takes on a sense of identity and gains clarity of purpose. By working together, it will build on relationships already established and increase the sense of trust and interdependence. But, as with most things, this takes time, and senior leaders who wish to create an adaptive organization must recognize this.

Once the relationships are sufficiently strong, the community learns to self-regulate. In fact, the most significant behavioral changes I have ever witnessed have occurred when peers and colleagues within the community give feedback and demand a change in behavior in each other. The power of the community to regulate the behavior of many must not be underestimated.

Pay attention to the value and benefits of the community

All too often once communities form in organizations, the members of that community are willing to go above and beyond to sustain it. Yet senior leaders fail to capitalize on this commitment and energy. They focus instead on the time and cost of sustaining the community and pay little attention to how they might leverage this strong network of relationships. Executives would better serve the organization by recognizing and acknowledging the existence of communities, and then exploring ways in which these communities can help transform the organization. A focus solely on the costs is reminiscent of a mechanistic way of thinking, doing little to create an adaptive organization.

WHAT DOES IT LOOK LIKE IN ACTION?

A group of cross-functional senior leaders that I worked with a few years ago developed into a strong community and stayed together for several years. The precipitating structure was an experiential leadership program for which a group of 15 was hand-selected by the executive. The first phase of their experience was to work with each other and collectively plan an experiential adventure involving a 70-foot sailboat. As part of this process, they had to make a business case to the executive as to why they should participate in this activity. They then gathered together for their adventure, saw it through to completion, and, before they returned to their jobs, selected an initiative they wanted to implement within the organization. They spent the next year implementing their new idea across the entire organization. In doing this, their relationships strengthened, their organizational knowledge increased, and they became a resource for others in the organization who were looking for a broad organizational perspective over and above the executive. They stayed as a community for some time, only dissipating when a few key members were transferred overseas and their sense of purpose no longer united them.

What made this community succeed? A few critical factors:

- There was a precipitating structure, namely the experiential adventure.
- Sufficient time was spent in the initial stages to cement the relationships and create a sense of identity. Norms of open communication and a non-hierarchical structure were established.
- The implementation of an initiative over an extended period of time gave the group a clear sense of purpose.
- The involvement of the executive in the initial phases ensured there was organizational support for the initial creation of the community.
- The executive then gave sufficient freedom for the group to meet and interact. In this case, all the community members were quite senior and had a considerable degree of autonomy. However, their desire to meet with each other was never questioned.
- The group ensured everyone in the organization knew of and, when appropriate, was involved in the implementation of the initiative. While the experiential adventure was not talked of to any great extent, the objectives of the initiative were made very public, as were the names of the members of the community.

How a community changes cultural norms

An interesting community in another organization was also formed through the process of leadership development. However, in this case, it was not an intact cohort that stayed together for the long term. Rather, it was certain individuals from a number of the different leadership cohorts.

In this case, the leadership development program was designed to change some deeply embedded cultural norms. The organization was very traditional and hierarchical; consequently, many of the ideas presented throughout the 18-month program seemed quite radical to many of the participants. However, a small number of participants embraced the ideas with great energy, recognizing the importance of the shift being proposed, and willingly worked to develop them themselves.

These participants found a way to connect outside of the regular program. From an initial group of just four, they invited other like-minded individuals to join them. The group soon grew to be well over a dozen. And while they worked in a variety of positions in different departments across the entire organization, they had a number of things in common. Primarily, they were united in their desire to both improve their own personal leadership and do the work that this demanded. However, they were also committed to changing the culture of the organization. Despite the fact they were such a small number, they knew they were widely respected throughout the organization and, consequently, had more influence than might be assumed, by simply reviewing the organizational chart.

They developed their own connecting structure. They consistently held monthly, off-site breakfast meetings. Whenever other members of the community who worked outside of head office came into town, they used it as an opportunity to get together. They also used each other as resource and frequently connected with each other via e-mail and phone.

In their meetings and interactions, they modeled the kind of culture they wanted to promote. Nothing was "off limits" and all conversations were candid and frank. This not only allowed them the practice to enhance their own leadership skills, but also allowed them to remain connected to the larger organization. As those they considered to be "like-minded" participated in the ongoing leadership program, the membership grew.

It was not long before the executive got wind of this group. However, the C-suite did not try to gain oversight of the program. Rather, the executive let it grow organically and ensured they kept out of the way. This was critical. Had the executive intervened and tried to assert control over it, this community would have floundered. Part of their identity was that of being a "rogue" group, set up without organizational endorsement. As this was a very hierarchical organization, this, in itself, was a radical move.

This community continues to flourish today. Interestingly, many of its members are now viewed as high potential and will likely find themselves on the executive sooner, rather than later. That bodes well for the future of the organization.

Why did this community thrive?

- The precipitating structure was once again a leadership development initiative.
- A common sense of purpose was key.
- Executive let it thrive and did not intervene.
- The boundaries of this group were soft. It was open to anyone who clearly demonstrated the willingness and ability to lead in a different, more effective manner.
- Norms were established early on that allowed individuals to create whatever structures they deemed appropriate for sustainability.

What the examples tell us

These and other examples offer some clear guidelines for executives who wish to connect individuals from across the organization and develop an adaptive organization. The role of those at the top lies in the following:

- Creating structures that can create ongoing relationships and networks across different parts of the organization. This involves an investment of time and money. However, the focus should be on recognition of the value of such networks, not on the costs of creation.
- Ensuring sufficient support exists to allow these communities to thrive organically. More often than not, this requires allowing members of the community sufficient freedom to do those things they deem important in maintaining the relationship.
- Not formalizing or taking control of these communities. To do so would simply reinforce the mechanistic nature of the organization.
- Use these communities as a resource when possible. Tap into them as information sources and as problem-solving bodies.

Communities are the mechanism that, particularly when built on a comprehensive leadership program for all, can overcome silos and traditional boundaries, creating an adaptable, organic, and competitive organization. But to do so requires both an appreciation of the value of communities and the commitment to initiate and support them by those at the top.

Chapter Sixteen Takeaways

1. Deliberate action to facilitate and support individuals in working outside of the traditional boundaries is necessary for organizational change to occur. When "communities" are established across the organization in which people can learn and solve problems together, the rigidity of a hierarchical organization is replaced by an organization in which people look not to the top for answers, but to each other.

2. In today's environment, effective organizations require structures that can span organizational boundaries and facilitate the development of a learning culture. The structures that are relevant in today's organizations and that allow traditional boundaries to be spanned can take several forms and are known by a variety of names. Networks, interest groups, and communities of practice are all based on the idea that people throughout the organization, who might not traditionally interact with each other, have ongoing relationships and collectively share information and solve problems.

3. Communities are different from teams. While they may initially come together as a result of some form of organizational intervention, the boundaries are less rigid and the processes less formal. Membership is not determined by hierarchy or position, but, instead, by common interest.

4. Adaptive organizations are created through the fostering of organizational communities. Through communities, connections and networks are developed among employees who may or may not work in the same area. Relationships are built that create a sense of trust and mutual obligation. A common language and context are shared by community members that can span silos and geographical constraints. It is through communities that the focus can transfer from those at the top of the organization to the entire organization.

5. Communities can be created through many structures such as a leadership development program based on a cohort model, the formation of a group to share a new process or knowledge, a cross-functional group that gathers together to address a challenge facing the organization, or organizational sponsorship of some form of community work.

6. To be successful, people must meet regularly, someone in an authority position will normally initiate and authorize the implementation of the initial structure, members of the future community need to have a shared experience together, and the structure must accommodate people beyond traditional organizational boundaries.

7. Executives can support communities by providing and allowing for opportunities in which members of the community can connect, allowing time and space for relationship building among individuals, paying attention to the value and benefits of the community.

PART FIVE

TELL PEOPLE HOW THEY'RE DOING

Change does not happen overnight and an individual's journey into different behaviors is oftentimes fraught with fear and uncertainty. Communication and a supportive community can certainly help, but on their own they are not enough. Employees venturing into new terrain without some form of feedback are likely to question the wisdom of the actions.

Unfortunately, while the importance of telling people how they are doing is acknowledged by many, appropriate action is taken by few. Senior executives do not always appreciate the importance of positive recognition and tend to rely too much on HR systems to manage the behavior and performance of employees. They assume that recognition programs and performance management systems will take care of things.

While such systems can help, those at the top cannot rely on them if they want to create a great organization. Senior executives have a critical role in managing the performance of employees. Employees want to know how they are doing, deserve to feel valued, appreciated, and understood, and need to know if they should do something differently. They want feedback. These things are not achieved by a formal performance management system, but by developing a culture that tells people how they are doing and recognizes and rewards them appropriately. Furthermore, those at the top cannot simply rely on other managers to do this. They must recognize the unique role of the executive and leverage this to the fullest extent. The starting point for this is to develop and demonstrate an appreciative mindset.

PAY ATTENTION TO WHAT'S WORKING

I was recently working with an organization that was trying to change the culture to one in which people spoke openly, meetings encompassed vigorous, unfiltered debate, and there was a degree of transparency in all conversations. Knowing this organization well, I knew that, for many employees, even those who were quite high up in the hierarchy, this was a radical move. It was a conservative organization and one in which people were very guarded in their conversations.

I was chatting with the CEO about how it was going. "Pretty well," he explained. "I think people realize I'm not going to kill them when they speak up."

"Have you given any positive feedback to those individuals who take what they feel is a risk?" I asked.

"No," he replied. He paused, reflectively. "I suppose I should," he added.

This is a classic example of what happens with alarming regularity in organizations. People make the change we are hoping for, but the only reinforcement they get is a lack of negative consequences. Those in charge assume that by "not being killed," employees realize they're doing the right thing.

While clearly the absence of negative consequences is a good thing, the lack of positive reinforcement points to a lost opportunity to cement and consolidate new behaviors. In the example cited above, I know that individuals felt it was a significant risk to speak up. Was it worth it? If the only benefit to them is not being killed and they can see no positive outcome, the chances are high that they will choose not to take this risk again.

In just about every organization I know, a passionate focus on what is working is sorely missing. Unfortunately, it is part of our culture to focus more on mistakes rather than on what is going well. Of course, great success rarely goes unnoticed, but what about the small day-to-day things that happen on a regular basis? Often these things are invisible.

It's something that is deeply embedded into our culture and, for many of us, starts in childhood. For example, when my 13-year-old daughter comes in from school, she often prepares herself a snack. If she fails to put away the cheese, the milk, or the crackers, my husband and I will almost certainly notice and nag her. However, if she prepares herself a snack and puts everything away, it is unlikely that we will make a positive remark to her.

The same is also true in organizations. We focus on those employees who are not performing and assume those who are doing well do not need our attention. We spot errors and typos on reports, but will be unlikely to comment if there are none. We assume work will be completed by a deadline and only comment if it is late.

Any executive who wishes to create a great organization has to change this focus on the negative. This can be done by developing what is known as an "appreciative mindset." With its origins in the principles of appreciative inquiry, the concept of appreciative mindset is quite simple—pay attention to what is going well and recognize and support it.

The CEO I referenced earlier was quite happy that the quality of conversation was changing in the meetings. However, it did not occur to him to overtly give some positive feedback to those who were making the required changes. If he were to do so, those individuals would likely repeat this behavior. When any action we do solicits a positive response from others, we are inclined to repeat it. Consider meals you have cooked or new recipes you've tried. If those you respect comment positively, you will likely make that meal again. This may not be the case if your cooking receives no comment.

Developing an appreciative mindset requires three things—find it, track it, fan it.

"Finding it" simply means looking for those things that are going well. It requires a shift in mindset away from the cultural biases we have to the negative. It means paying attention to the things that are working and noticing shifts in behavior, however small.

"Tracking it" means paying attention to the bigger picture. It requires paying close attention to positive shifts, and monitoring trends and systemic changes.

Once you notice the positive changes and are aware of how these trends fit into the big picture, you must do whatever it takes to keep it going. You must "fan the flame" by giving positive encouragement and recognition. This practice is critical and ensures the behavior is sustained.

Perhaps this is not new. After all, the concept of "catch someone doing something right" has been around for some time. However, I continue to be astounded by how often executives fail to adopt an appreciative mindset. And with this failure, they lose a unique opportunity to leverage the power that, rightly or wrongly, employees continue to invest in them.

Throughout this book I have emphasized the importance of moving away from a hierarchical, power-based model of leadership to one that is more collaborative and adaptive. However, if truth be known, many employees still consider the executives to be the untouchables at the top. The irony is that this affords an opportunity for executives to have a great impact and thereby transform the organization to one where people look to themselves more than executives for the answer. Many employees continue to hang on every word an executive says—a fact that can be leveraged by those at the top who are aware of how they can use old paradigms to create new organizations.

The impact of an executive acknowledging and appreciating a change in behavior can be dramatic and change the culture very quickly. Therefore, a critical role of executives who want to create great organizations is to recognize and reward people for the desired behaviors. This doesn't require a big event; people appreciate a signal of appreciation for small accomplishments.

But don't ignore the negative. Does having an appreciative mind-set mean ignoring things that are not right? Absolutely not. Most employees I know are yearning for feedback. They want to do a good job and, often, simply don't have the information they need to know to do it. If they do something "wrong," they would rather know about it in order to improve.

I remember many years ago learning to fly. It was a new experience for me and, certainly in the initial stages, quite terrifying. Coming in to land, I had to pull the stick back to nudge the nose of the airplane up, resulting in a stall at the perfect moment of touch-down. I remember pulling back on the stick and encountering incredible resistance. I had no idea landing was going to be so physically exhausting, but I knew I had to get the nose of the plane up, so with all my might I pulled back on the control stick. After many, many landings like this, I relaxed enough to look across to my instructor. There he was, knuckles white, pushing the control stick forward as hard as he could in an attempt to prevent me from pulling the nose of the plane up too far. He was fighting the efforts I was making every step of the way. I suddenly realized all I had been doing was working against his pressure—and all he was doing was trying to prevent a disaster. In hindsight, it was laughable. To this day, I have no idea why he didn't tell me what was happening. Perhaps he thought I'd figure it out on my own—which is what I did.

This is also true in organizations. For whatever reason, we often fail to give employees the information they need to do a good job. Perhaps we don't want to hurt their feelings, perhaps we feel we don't have the skills to do it, or we don't want to be demotivating. All are valid reasons and all are irrelevant when it comes to creating a great organization.

The challenge lies in how to give employees information that they could, or should, be doing something differently, while at the same time spurring them on to greater achievement. The answer lies in first ensuring you have the skills to do this. Hopefully, those at the top have, during the course of their career, learned how to give feedback in a way that inspires future performance, rather than disengages an individual from the organization. Feedback, even when it is critical, accompanied by an appreciative mindset and a recognition of the value and contribution of the employee, is likely to be welcomed and heard, particularly when delivered by a senior executive. Remember that one of the primary drivers of employee engagement is the extent to which employees feel senior managers care about them. Giving quality feedback is one way to demonstrate this.

THE INSTITUTIONALIZATION OF FEEDBACK

Every executive or manager in an organization has a responsibility to tell employees how they are doing. In a great organization defined by collaboration and adaptiveness, such behaviors will be embedded into the culture. However, we know that many organizations continue to be dominated by the mechanistic paradigm in which employees are viewed more as parts of the machine rather than emotional humans. In such organizations, the assumption that there will be free-flowing feedback on employees' performance is naïve at best. However, in response to an acknowledgment that even in a mechanistic organization employees need to receive feedback, formal processes have been established. These processes are now considered common practice in any organization and include such things as recognition programs and performance management systems.

While one could argue that these programs are not relevant in organizations that have made the transition from the mechanistic model, in reality, they do provide a safety net for cases where individual managers are struggling to communicate effectively with their employees. Furthermore, if designed and implemented appropriately, they can be used to drive the behavior that, ultimately, will lead to these programs' redundancy. However, the opposite is also true and, unfortunately, all too often performance programs recognize and reward behaviors that the organization needs to discourage. For example, an organizational change away from silos to collective action may be desired, yet employees are recognized for individual performance.

The challenge for today's executive is to understand how to best leverage recognition and performance management programs in ways that achieve organizational greatness.

RECOGNITION PROGRAMS

There is no doubt that all employees need and want recognition. In fact, recognition is key to organizational success. A report of the Office of the Auditor General of British Columbia stated: "Recognition has been shown to motivate staff, increase morale, productivity, and employee retention, and decrease stress and absenteeism."[1] The authors indicated that "individual recognition" was one of the top three factors for improving the levels of employee satisfaction and employee engagement in the B.C. public service.

Today's employee relies and depends upon recognition as the means of defining what is valued by the organization. Therefore, praise and recognition are communication vehicles for what is deemed as important. Ultimately, it is a manager's responsibility to ensure that appropriate praise and recognition are regularly communicated. However, this does not always happen and, consequently, executives tend to rely on organizational recognition programs to formalize this form of communication.

Such programs require the same executive oversight as other strategic interventions. As Globoforce, a consulting company that provides strategic employee recognition programs for 2,000 global companies, suggests, "Recognition programs, properly and strategically executed, have the potential to support an organization's financial objectives, improve talent outcomes and reinforce cultural values for a low cost with a high return on investment."[2]

The key element here is the concept of "properly and strategically" executed. Unfortunately, many organizations fall down in this regard. For example, from the same report from the Office of the Auditor General of B.C. quoted above, it was found that only 29 percent of employees were satisfied with the recognition they receive and only 20 percent agreed that recognition and rewards were based on merit.[3] In a 2004 survey, Gallup reported 65 percent of American employees received no recognition for their efforts.[4]

The issue is not a lack of recognition programs. Most organizations have comprehensive and often expensive recognition programs. But do not confuse a complex, comprehensive, and costly program with effectiveness. In a study conducted by Globoforce, senior HR leaders reported that their programs fell short in impact; one-third (33 percent) said their CEOs did not believe their programs drove bottom-line results, and 45 percent of the HR leaders agreed.[5] As those at Globoforce suggest, "Most companies are already investing significantly in an incentive or recognition program of some sort, but the majority of those programs are disparate, unfocused, and do not deliver the full return on investment possible with strategic recognition."[6]

So here's a question for you. How much does your organization spend on recognition programs? And what kind of return do you get for that outlay? Can you honestly say it is money well spent? A recent study showed an astounding 42 percent of organizations are not measuring the results of their recognition program in any way, leaving CEOs in the dark on program effectiveness and wasting the money invested.[7] Such facts are disturbing at best. Although recognition has been shown to directly impact the bottom-line results and recognition programs can consume a huge amount of resources, most executives appear to have little awareness as to the effectiveness of this strategic investment. Any senior executive interested in creating a great organization would be well advised to pay attention to their organization's recognition programs.

When it comes to recognition programs, executives do not need to be authorities any more than they need to be experts in other strategic initiatives outside of their own expertise. There is, hopefully, sufficient recognition program expertise residing in the HR department. However, today's executive needs to ensure that such programs represent a modern organizational paradigm and are effective in supporting the required organizational change.

Recognition programs must reward people for actions and behaviors that reinforce company values, advance the company's mission, and execute on the strategy. Organizations that do well at employee recognition have a recognition strategy and framework that are integrated, multi-faceted, and multi-tiered. Effective programs must be values-based, frequent, timely, relevant, available to all, and measurable.

Ultimately, recognition programs must make employees feel valued, appreciated, and understood. These are guidelines that executives must bear in mind when assessing the quality of recognition programs. All too often, harm is done by failing to deliver a thoughtful and relevant program. Some common mistakes include these:

- Assuming one size fits all. If you really understand your employees, you will recognize that they have different needs.
- Rewarding exceptional performance with more work. How often do you load up your star performers with more work because you can trust them to get it done? Hardly a way to demonstrate that you appreciate what your employees have done.
- Confusing recognition with performance incentives. Michael T. Williams of the Inergy Marketing Group suggests, "Employee recognition is the timely, sincere, and visible gestures of respect and recognition that are offered directly to an employee for his or her contribution to a job well done."[8] It is based on the work that has been done in the past and not on future performance expectations. When recognition is confused with incentives, you will not help employees feel valued, appreciated, or understood.

- Making it too big. Organizations tend to do a great job of recognizing superhuman efforts by employees. Yet often, the employee who is changing their behavior and quietly contributing in increasingly effective ways to the organization is ignored. The most effective recognition programs pay attention to little changes as well as big ones.
- Assuming financial rewards are the best rewards. I once worked with an organization that chose to reward its employees through experiences. For example, one up-and-coming young manager was given responsibility to oversee the construction of the largest on-hill restaurant ever built at a ski resort. He was just 30 years old at the time and, without a doubt, this was a stretch assignment for him. However, it was one that he was not only capable of delivering on, but would also propel his career in a significant manner. He clearly saw that by giving him this assignment, the company was recognizing his performance.
- Rewarding an absence of bad behavior. As Aubrey Daniels points out, "As unorthodox as it sounds, every day organizations reward things a dead man can do. A million hours without an accident, a reduction in errors, or perfect attendance, can all be accomplished by a corpse. This doesn't qualify as valuable behavior and deserves no celebration. In addition, the same error occurs when any perk or benefit is given across the board. That way, employees will want to do just enough to remain on the payroll. Where poor performers are rewarded, it is punishing to all those who do a good job."9

The purpose of recognition programs is to let people know, in a formal manner, what they are doing well. Done effectively, such programs can be very helpful in communicating and cementing changes in behavior. But done poorly, they can create a significant stumbling block to organizational change. Consequently, those at the top would be well-advised to ensure that recognition programs are leveraged in the most effective ways possible. They are, without doubt, a strategic executive responsibility.

PERFORMANCE MANAGEMENT PROGRAMS

Just as recognition programs are formal communication tools that can guide and direct individual behavior, so are performance management programs. In much the same way, while individual executives do not have to be experts, they must ensure that these programs facilitate the desired organizational change and do not work against it.

Performance management is defined as "the strategy and sets of methodologies and processes that an organization uses to direct its employees, partners, suppliers, and customers to achieve a common set of goals and objectives."[10] It is a process that provides feedback, accountability, and documentation for performance outcomes. While the term "performance management" has a distinctive mechanistic ring, the notion that a process exists to help direct employees is, I believe, a good one.

Within organizations, performance management is widely defined. In some organizations it can refer simply to performance appraisals, while in others, it represents a much more comprehensive process to ensure that employees' outputs are relevant to the organizational goals.

Performance management systems, when appropriately implemented, can prevent misalignment of individual actions with purpose, strategy, and goals. Unless this misalignment is appropriately addressed in some systematic fashion, the creation of a high-performance organization will remain a pipe dream. A performance management system is a process that has the potential to ensure such alignment. Executives who do not hold the responsibility for the HR function do, nevertheless, have the responsibility to ensure that every element of the performance management system aligns to the organizational strategy.

I once worked with an organization that had a very formal performance management system. Each year, individual objectives were established for employees and tracked on a quarterly basis, and bonuses were paid out on performance-based objectives. At the same time, a leadership development program was underway that was advocating some new and different behaviors.

The problem was that the objectives set through the performance management system bore no relationship to the leadership behaviors being advocated through the leadership program. In fact, in many cases, they actually contradicted the desired behavioral change. For example, the performance management system rewarded those managers who achieved results at any cost. It did not matter that these managers alienated everyone on their team and nobody wanted to work with them, even though one of the articulated competencies was to create and sustain a sense of trust.

As demonstrated by this example, an organization's performance management system must be designed in a way that will support and facilitate the development of new behaviors. It is another formal organizational tool to tell people how they are doing. The context for this conversation must be the organizational vision, not the currently embedded culture.

Unless they are in HR, no executive needs to be an expert on recognition programs or performance management processes. However, it's important that they're aware of these tools and how the performance management process is either a facilitator or a barrier to organizational change. Any executive who wants to create a great organization can only do this through individual behavior change and, regardless of his or her formal responsibilities, the executive must leverage their position as a senior leader to tell employees how they are doing. Given that this is the ultimate goal, executives must ask themselves the following:

- To what extent do employees know how they're doing?
- What processes do we have to support the desired changes on a timely and regular basis?
- To what extent am I abdicating this to the HR department?
- How can I better use formal recognition and performance management processes to communicate and appreciate employees?
- Is the way we are recognizing, rewarding, and giving feedback to employees creating a great organization? If not, what do I need to change? If so, what can we do more of?

Chapter Seventeen Takeaways

1. Senior executives have a critical role in managing the performance of employees. Employees want to know how they are doing; feel valued, appreciated, and understood; and know if they need to do something differently. These things are not achieved by a formal performance management system, but rather by developing a culture that tells people how they are doing, and recognizes and rewards them appropriately. Those at the top must recognize the unique role of the executive in providing feedback to employees and leverage this opportunity to the fullest extent.

2. Most organizations and senior leaders have a tendency to focus more on mistakes than what is going well. A passionate focus on what is working is sorely missing. While great success is often appreciated, small day-to-day things that happen on a regular basis typically go unnoticed. Any executive who wishes to create a great organization has to change this focus

on the negative and should pay attention to what is going well, and recognize and support it.

3. The impact of an executive acknowledging and appreciating a change in behavior can be dramatic and change the culture very quickly. Therefore, a critical activity of executives who want to create great organizations is to catch people doing something right, and recognize and reward them. Senior leaders should not wait until the big events, but instead look for small actions that are indicative of what is desired.

4. The assumption that there will be free-flowing feedback on employees' performance is naïve at best. In response to an acknowledgment that even in a mechanistic organization employees need to receive feedback, formal processes have been established. These processes are now considered common practice in any organization and include such things as recognition programs and performance management systems. All executives have a responsibility to ensure that such programs support the creation of a great organization and do not work against the desired transformation.

5. Today's employee relies and depends upon praise and recognition as the means of defining what is valued by the organization. Praise and recognition are therefore communication vehicles for what is deemed as important. Ultimately, it is a manager's responsibility to ensure that appropriate praise and recognition are communicated. However, this does not always happen and, consequently, executives tend to rely on organizational recognition programs to formalize this form of communication. Such programs require the same executive oversight as other strategic interventions.

6. Performance management systems, when appropriately implemented, can prevent misalignment of individual actions with purpose, strategy, and goals. Unless this misalignment is appropriately addressed in some systematic fashion, the creation of a high-performance organization will remain a pipe dream. A performance management system is a process that has the potential to ensure such alignment. Executives who do not hold the responsibility for the HR function do, nevertheless, have the responsibility to ensure that every element of the performance management system aligns to the organizational strategy.

PROMOTE FOR THE FUTURE

An organization can only be great if people in the organization are behaving in ways that facilitate greatness—both now and in the future. Hence, a critical part of an executive's responsibility is to look ahead to ensure there is a healthy pool of people with the necessary skills and capabilities to lead the organization into the future. Regardless of whether it is called succession planning, talent management, or some other trendy term, developing a system to ensure that the organization is sustainable for years to come is not only a critical strategic initiative, but also a key communication tool. As with many other people-related responsibilities, it is one that can no longer be left solely in the hands of HR. Rather, those at the top must take collective responsibility for assessing, developing, and promoting future talent.

For many, this is not a new idea. However, despite knowing this is a critical process, few organizations get it right. Not only are organizations failing to ensure a ready supply of talent for the future, the manner in which they implement succession planning often does more harm than good to organizational effectiveness.

Succession planning demands excellence at the most senior level, something that is not always fully appreciated by today's executive. It requires the following:

- The executive to be a highly functioning collaborative team.
- Individual executive members must be able to distinguish between filtered and authentic communication.

- All on the executive team must be prepared to abandon old paradigms and preconceived beliefs regarding an individual's competence and reputation.
- The top team must be clear on the talents, skills, and abilities the organization needs to implement the vision.
- In implementing the succession process, the executive must model the organizational values every step of the way.

Unfortunately, these preconditions are not always present, ultimately resulting not only in a flawed succession planning process but also in a loss in organizational credibility.

Despite the fact that planning for the future is a critical strategic task, executives at the top, time and time again, make errors in two critical areas—the assessment of their people and the manner in which the process is communicated.

SIZING UP YOUR TALENT: MISTAKES EXECUTIVES MAKE

You have hundreds, thousands, or perhaps hundreds of thousands of employees in your organization. How do you know who in this vast group "has what it takes" to guide your organization now and in the future? Clearly, some form of assessment is required. Unfortunately, assessment processes are fraught with problems and those at the top make erroneous judgments about people.

The life of an executive is a busy one. Demands external to the organization typically limit executives' time to observe and interact with employees. As a result, they risk painting a distorted picture about how employees are performing. Often, a senior leader's view of an individual's competence is based more on a reputation established in years gone by than current realities. The situation is compounded in a culture where information is filtered to those at the top.

A few years ago I was working with a vice president at a company. He was a pleasant fellow, and whether I was coaching or observing him as a participant in a leadership program I was running, he certainly gave the appearance of being a great leader. His senior vice president held a similar view. However, I was also coaching many of his direct reports and the story I got from them was significantly different. They found this VP to be controlling and disrespectful, and they detested working for him. I had no idea about this and neither did his boss. It was only when I alerted the senior vice president to the fact that there may be a problem that the real truth of the matter was unearthed. To his credit, the senior VP acted immediately. This vice president was quickly removed from the list of future successors, and it wasn't long before he left the organization.

This is just one example, yet I've seen similar occurrences on numerous occasions. Indeed, I've even been fooled myself. A few years ago, I had a manager reporting to me who had me convinced he was mostly competent. From where I sat, his team enjoyed working for him and he supplied me with information to suggest he was on top of everything. While we weren't getting the results we wanted, his rationale for this failure always seemed to make sense. He was confident and so was I. So much so, that I allowed him a free rein of the organization. I soon found out this was a big mistake, one that almost ended in the downfall of the company. A couple of complaints from clients caused me to question my judgment and I started digging into what was really going on. What I found was a serious case of narcissistic leadership and managerial incompetence. Yes, I had been duped!

One of the worst misjudgments that an executive can make in assessing talent is to do what I did—mistake narcissism for competence. It's easily done, as on the surface, these individuals' energy, charm, and self-confidence can manifest as effective leadership. As R. Hogan, R. Raskin, and D. Fazzini suggest in their essay "The Dark Side of Charisma": "Narcissists typically make judgments with greater confidence than other people . . . and, because their judgments are rendered with such conviction, other people tend to believe them and the narcissists become disproportionately more influential in group situations. Finally, because of their self-confidence and strong need for recognition, narcissists tend to 'self-nominate'; consequently, when a leadership gap appears in a group or organization, the narcissists rush to fill it."[1]

However, be aware that narcissists are terrible managers. Make no mistake, narcissists likely have an Opportunist action logic, masked with an ability to project more as a Strategist. These individuals resist accepting suggestions, thinking it will make them appear weak, and don't believe that others have anything useful to tell them. Hogan and his co-authors write, "Narcissists are biased to take more credit for success than is legitimate, and biased to avoid acknowledging responsibility for their failures and shortcomings for the same reasons that they claim more success than is their due."[2] The net result is that they look good to their peers and their bosses, but turn out to be a negative force in their companies.

Unfortunately, senior executives who are often overloaded or distracted by external demands often fail to pick up the warning signs that there is a narcissist in their midst. Worse, they view such an individual as a superstar and promote him or her into positions of greater responsibility. This can be a critical error for any executive who wants to create a great organization.

Another error occurs when future talent is identified based on criteria that, while pertinent in the past, are irrelevant for the future. I worked with a company that, despite huge investments in leadership development, consistently promoted individuals who were good technical experts, but terrible at working with people. In this case, it simply didn't matter how much effort the CEO expended promoting the virtues of effective leadership. The old adage that actions speak louder than words clearly applied in this case, and the CEO soon lost all organizational credibility.

Often, individuals are assessed based on outcomes. This makes sense—after all, we pay people to get things done. However, this assumes that the employee has complete control over an outcome. In today's boundary-less world this is not always the case and, frequently, our assessment of an individual's performance does not take into account the variables that might influence the outcome. Furthermore, in a collaborative organization, we need to be more concerned with the performance of the collective, rather than one individual. A focus on individual output flies in the face of everything we now know about effective organizations and this focus hardly does anything to promote a collaborative, rather than competitive, organization.

Those deemed "talented" are often moved from job to job very quickly. Yet often, achievements (or lack thereof) cannot be properly assessed in a short period of time. Relying instead on our own beliefs that they are high performers, we look for evidence to confirm this, often disregarding indications that this might not be the case. At Enron, for example, annual turnover from promotions was close to 20 percent. People deemed "talented" were constantly being pushed into new jobs and given new challenges. As Malcolm Gladwell in his article "The Talent Myth" points out, "How do you evaluate someone's performance in a system where no one is in a job long enough to allow such evaluation?"[3]

With struggles in assessing performance, we sometimes make assumptions that those with a high IQ will likely be the best performers. Not so. R. Wagner has determined that the correlation between IQ and occupational success is between 0.2 and 0.3. A high intelligence does not necessarily equate with a high level of common sense, something that is critical for high performance.[4]

Some organizations have turned to multi-rater feedback such as 360 assessments to provide a more rigorous form of evaluation, given that it takes into account the views of many. Yet as described in Chapter Six, these questionnaires are susceptible to several types of bias and error, and should in no way be viewed as absolutes.

Furthermore, problems exist when 360s are used for assessment rather than development. While they may have initially been implemented as a developmental tool, sooner or later someone in senior management suggests using them as a guide to evaluate performance. At first blush this would seem to make total sense, but in reality, such a change in use will impact how people rate each other. Research has shown that when the ratings become evaluative rather than purely developmental, some raters (up to 35 percent) change their ratings.[5] Therefore, great care should be taken when considering using 360 feedback for performance evaluation.

A BETTER ASSESSMENT PROCESS

Given these problems, what is the best way to go about identifying future talent? In particular, how can you assess your employees in a way that is reflective of today's organizations and not outdated paradigms? Executives today do not need to be the experts on the intricacies of the succession planning process. However, in order to ensure that succession planning helps rather than hinders the development of a great organization, those at the top need to ensure the following principles are firmly embedded in the process.

Use multiple data sources

Given the problems outlined above with assessment, do not rely on a single data source. Walk around, ask questions, and be curious. Solicit the views of others on who they believe has the potential to be an effective leader in the future. Try and gather some differing views. Don't dismiss people simply because they have not got the experience. Increasingly, we are seeing younger generations demonstrate the behaviors that we need for the future. Remember, experience is no guarantee of future success. Be aware of your own paradigms and design a process that will help you see different realities. At this point, look for strengths and disregard weaknesses. Use the action logic framework to find those who have a Strategist frame.

Future orientation

As described in Chapter Three, it is important to get a picture of what you want in the future. Rather than getting bogged down with semantics or the wordsmithing of competencies, you need to identify those talents that will be key as you move forward. For instance, given that the future is an unknown, it will be critical that those charged with responsibility for leading the organization have both a willingness and ability to learn new ways. They must be comfortable with change and taking the initiative.

Look for people's strengths

It now becomes a matter of identifying those who best model what you will need in the future. In particular, who has real strengths in these areas?

It is at this point that you must make sure you're not being governed by old paradigms. Look across the organization—in every place and at every level. Look in places you previously would never have looked. In the traditional organization, you may have only looked at certain hierarchical levels. In today's organization, such an approach may well fail to identify your most talented future leaders. Try to clear your mind of preconceived ideas and assess solely on what is required for the future.

Assess their weaknesses

We all have strengths and weaknesses. The question that must be asked is whether the weaknesses are "showstoppers," or is it possible to manage around them? For those who will lead the organization there are some weaknesses that Zenger and Folkman describe as fatal flaws. These are described as the

- Inability to practice self-development, specifically by failing to learn from mistakes;
- Lack of core interpersonal skills and competencies;
- Lack of openness to new or different ideas, resulting in a failure to innovate or lead change;
- Lack of accountability or failure to focus on results; and
- Failure to take initiative.[6]

Regardless of the strengths an individual may have, any one of these fatal flaws should exclude someone from being part of the talent pool destined to assume the leadership of the organization. While few would argue with this, in reality, it is very difficult to implement. The first point, the inability to practice self-development, is disturbingly prevalent at the top of organizations. Therefore, in assessing the organization's talent, be careful not to make assumptions that those currently in positions of responsibility are free and clear of these fatal flaws.

Make it a collaborative process

Traditional succession planning has evolved in organizations dominated by silos and clear boundaries between departments. Managers in departments have identified their successors and supplied lists to HR, who merrily put names into boxes. While making everyone feel good, such a process was typically quite ineffective and certainly makes little sense in today's dynamic and collaborative environment.

Effective succession planning must be done as a team. It is a critical strategic task that must be undertaken by the executive as a whole. Organizations that rely on individual decisions with limited, if any, group consultation are at risk of destroying organizational credibility and trust.

The manner in which this collaboration happens can vary depending on the circumstances. The most effective way is typically to have individual executives bring names of identified talent to the executive table for discussion. It is this discussion that is perhaps one of the most critical elements of any succession planning process and, as such, it is essential that the executive team is highly functioning and extremely collaborative. This discussion must be no-holds-barred and with no agenda except what is in the best interests of the organization.

The discussion must focus on strengths and fatal flaws. Integrating discussions of individuals' action logic frames is invaluable. An investment in confirming key individuals' present frames by commissioning a Leadership Development Profile (as described in Chapter Four), is a wise and cost-effective option. Remember, organizational transformation requires Strategists.

Executive team members must challenge, debate, and discuss who best fits the bill in terms of future needs. Typically, pools are created of As, Bs, and Cs. The As are those who are seen as having what it takes to move the organization forward. Bs are valuable employees to be retained, but not necessarily given any additional responsibility. Cs are those whose performance gives rise for concern.

WHEN THE RUBBER HITS THE ROAD: TALKING ABOUT YOUR SUCCESSION DECISIONS

We now come to the second area in which many organizations fall short with respect to succession planning—communication. By definition, the succession planning process demands that some individuals be selected over others. There must be some differentiation or, as Diane Rabbani, a former provincial deputy minister, once told me, "we'll all be average together."

The transparency of the process and, in particular, how this selection takes place, is articulated, and the different tiers are treated speaks volumes about organizational values. Executives can leverage this to both transform an organization and firmly cement the values. Alternatively, if not done well, the succession planning process can make a mockery of espoused values and destroy organizational integrity and trust.

For years, succession planning has been an "underground" process. Rather than risking offending anyone, organizations have adopted a philosophy of secrecy as the succession process unfolds. Such an approach does little to engender trust throughout the organization. Furthermore, it demonstrates that those in positions of influence in the organization lack the strength and courage to step up to the leadership challenges of the future.

I once worked with an organization desperately trying to transform from a rigid bureaucracy to a much more nimble and enlightened organization. They recognized that they needed a different quality of leadership at every level and set about identifying those individuals they believed could challenge the status quo, speak up, take the initiative, and make decisions. But when it got to the point of informing these individuals that they were seen as the future, the senior executives backed down and the entire process ground to a halt. Ultimately, the selected individuals only learned they were seen as high potential during their exit interviews; ironically, many of them chose to go and work for other organizations where their talents were better appreciated.

The simple act of sitting down with employees and having an honest two-way conversation about the organization's hopes and expectations, and the alignment of these to an individual's career aspirations, can, in itself, transform many organizations. Those senior leaders who, for years, have articulated a desire to develop a culture of openness now have a unique opportunity to "walk the talk" and insist that their managers do likewise. It is critical that not only senior executives do this, but also those who report to them. Some training and development may be required on how to conduct these conversations, but that should not prevent them happening.

The A players

Although these are your stars, it is critical you do not give them superstar status. Any attempts to disproportionately reward them will reinforce the notion of individualistic and heroic leadership, while at the same time de-motivate all others within the organization. Yes, those to whom you will entrust the future of the organization need to be rewarded and recognized, but not at the outrageous levels we've seen in many North American corporations.

Perhaps the most important thing is to talk to those who have been collectively identified by executives at the top as being key to the future of the organization. There is no blueprint for this conversation, but consider the following:

- The person you're talking to needs to hear directly from you that you believe they have the talent to take the organization into the future.
- Ask them about their plans, dreams, and ambitions. Remember, if they are not interested in greater responsibility, it does not matter that you have them down as a successor.
- Whatever you do, don't promise them a particular position. The future is unknown and, thus, commitment to a particular promotion may be wishful thinking at best.
- Ask them what they need in the way of development or support.

The B players

It is the conversations with those who are not in the top pool that often present the greatest challenge for managers. Too concerned with hurting feelings or de-motivating these individuals, managers choose instead to say nothing. What they fail to realize is that this lack of communication is even more disengaging. These conversations are important and, often, not as hard as anticipated. Consider this:

- While promotion to a greater level of responsibility may be viewed as desirable by some, this is not the case for all. Indeed, in these crazy days of 24/7 work, overfilled schedules, and lack of a decent work-life integration, many have looked to the top and decided they have no ambition to be there. It may be through your conversation with those in the B pool that you find they are more than happy with where they are at the present time.
- The boundaries between the different pools are open and not closed. Therefore, if someone in the B pool has a desire to be in the A pool, there may be nothing to stop them from getting there. Your role in the conversation is then to work out a development plan and support their ambitions.
- For some, although they may have a desire for greater responsibility, it may be clear to you and others that they do not have the raw talent. In this case, an honest conversation is called for. While difficult, it is essential, for unless this

discussion occurs, the individual will increasingly disengage from the organization as his or her ambitions are thwarted. The challenge for you, or whoever is having the conversation, is to identify ways in which this person can become engaged and fulfilled at work while not climbing the ladder of advancement. Together, you need to find alternative challenges and goals.

- It is frequently the B players that are overlooked. Those in the A pool garner great attention from those at the top, as do those in the C pool, albeit for different reasons. The B players are the backbone of an organization, yet they are often the ones that are neglected. A discussion with them can motivate, affirm, and encourage them in ways they have never felt before.

The C players

Typically, there has been no shortage of conversations with those employees whose performance is less than satisfactory. Indeed, these individuals often consume vast amounts of time, often at the expense of the more engaged and talented employees. However, as part of the succession planning process, it is important to have conversations with C players, but with a view to resolution. Ultimately, poor performance is an indication that neither party is happy. Again, a few points to consider:

- Don't be afraid to make a decision that the situation is irretrievable. Consider not only the cost of acting, but also the cost of *not* acting. To what extent is this individual impacting more motivated employees? What does it say about your culture if you continue to tolerate poor performance?
- Try to get to the root cause of poor performance. I believe most people want to do a good job. They certainly show up that way on their first day of work. From this first day, organizations then systematically go about disengaging these motivated employees. If it's not working out, ask yourself (and them) what's getting in the way.
- Make sure that you act in ways that honor your organizational values. Such things as respect and integrity should not only apply to your A and B players. The process by which you address concerns you have with C players will speak volumes about your organization.

Succession planning, done properly, is a powerful communication tool for any executive. Much can be gained by implementing a transparent process in which organizational values are apparent to all.

Conversely, much harm can be done when executives fail to recognize the strategic importance of the process, make naïve assumptions about performance, or make succession decisions that do not align with their articulated priorities.

Chapter Eighteen Takeaways

1. A critical part of an executive's responsibility is to look towards the future to ensure there is a healthy pool of people with the necessary skills and capabilities to lead the organization into the future. Regardless of whether it is called succession planning, talent management, or some other term, developing a system to ensure that the organization is sustainable for years to come is not only a critical strategic initiative, but also a key communication tool. Those at the top cannot abdicate this responsibility to HR, but must instead take collective responsibility for assessing, developing, and promoting future talent.

2. Succession planning demands excellence at the most senior level. It requires that the executive be a highly functioning collaborative team; individual executive members be able to distinguish between filtered and authentic communication; everyone on the executive team be prepared to abandon preconceived beliefs regarding an individual's competence; the top team be clear on the talents, skills, and abilities the organization needs to implement the vision; and the executive recognize that in implementing the succession process they must model the organizational values.

3. One of the worst misjudgments that an executive can make in assessing talent is to mistake narcissism for competence. This can easily occur as, on the surface, these individuals' energy, charm, and self-confidence can manifest as effective leadership. Senior executives often fail to pick up the warning signs that there is a narcissist in their midst. This can be a critical error for any executive who wants to create a great organization, as narcissists are terrible managers.

4. Another error occurs when future talent is identified based on criteria that, while pertinent in the past, are irrelevant for the future. This is particularly common in situations where technical expertise is given weight over people skills.

5. Assessment is made all the more challenging because employees do not always have complete control over an outcome or move between various jobs so quickly that there is insufficient time to properly assess individual performance. Furthermore, in a collaborative organization, we need to be more concerned with the performance of the collective rather than one individual. In addition, 360 assessments are susceptible to several types of bias and error, and should only be used for assessment with great caution.

6. To ensure that succession planning helps rather than hinders the development of a great organization, executives must ensure that assessment takes place with a future orientation, individuals' strengths are identified, and the relevance of weaknesses are assessed to determine if they can be managed around, or whether such weaknesses are "fatal flaws." In addition, multiple data sources should be used.

7. Effective succession planning must be done as a team. It is a critical strategic task that must be undertaken by the executive as a whole. Organizations that rely on individual decisions with limited, if any, group consultation are at risk of destroying organizational credibility and trust.

8. The transparency of the process and, in particular, how this selection takes place and is articulated, and how the different tiers are treated speaks volumes about organizational values. Executives can leverage this to both transform an organization and firmly cement the values. Alternatively, if not done well, the succession planning process can make a mockery of espoused values and destroy organizational integrity and trust. The simple act of sitting down with employees and having an honest two-way conversation about the organization's hopes and expectations, and how these align with an individual's career aspirations, can, in itself, transform many organizations.

PRINCIPLE #19:

INTEGRATE THE HARD AND THE SOFT

Traditionally, we have assumed that the skills required of those who lead organizations fall into two categories—hard and soft. Hard skills are those we consider to be more tangible and are usually easy to observe, quantify, and measure. Activities such as account management, data management, project management, financial management, product development, and business analysis are typically thought to demand hard skills. In contrast, soft skills are much more nebulous. Harder to quantify and measure, soft skills have to do with how people relate to each other and include such things as communicating, listening, engaging in dialogue, giving feedback, collaborating as a team member, solving problems, contributing in meetings, and resolving conflict.

Simple, right? Not so. As with much of organizational life, while straightforward differentiation may appeal to us, it is a gross over-simplification of what actually happens within organizations. The hard and soft elements of an individual's behavior are not unique and separate, but are instead integrated.

Why should this concern an executive trying to build a great organization? Is this simply semantics, or does it in some way impact the way today's executive builds a great organization?

It is, without doubt, the latter. When we act as though hard and soft skills are unique and separate, we are, in effect, treating them as events, distinct from processes. The message we send is that at certain times, hard skills are important, while at other times, it is the soft skills that matter. This mechanistic mindset does not reflect the reality of organizational life in which soft skills are inexorably intertwined with hard skills. Indeed, the notion that one can, at one minute, be working on a task requiring hard skills and, at another, be working on something requiring soft is folly. In reality, most tasks require both hard and soft.

The shortcomings associated with isolating the soft from the hard are evident in many aspects of organizational life. Some of the most significant, for today's executive, are apparent when we reflect on the differences between management and leadership, when we make decisions, when we engage in a strategic planning process, and when we implement training and development. A closer examination of these features of organizational life will bring such problems to light.

MANAGEMENT VERSUS LEADERSHIP

Perhaps nowhere is the distinction more pronounced than in discussions and debate regarding the separation between management and leadership. It's a debate that rages on in most leadership programs, is extensively explored in the literature, and has more than its share of cute phrases. You've likely heard them:

- "Management is doing things right; leadership is doing the right things." (Warren Bennis)
- "Management is efficiency in climbing the ladder of success; leadership determines whether the ladder is leaning against the right wall." (Stephen Covey)
- "The manager accepts the status quo; the leader challenges it." (Warren Bennis)
- "You cannot manage men into battle. You manage things; you lead people." (Grace Hopper)

Is there a difference between managing and leading? Often those in organizations confidently state that these are distinct processes. Managers are concerned with managing, which typically requires directing and controlling the work of others. Textbooks on management typically list five primary managerial responsibilities: planning, organizing, staffing, directing, and evaluating. Managers frequently find themselves focusing on operational details and procedures. Conversely, leaders are seen as rallying the troops, inspiring others, or articulating a powerful vision. Clearly, this is something that is different to management.

To illustrate the differences, academics create charts and tables stating the differences, such as the one following, which was produced by J. Kotterman.[1]

Process	Management	Leadership
Vision establishment	• Plans and budgets • Develops process steps and sets timelines • Displays impersonal attitude about the vision and goals	• Sets the direction and develops the vision • Develops strategic plans to achieve the vision • Displays very passionate attitude about the vision and goals
Human development and networking	• Organizes and staffs • Maintains structure • Delegates responsibility • Delegates authority • Implements the vision • Establishes policy and procedures to implement vision • Displays little emotion • Limits employee choices	• Aligns organization • Communicates the vision, mission, and direction • Influences creation of coalitions, teams, and partnerships that understand and accept the vision • Displays driven, high emotion • Increases choices
Vision execution	• Controls processes • Identifies problems • Solves problems • Monitors results • Takes low-risk approach to problem solving	• Motivates and inspires • Energizes employees to overcome barriers to change • Satisfies basic human needs • Takes high-risk approach to problem solving
Vision outcome	• Manages vision order and predictability • Provides expected results consistently to leadership and other stakeholders	• Promotes useful and dramatic changes, such as new products or approaches to improving labor relations

Although at first blush this appears to make good sense, a closer look reveals that such a distinct separation rarely reflects the reality of organizational life. While those in managerial positions have to perform certain tasks, the way they do this is governed by the kind of leader they are.

The separation between management and leadership appears to be clear when we have leaders who are charismatic and inspirational. The chart above assumes that all motivation, emotions, and influence fall under the jurisdiction of the leader. A manager is an unemotional workhorse. The manager deals with the boring task-oriented work, while the enigmatic, larger-than-life leader rallies the troops.

Such a belief takes us back to the era of heroic leadership in which strong leadership was the domain of just a few. Organizations today demand something different and, I believe, require that those who are responsible for others in the organizational hierarchy lead through the application of the managerial role. In other words, in doing the work of management, such as planning, implementing, or problem solving, they must inevitably interact with people. This interaction is where leadership can occur. It is not hard *or* soft. It is hard *and* soft.

The work of management, by definition, demands that a manager deals with people. In such dealings, a manager must have well-developed soft skills of the kind we see in leaders. I do not believe that an individual can, at one moment, be a manager and, the next moment, a leader. While the managerial roles defined as "task" provide the context, the manner in which others are engaged in this task and giving their best effort is determined by a manager's leadership effectiveness. To assume that a manager deals with tasks and a leader deals with people is a gross oversimplification of organizational reality.

The idea that leadership is something separate from management reinforces the notion that leadership resides in just a few. However, if we accept that it is integrated into the very fabric of organizational life, then executives are justified in demanding that effective leadership takes place at every level, and on every occasion, throughout the organization.

DECISION-MAKING

One of the areas where the separation between hard and soft is most harmful is in the realm of decision-making. A significant part of the job of a manager is to solve problems and make decisions. Thus, managers are given training to help them make decisions in a timely and effective manner. Whether it is through an MBA program or internal management training courses, those who are in management positions learn about the decision-making methods and techniques that vary in degrees of autonomy, consultation, and participation. With the presentation of clear-cut formulas as to when and where to apply the various decision-making techniques, managers often come to see decision-making as a hard skill.

However, the manner in which decisions are made, and the way the decision-maker interacts with those impacted by the decision, is clearly a soft skill. When it is approached more as an absolute hard skill than an integrated soft, people-oriented skill, opportunities to leverage both the soft and the hard are lost and with the lost opportunities, the capacity to ensure that not only are good decisions made, but are also followed through on and implemented.

This separation between hard and soft in the arena of decision-making significantly impacts an organization's effectiveness. For example, studies of 356 decisions in medium- to large-sized organizations in the United States and Canada revealed that half of these decisions failed. These failures were traced to managers who imposed solutions, limited the search for alternatives, and used power to implement their plans—all tactics that indicate poor soft skills. Indeed, researcher P. Nutt found that processes that were likely to lead to a failure in decision-making were used in two of every three decisions that were studied.[2] In addition, a survey of 350 global companies revealed only 15 percent said they have an organization that helps the business outperform competitors. What set those top performers apart was the quality, speed, and execution of their decision making.[3]

This research suggests that, despite the fact decision-making is typically taught to organizational managers, the skill is not being well applied. I propose that one key reason for this is the separation of hard and soft skills. A good decision (i.e., one that is the best decision given the circumstances and is followed through and implemented) requires an emotionally intelligent application of decision-making skills. Nutt proposes that in order for decisions to succeed within organizations, those responsible for the decision must employ a number of "soft-skilled" tactics. These include self-management, reflection, an understanding and appreciation of the larger process, and a willingness to explore creative options and implementation ideas.

However, more recent research suggests that another challenge is the fact that as an individual progresses up through the organizational hierarchy, so his or her decision-making style needs to evolve. As Brousseau, Driver, Hourihan, and Larsson state: "Somewhere between the manager and director levels, executives hit a point where approaches that used to work are no longer so effective."[4] This research, based on a study of the decision-making profiles of more than 120,000 executives, found that as they rose through the hierarchical ranks, to be successful managers and executives they needed to become increasingly open and interactive in their leadership styles, and more analytic in their thinking styles. The research shows that decision-making profiles do a complete flip over the course of a career; that is, the decision profile of a successful CEO is the opposite of a successful first-line supervisor's.

This research highlights how the hard and soft skills are so clearly intertwined. The authors found that people make decisions very differently in public than they do in private. In public, senior leaders strive to be seen as open and interactive. It is important to them that they gather as much information as possible. Knowing that some individuals are typically reluctant to fully disclose to executives at the top, successful executives consciously present a willingness to consider options and alternatives. The information-hungry executive invites input and leads in a way that encourages the free flow of information.

However, in private, they adopt a different style. No longer concerned with how they are necessarily perceived by others, successful executives become increasingly analytical and use the information they have gathered to make a decision or, at a minimum, narrow the options down to a workable strategy. In private, they do not follow the same style as others see in public, but rather follow a more autocratic process in which they are focused to find a single right answer.

One could argue that, in this case, the external process is leadership, while the internal is management. But such a categorization hardly does justice to the complexities of the process. Furthermore, at the lower levels, a successful manager uses a different process. In these cases, supervisors will tend to be more overtly decisive and combine the use of minimal information in a single option. In private, supervisors may adopt a more exploratory, creative thinking approach, rather than their focused directive style.

Clearly, the decision-making process is a complex one and, as such, it involves a complex interaction between the skills we regard as hard and those we consider to be soft. In other words, effective decision-making is a function of effective management and leadership.

PLANNING STRATEGY

Every executive knows that strategic planning is important. Gaining clarity concerning the future direction of the organization and how this is to be achieved is often regarded as a priority by many executives.

I cannot count the number of organizations that I have worked with that invest enormous amounts of time and money into a comprehensive strategic planning process. Retreats are held, possible options are debated, and documents produced. The binders are distributed, verified, and everyone relaxes knowing the work has been done.

And then what happens? Nothing! Plans remain as simply words on paper and the business carries on as always. Why does this happen? Because the soft skills are not integrated with the hard. Assumptions abound that clearly articulated plans will change people's behavior, the future is a known, and there are no hidden agendas. Time and time again we see that this is simply not the case.

Strategic planning is a process through which organizations determine exactly where they are going over the next year or more, and how they are going to get there. A strategic plan is a coordinated and systematic way to develop a course and direction for an organization. As described by the Business Development Bank of Canada, "Basically, if you don't have a strategic plan, it's akin to navigating unknown territory without a map. And without a map, you're lost in a highly competitive business environment that will inevitably throw these challenges your way: increasing globalization, unpredictable investment patterns, more demanding clients, and the dizzying speed of technology. A rule of thumb is that if there's uncertainty on the horizon, which there always is today, the greater the need for strategic planning."[5]

Unfortunately, despite the recognized importance of the strategic planning process and the considerable resources spent on it, strategic planning often fails to produce anything of use. In a survey conducted by McKinsey in 2006, fewer than half of the executives who responded to an online survey indicated that they were satisfied with their company's approach to planning strategy. Further, although more than three-quarters of the respondents reported that their company had a formal strategic planning process, fewer than a quarter suggested that the process was key to making their most important decisions.

In his empirical study of the strategic planning process of 100 German companies, A. Huber (2006) found that 95 percent of the participants of this survey believed it was very important to implement and execute a strategic planning process. Yet despite this belief, 39 percent of participants were not able to differentiate the terms "strategy," "strategic planning," and "strategy development."[6] Participants stressed the need to improve implementation and executing monitoring.

Why the problem? Rothschild et al. suggest that, often, strategic planning takes the form of blue sky visioning with little attention paid to rigorous homework. The outcome is a confusing set of statements that fall into the no man's land between vision statement and concrete action. The strategy is described as vague, hence, it does not force the organization to establish commitment.[7]

Other organizations avoid this trap and conduct what Rothschild et al. call "strategy by spreadsheet," in which organizations run their strategic planning as a sterile budgeting exercise with a very strong focus in financial details. Those organizations fail to anticipate changes in the competitive environment and in customer expectations.

These illustrate the two extremes of planning—from blue sky to financial spreadsheets. The struggle lies in the fact that the future is unknown. Some choose to react to this by allowing boundless imagining, while others focus on irrelevant concreteness. Neither is particularly helpful.

What matters most is some general directions and guidelines, and an ability to adjust and change as the future unfolds. In other words, the "hard" plans are important, but only when supported by the "soft" process. The quality and usefulness of any strategic plans are not governed by an ability to see into the future or, at the other end of the spectrum, develop a finely crafted financial modeling process. Rather, success is determined by the ability of those charged with planning for the future to build relationships, overcome politics, foster honest and effective communication, and build and nurture highly functioning teams. Furthermore, plans must recognize that they are to be implemented by people. As O. Recklies suggests, "Most planning models also do not consider the irrational behavior of employees, groups, and organizations."[8]

The people side of the equation is not always fully appreciated in the strategic planning process. Farrell and Associates suggest that "strategic planning is more often than not an internal battle ground for inter-departmental conflicts; negotiations and bargaining take place to achieve 'organizational peace until the next planning session.'"[9] Thommen and Achleitner state that, in practice, the allocation of organizational resources is based more on the distribution of power than developed corporate strategies.[10] M. Kearns observes, "Unfortunately, most plans are filled with horrible mistakes, unrealistic expectations of the ability to control variables beyond the control of group, and a level of 'me first' thinking."[11]

While a comprehensive strategic plan may assure the board and senior executives alike that the organization is in good hands, unless such plans have been developed with an effective process that takes into account the idiosyncrasies and realities of humans, it is likely to remain only wishful thinking. To ensure that the resources that are committed to strategic planning are leveraged fully, soft and hard skills must be integrated. Specifically, consider the following:

- Don't even bother conducting a strategic planning process unless the team at the top is highly functional as described in Chapters Nine, Ten, and Eleven. Unless this team is able to make decisions that serve the greater good, can be completely transparent in their communication, and are able to overcome the power dynamics that exist at the top, any strategic plan that is produced will be built upon political agendas and faulty assumptions.

- Pay careful attention to the manner in which information is gathered and decisions are made. All too often a senior team, who are typically out of touch with the realities of the business, separate themselves even further when developing a strategic plan. While some time away is often required, any planning process should be based more on inclusion than isolation.

- Production of the plan is the easy part. Therefore, the planning process must include realistic discussions concerning how it is to be implemented. If employees are required to change their behavior (and most strategic plans do demand this, at least in some degree), do not expect this to happen by producing a document. Behavioral change implies organizational transformation, which, in turn, means you will need to focus on many of the ideas presented in this book.

OTHER EVIDENCE OF THE HARD-SOFT SEPARATION

Aside from the manner in which we approach such things as decision-making and strategic planning, the separation between hard and soft skills is evident in many organizational cultural artifacts. Performance appraisals typically separate hard skills and soft skills. The hiring process, more often than not, overemphasizes the hard, technical skills and fails to recognize soft skills.

This separation is clearly apparent when it comes to developing and training employees. Hard skills programs and courses are abundant in organizations. Rarely questioned, these more technically oriented courses are seen as essential within organizations. They teach people how to perform the required task and include development of managerial skills such as planning, problem solving, and budgeting. On the other hand, soft skills courses are viewed as something quite different from hard skills. While most organizations recognize their importance, soft skills are not given the same priority as hard skills. When times get tough, it is soft skill development that falls by the wayside, while the hard skills remain.

This approach assumes that hard and soft skills are unique and separate. But, as I have argued, they are not and to teach hard skills with no reference to soft makes no sense. As a result, there is a lost opportunity to apply hard skills in a way that is aligned to the transformation to a great organization. Furthermore, such separation sends an implicit message that when applying the hard skills, it is not important to pay attention to the "softer" and people side of the business. That occurs at another time when one is leading.

Any executive wishing to create a great organization must consider ways to integrate hard and soft skills. Do you run management training and leadership development as separate programs? If so, consider integrating them. Look at all training, development, and other organizational processes and identify opportunities for a greater integration. Ultimately, such a strategy is essential if you are to eliminate disconnects, inefficiencies, and divisions within your organization.

Chapter Nineteen Takeaways

1. Traditionally, we have assumed that the skills required of those who lead organizations fall into two categories—hard and soft. Hard skills are those we consider to be more tangible and are typically easy to observe, quantify, and measure. In contrast, soft skills are harder to quantify and measure and have to do with how people relate to each other. This is a gross oversimplification of what actually happens within organizations. The hard and soft elements of an individual's behavior are not unique and separate, but are instead completely integrated with each other.

2. When we act as though hard and soft skills are unique and separate, we are, in effect, treating them as events as distinct from processes. The message we send is that, at certain times, hard skills are important, while at other times, it is the soft skills that matter. This mechanistic mindset does not reflect the reality of organizational life in which soft skills are inexorably intertwined with hard skills. In reality, most tasks require the application of both hard and soft skills.

3. This separation of hard and soft skills should be a concern for any executive wanting to create a great organization. The integration of hard and soft skills can guide executives and

their work of organizational transformation. The idea that leadership is something separate from management reinforces the notion that leadership resides in just a few. However, if we accept that it is integrated into the very fabric of organizational life, executives are then justified in demanding that effective leadership takes place at every level and on every occasion throughout the organization.

4. The separation between hard and soft skills in the arena of decision-making significantly impacts an organization's effectiveness. The manner in which decisions are made and the way the decision-maker interacts with those impacted by the decision is clearly a soft skill. When decision-making is approached as an absolute hard skill rather than an integrated soft, people-oriented skill, opportunities to leverage both the soft and the hard skill are lost, along with the capacity to ensure that not only are good decisions made, but they are also followed through on and implemented. The net result is that many organizations have a poor and ineffective decision-making process.

5. As an individual progresses up through the organizational hierarchy, his or her decision-making style needs to evolve. To be successful, managers and executives need to become increasingly open and interactive in their leadership styles and more analytic in their thinking styles. Decision-making profiles do a complete flip over the course of a career; that is, the decision profile of a successful CEO is the opposite of a successful first-line supervisor's.

6. Many organizations fail to implement ideas determined through a strategic planning process. Despite a rigorous process, plans remain words on paper and the business carries on as always. This occurs because the soft is not integrated with the hard. Assumptions abound that clearly articulated plans will change people's behavior, the future is a known, and there are no hidden agendas. Time and time again we see that this is simply not the case.

7. While a comprehensive strategic plan may assure the board and senior executives alike that the organization is in good hands, unless such plans have been developed with an effective process that takes into account the idiosyncrasies and realities of humans, it is likely to remain only wishful thinking.

8. Any executive wishing to create a great organization must consider ways to integrate hard and soft. In particular, he or she should ensure management training and leadership development are not separate programs, but are integrated. Identify opportunities for a greater integration of all training, development, and other organizational processes. Ultimately, such a strategy is essential if you are to eliminate disconnects, inefficiencies, and divisions within your organization.

PRINCIPLE #20:

NEVER STOP

If you take the lessons from this book to heart, your organization will be well positioned to become more organic, responsive and, yes, a great organization. Your employees will be more engaged, your executive team more united and collaborative, and, on a personal level, you will be more aware and effective as a leader. Bottom line—you will be leading a more profitable and sustainable organization.

So, is the job done? Absolutely not. In fact, those who believe organizational transformation is an event with a defined beginning and end are still embedded in the mechanistic mindset. Unfortunately, many models of organizational change reinforce this belief. Whether it be W. Bridges's model of the three phases of change (ending, neutral, and new beginnings),[1] K. Lewin's model of transformation (unfreeze, change, and refreeze),[2] or J. Kotter's eight-step model (establish a sense of urgency, create the guiding coalition, develop a vision and strategy, communicate the change vision, empower employees for broad-based action, generate short-term wins, consolidate gains and produce more change, and anchor new approaches in the culture),[3] all suggest there is a start and an end to change.

While these models are helpful in navigating the various elements of the change process, it is naïve to assume that there comes a point in time when change is complete. Today's executive would do better to acknowledge that change, whether personal or organizational, is an ever-evolving process. It may vary its nature and area of focus, but change is better regarded as a normal part of business, rather than something that one has to "get through" before life returns to status quo and normalcy.

Organizational change is contextual. In other words, changes in the external environment influence organizational change—and vice versa. Given that the external environment is forever changing, the same holds true with any organization. There is no such thing as status quo. Organizations that are not changing and evolving are not standing still, but going backwards.

This is not to say that one must continually focus on the same areas of change—these will vary just as the external environment does. Nor does this mean I am advocating change for the sake of change. I worked with an organization once that adopted this philosophy, and it wasn't long before all change initiatives lost credibility. Employees simply couldn't see the rationale for the changes being advocated, other than making their lives miserable and wasting effort and energy.

What I am suggesting is that executives at the top introduce a discipline and develop a culture in which an ever-constant desire to find ways to improve is normalized. The principles introduced in this book will help in this regard:

- Principle #1: Face the Facts
- Principle #2: Break the Mold
- Principle #3: Define a Better Way
- Principle #4: Figure Out if You Have What It Takes
- Principle #5: Give Yourself a Leadership Reality Check
- Principle #6: Conduct a Personal Leadership Audit
- Principle #7: Embark On a Leadership Makeover
- Principle #8: Put Yourself First
- Principle #9: Understand What Could Be Amiss with Your Top Team
- Principle #10: Recognize How Executive Team Dynamics Promotes Mediocrity
- Principle #11: Get the Top Team Working
- Principle #12: Get the Board on Board
- Principle #13: Develop Everyone's Leadership
- Principle #14: Get Other Executives on Board (Or Out of the Way)
- Principle #15: Figure Out Communication
- Principle #16: Create Communities
- Principle #17: Tell People How They're Doing
- Principle #18: Promote for the Future
- Principle #19: Integrate the Hard and the Soft
- Principle #20: Never Stop

Each one of these principles requires a similar process:

- Some deep reflection into the current state of affairs and how an outdated mechanistic mindset contributes to personal and organizational ineffectiveness.
- Identification of new and better ways to lead that will result in a more effective organization.
- Implementation of new and more relevant actions and behaviors.

But it doesn't stop there. As behaviors change, initiatives are implemented, and structures introduced, new knowledge is attained. This, in turn, requires another cycle of reflection in which the new knowledge is integrated with the old. From this integration, new strategies will merge which will then dictate different actions—and so it continues.

While few would argue with this process, all too often the energy for change and the required cycle of learning fall by the wayside as the pressures of day-to-day business increase. To a large extent, this is inevitable and to be expected. However, it must not be tolerated. Any executive wishing to create a great organization must ensure the cycle for constant learning and change is ever present. At some point in time it will become engrained in the culture, but until then, the focus on change must continually be on the executive agenda.

As I suggested in Chapter Sixteen, structures can be invaluable tools for supporting and driving desired behaviors, and used to maintain a focus on change. Whether it is regularly scheduled meetings to review organizational transformations, one-on-one discussions with peers or direct reports to review personal development efforts, or a standing item regarding team development on the senior team meeting agenda, any structure can introduce a discipline that will ensure change becomes normalized within the organization.

The challenge for any executive keen to continually strive for organizational greatness is not to fight, but rather embrace change. The introduction of structures to keep personal and organizational change front and center is not an option. Furthermore, a welcoming and positive attitude to change will go a long way to helping employees understand that "business as normal" and "change" are one and the same. Those with a Strategist action logic frame will find this easier than those with action logics from earlier stages. But regardless, change must be embraced by all employees if organizational greatness is to become a reality.

* * *

Mechanistic thinking pervades every aspect of organizational life. It is more than just how we show up as leaders. It is how we organize, interact, implement structures, and guide the organization. Few are aware of the impact of such mechanistic thinking. As a result, employees are disengaged, senior executives are mistrusted, unhealthy conflict is ever present, and organizations are a long way from being effective.

But the solution is clear and obvious. We know how to create great organizations. However, a willingness to do the work it takes is sorely lacking at the senior level. Instead, those at the top often prefer to direct their energies into planning processes that do little more than make them feel good, leadership programs that are not supported either by other leaders or organizational processes, or a litany of surveys that provide nothing more than confirmation that all is not well.

Senior executives who are willing to move beyond lip service and create great organizations must be prepared to roll their sleeves up and get to work. They must be willing to shake off the old paradigms, take a long hard look in the mirror, be vulnerable and real, and, at least for a short time, put their own developmental needs ahead of the organization. Ultimately, those at the top must recognize the world has changed and what got them to the top may now be keeping the organization embedded in mediocrity. They must be willing to change.

Those executives that are able to embrace the lessons of this book will lead their organization into a healthy, sustainable, and profitable future. Those who are unwilling to put their egos on the line are dooming their organization to poor performance on every measure.

What will it be—mediocrity or greatness? The choice is yours.

ENDNOTES

PREFACE

1   Towers Perrin. *Closing the Engagement Gap: A Road Map for Driving Superior Business Performance.* Towers Perrin Global Workforce Study, 2007–2008.
2   Ibid.
3   Rosen, R., & Adair, F. "CEOs Misperceive Top Teams' Performance." *Harvard Business Review* September 2007: 1–2.

CHAPTER ONE

1   Hay Group. "The War for Leaders: How to prepare for battle." Hay Group Report, 2007.
2   Donlan, J.P. "Best Companies for Leaders," Chief Executive Group, December 2007.
3   "Creating Leaders." *The Economist* Supplement: "A Survey of Corporate Leadership." October 25, 2003: 7–11.
4   Towers Perrin. "Closing the Engagement Gap: A Road Map for Driving Superior Business Performance." Towers Perrin Global Workforce Study, 2007–2008.
5   www.hewittassociates.com/Intl/NA/en-US/Consulting/ServiceTool. aspx?cid=2256. (Accessed February 13, 2010.)
6   BlessingWhite. "The State of Employee Engagement 2008." Blessing-White Study.
7   Rutledge, T. *Getting Engaged the New Workplace Loyalty.* Toronto: Mattanie Press, 2005.
8   Hay Group. "Brighter Skies Ahead: How Employee Engagement and Enablement Can Improve Performance During the Economic Storm and Beyond." The Hay Group Report, May 2009.
9   Towers Perrin. "Closing the Engagement Gap: A Road Map for Driving Superior Business Performance." Towers Perrin Global Workforce Study, 2007–2008.

10   Gallup Inc. "Employee Engagement: What's Your Engagement Ratio?" Gallup Inc. Study, 2008.

11   Hewitt Associates. "Employee Engagement Higher at Double-digit Growth Companies." Hewitt Associates Study, 2004.

12   Towers Perrin. "Closing the Engagement Gap: A Road Map for Driving Superior Business Performance." Towers Perrin Global Workforce Study, 2007–2008.

13   BlessingWhite. "The State of Employee Engagement." BlessingWhite Study, 2008.

14   ASTD. "Learning's Role in Employee Engagement." An ASTD Research Study, 2008.

15   Ott, B., & Kilham, E. "Would You Fire Your Boss?" *Gallup Management Journal*, 2007.

16   Wheatley, M. *Leadership and the New Science: Learning About Organization from an Orderly.* San Francisco: Berrett-Koehler, 1992.

17   Hoffler, D. "Organic Organizations." *Encyclopedia of Management*, Ed. Marilyn M. Helms. Gale Cengage, eNotes.com. 2006. January 23, 2010. www.enotes.com/management-encyclopedia/organic-organizations.

CHAPTER TWO

1   Bass, B. *Bass & Stogdill's Handbook of Leadership: Theory, Research, & Managerial Applications*, 3 ed. New York City: Free Press, 1990. p. 11.

2   Kotter, J. "What Do Leaders Really Do?" *Harvard Business Review*, May–June 1990: pp. 103–111.

3   Knowles, H., & Saxberg, B. *Personality and Leadership Behavior.* Reading, MA: Addison-Wesley, 1971.

4   Hogan, R., Curphy, G., & Hogan, J. "What We Know About Leadership." *American Psychologist*, 49–6 (June 1994): p. 493.

5   Bryman, A. *Charisma and Leadership in Organizations.* London: Sage Publications, 1992.

6   Locke, E. *The Essence of Leadership.* New York: Lexington Books, 1991. p. 2.

7   Conger, J. A. *Learning to Lead: The Art of Transforming Managers into Leaders.* San Francisco: Jossey-Bass, 1992. p. 18.

8   Smith, R. "A Born Leader?" *Management Accounting* 71–4 (1993): pp. 36–37.

9   Martin, Dean Roger. "Death of Heroic Leadership." *Rotman Management*, Fall 2000.

10   Heifetz, R., & Laurie, D. "Learning to Lead: Real Leaders Say, 'I Don't Have the Answer.'" *Ivey Business Journal* 67–3 (January 2003): p. 1.

11   Cherniss, C., & Goleman, D. *The Emotionally Intelligent Workplace: How to Select For, Measure, and Improve Emotional Intelligence in Individuals, Groups, and Organizations.* San Francisco: Jossey-Bass, 2001. p. 4.

12 Towers Perrin. "Closing the Engagement Gap: A Road Map for Driving Superior Business Performance." Towers Perrin Global Workforce Study, 2007–2008.

CHAPTER THREE

1   Intagliata, J., Ulrich, D., & Smallwood, N. "Leveraging Leadership Competencies to Produce Leadership Brand: Creating Distinctiveness by Focusing on Strategy and Results." *Human Resource Planning* 23.4 (Winter, 2000): 12–23.

2   Low, J., & Seisfeld, T. "Measures That Matter: Wall Street Considers More Than You Think." *Strategy and Leadership* (March–April 1998): 24–30.

3   Intagliata, J., Ulrich, D., & Smallwood, N. "Leveraging Leadership Competencies to Produce Leadership Brand: Creating Distinctiveness by Focusing on Strategy and Results." *Human Resource Planning* 23.4 (Winter, 2000): 12–23.

4   Ulrich, D., Smallwood, N., & Snyder, S. "Leadership Brand." *Executive Excellence* (March 2001): 14.

5   Collins, J., & Porras, J. *Built to Last: Successful Habits of Visionary Companies*. New York: Harper Business, 1994. p. 48.

6   Berry, L. *Discovering the Soul of Service: The Nine Drivers of Sustainable Business Success*. New York: The Free Press, 1999.

7   Kouzes, J., & Posner, B. *Credibility: How Leaders Gain It and Lose It, Why People Demand It*. San Francisco: Jossey-Bass, 2003.

8   Harmon, F. *Playing for Keeps*. New York: John Wiley & Sons, Inc., 1996. p. xiv.

9   Lucia, A., & Lepsinger, R. *The Art & Science of Competency Models*. San Francisco: Jossey-Bass, 1999.

10 Intagliata, J., Ulrich, D., & Smallwood, N. "Leveraging Leadership Competencies to Produce Leadership Brand: Creating Distinctiveness by Focusing on Strategy and Results." *Human Resource Planning* 23.4 (Winter, 2000): 12–23. p. 13.

11 Denning, S. "Telling Tales," *Harvard Business Review* 82, No. 5 (May 2004): 12–19.

12 Tichy, N. *The Leadership Engine: How Winning Companies Build Leaders at Every Level*. New York: HarperCollins, 1997.

13 www.storytellings.com/power.htm. ©2004–2009 StoryTellings™ Consulting.

CHAPTER FOUR

1   Piaget, J. *The Psychology of the Child*. New York: Basic Books, 1966.

2   Loevinger, J. *Ego Development: Conceptions and Theories*. San Francisco: Jossey-Bass, 1976.; Torbert, W. *Action Inquiry: The Secret of Timely and Transforming Leadership*. San Francisco, CA: Berrett-Koehler Publishers, 2004;

Cook-Greuter, S. *Transcendence and Mature Thought in Adulthood.* Lanham: Rowman & Littlefield Publishers, Inc., 1994; Kegan, R. *The Evolving Self: Problem and Process in Human Development.* Cambridge: Harvard University Press, 1982; Harthill Consulting Ltd, The Grange, Hewelsfield, Lydney, Gloucestershire, England, GL15 6XA, www.harthill.co.uk, 2006.

3   Rooke, D. "Organizational Transformation Requires the Presence of Leaders Who Are Strategists and Alchemists." First published in *Organizations and People* 4.3 (1997). Amended October 2001. p. 3.

4   Harthill Leadership Development Framework, Harthill Consulting Ltd. June 2009. p. 3.

5   Ibid. p. 10.

6   Rooke, D., & Torbert, W. "Seven Transformations of Leadership." *Harvard Business Review*, April 2005: p. 67.

7   Rooke, D. "Organizational Transformation Requires the Presence of Leaders Who Are Strategists and Alchemists." First published in *Organizations and People* 4.3 (1997). Amended October 2001. p. 34.

8   Ibid. p. 4.

9   Rooke, D., & Torbert, W. "The CEO's Role in Organizational Transformation." *The Systems Thinker* 10, no. 7 (1999): 1–5.

CHAPTER FIVE

1   Rooke, D., & Torbert, W. "Seven Transformations of Leadership." *Harvard Business Review*, April 2005: 66–76.

CHAPTER SIX

1   Yukl, Gary. *Leadership in Organizations.* Seventh Edition. Alexandria, VA: Prentice Hall, 2009.

2   Van der Heijden, B., & Nijhof, A. "The Value of Subjectivity: Problems and Prospects for 360-degree Appraisal Systems." *International Journal of Human Resource Management* 15–3 (May 2004): 493–511.

3   Arnold, J., & MacKenzie Daveys, K. "Self-Ratings and Supervisor Ratings of Graduate Employees' Competences during Early Career." *Journal of Occupational and Organizational Psychology* 65 (1992): 235–50; Harris, M., & Schaubroeck, J. "A Meta-Analysis of Self-Supervisor, Self-Peer, and Peer-Supervisor Ratings." *Personnel Psychology* 41 (1988): 43–62; Hoffman, C., Nathan, B., & Holden, L. "A Comparison of Validation Criteria: Objective versus Subjective Performance Measures and Self- versus Supervisor Ratings." *Personnel Psychology* 44 (1991): 601–619; Holzbach, R. "Rater Bias in Performance Ratings: Superior, Self-, and Peer Ratings," I, 63-5 (1978): 579–88.

4   van Hooft, E., van der Flier, H., & Minne, M. "Construct Validity of Multi-Source Performance Ratings: An Examination of the Relationship of Self-, Supervisor-, and Peer-Ratings with Cognitive and Personality

Measures." *International Journal of Selection & Assessment* 14–1 (March 2006): 67–81.

5   Conway, J., & Huffcutt, A. "Psychometric Properties of Multisource Performance Ratings: A Meta-analysis of Subordinate, Supervisor, Peer, and Self-ratings." *Human Performance* 10 (1997): 331–360.

6   Stewart, J. "Intervention and Assessment: The Ethics of HRD." *Human Resource Development International* 1–1 (1998): 9–12.

7   Van der Heijden, B., & Nijhof, A. "The Value of Subjectivity: Problems and Prospects for 360-degree Appraisal Systems." *International Journal of Human Resource Management* 15–3 (May 2004): 493–511.

8   Longenecker, C.O., & Fink, L.S. "How Top-level Managers Develop: A Field Study." *Development and Learning in Organizations* 20–5 (2006, September): 18–20.

9   Kaplan, R. "What to Ask the Person in the Mirror." *Harvard Business Review* 85–1 (January 2007): 86–95.

10 Cashman, K. "Being a Leader." *Leadership Excellence* 26–1 (January 2009): p. 8.

CHAPTER EIGHT

1   Kahn, R., Wolfe, D., Quinn, R., & Snoek, J. D. *Organizational Stress: Studies in Role Conflict and Ambiguity.* New York: Wiley, 1964.

2   HR Agenda. "Managers Recognize Heavy Workloads." *HR Briefing*, May 1, 2002.

3   Cummings, B. "Sales Ruined My Personal Life." *Sales and Marketing Management* 153 (November 2001): 44–51.

4   Bandura, A. *Self-efficacy: The Exercise of Control.* San Francisco: Freeman 1997; Locke, E., & Latham, G. *A Theory of Goal-setting and Task Performance.* Englewood Cliffs, NJ: Prentice Hall, 1990.

5   Brown, S., Jones. E., & Leigh, T. "The Attenuating Effect of Role Overload on Relationships Linking Self-efficacy and Goal Level to Work Performance." *Journal of Applied Psychology* 90–5 (September 2005): 972–979.

6   Jex, S. *Stress and Job Performance: Theory, Research, and Implications for Managerial Practice.* Thousand Oaks, CA: Sage, 1998.

7   Britt, T. "Black Hawk Down at Work." *Harvard Business Review* 81 (January 2003): 16–17; Jex, S., & Adams, G. (in press). "Organization-based Self-esteem as a Moderator of Reactions to Role Stressors: The Influence of Employee of Job Involvement." *Journal of Social Behavior and Personality.*

8   Hallowell, E. "Overloaded Circuits: Why Smart People Underperform." *Harvard Business Review* 83–1 (January 2005): 54–62.

9   Argyris, C., & Schon, D. *Organizational Learning: Theory, Method, and Practice.* First Edition. Reading MA: Addison-Wesley, 1978.

10 Heifetz, R., & Laurie, D. "Learning to Lead: Real Leaders Say, 'I Don't Have the Answer." *Ivey Business Journal* 67–3 (January 2003): 1–7.

11 Argyris, C., & Schön, D. (1978) *Organizational Learning: A Theory of Action Perspective.* Reading, Mass: Addison-Wesley.

12 Covey, S.R., Merrill, R.A., & Merrill, R.A. *First Things First: To Live, to Love, to Learn, to Leave a Legacy.* New York: Free Press, 1996.

13 Loehr, J., & Schwartz, T. *The Power of Full Engagement: Managing Energy, Not Time, Is the Key to High Performance and Personal Renewal.* New York: Free Press, 2004.

CHAPTER NINE

1 Senge, P. *The Fifth Discipline: The Art & Practice of The Learning Organization.* New York: Currency, 2006.

2 Nadler, D., & Spencer, J. *Executive Teams.* First Edition. San Francisco: Jossey-Bass, 1997. p. 19.

3 Burruss, J., Hackman, J., Nunes, D., & Wageman, R. *Senior Leadership Teams: What It Takes to Make Them Great* (Center for Public Leadership). New York: Harvard Business School Press, 2008. p. 7.

4 Pearce & Conger, 2003 In C.L. Pearce & J.A. Conger (Eds.), *Shared Leadership: Reframing the Hows and Whys of Leadership.* Thousand Oaks, CA: Sage, 2003.

5 O'Reilly, C., Snyder, R., & Boothe, J. "Executive Team Demography and Organizational Change." In G. P. Huber & W. H. Glick (Eds.), *Organizational Change and Redesign: Ideas and Insights for Improving Performance.* New York: Oxford University Press, 1993. 147–175.

6 Edmondson, C., Roberto, M., & Watkins, M. "A Dynamic Model of Top Management Team Effectiveness: Managing Unstructured Task Streams." *The Leadership Quarterly* 14–3 (June 2003): 297–325. p. 298.

7 Burruss, J., Hackman, J., Nunes, D., & Wageman, R. *Senior Leadership Teams: What It Takes to Make Them Great* (Center for Public Leadership). New York: Harvard Business School Press, 2008. p. xiii.

8 Janis, I. L. *Victims of Groupthink.* Second Edition. Boston, MA: Houghton-Mifflin, 1982.

9 Ross, J., & Staw, B. "Expo 86: An Escalation Prototype." *Administrative Science Quarterly* 31–2 (1986): 274–297; Ross, J., & Staw, B. "Organizational Escalation and Exit: Lessons from the Shoreham Nuclear Power Plant." *Academy of Management Journal* 36–4 (1993): 701–732.

10 Ibid.

11 Edmondson, C., Roberto, M., & Watkins, M. "A Dynamic Model of Top Management Team Effectiveness: Managing Unstructured Task Streams." *The Leadership Quarterly* 14–3 (June 2003): 297–325. p. 298.

12 Amason, A. "Distinguishing the Effects of Functional and Dysfunctional Conflict on Strategic Decision Making." *Academy of Management Journal* 39–1 (1996): 123–148.

13 Wooldridge, B., & Floyd, S. W. "The Strategy Process, Middle Management Involvement, and Organizational Performance." *Strategic Management Journal* 11(3) (1990): 231–241.

14 Eisenhardt, K. "Making Fast Strategic Decisions in High-velocity Environments." *Academy of Management Journal* 32-4 (1989): 543–576.

15 Rosen, R., & Adair, F. "CEOs Misperceive Top Teams' Performance." *Harvard Business Review*, September 2007: 1–2.

16 Murray, A. "Top Management Group Heterogeneity and Firm Performance." *Strategic Management Journal* 10 (1989): 125–141; Eisenhardt, K. M., & Schoonhoven, C. "Organizational Growth: Linking Team Founding, Strategy, Environment, and Growth Among U.S. Semiconductor Ventures, 1978–88." *Administrative Science Quarterly* 35-3 (1990): 504–529; Murmann, J. P., & Tushman, M. "The Effects of Executive Team Characteristics and Organizational Context on Organizational Responsiveness to Environmental Shock." Working Paper, Columbia Business School. (1997).

17 Williams, K., & O'Reilly, C. "Demography and Diversity in Organizations: A Review of 40 Years of Research." In B. Staw & R. Sutton (Eds.), *Research in Organizational Behavior*. Greenwich, CT: JAI Press, 1998: 77–140; Hambrick, D. C., Cho, T. S., & Chen, M. J. "The Influence of Top Management Team Heterogeneity on Firms' Competitive Moves." *Administrative Science Quarterly* 41-4 (1996): 659–684; Wagner, W., Pfeffer, J., & O'Reilly, C. "Organizational Demography and Turnover in Top Management Teams." *Administrative Science Quarterly* 29-1 (1984): 74–92.

CHAPTER TEN

1 Nadler, D. "High Performance Executive Teams." *Corporate Boar* 13–75 (July 1992): p. 20.

2 Lax, D., & Sebenius, J. *The Manager as Negotiator: Bargaining for Cooperation and Competitive Gain*. New York: Free Press, 1986.

3 Nadler, D. "High Performance Executive Teams." *Corporate Boar* 13–75 (July 1992): p. 20.

4 Janis, I.L. "Groupthink: The Desperate Drive for Consensus at Any Cost." *Psychology Today* 12 (1971): pp. 43–76.

5 Baron, R. S. "So Right It's Wrong: Groupthink and the Ubiquitous Nature of Polarized Group Decision Making." In Zanna, Mark P. (Ed.) *Advances in Experimental Social Psychology*. Vol. 37. San Diego. Elsevier Academic Press. (2005): 219–253.

CHAPTER ELEVEN

1 Burruss, J., Hackman, J., Nunes, D., & Wageman, R. *Senior Leadership Teams: What It Takes to Make Them Great*. (Center for Public Leadership). New York: Harvard Business School Press, 2008.

2 Ibid.

CHAPTER TWELVE

1   Meyer, K., & Rollo, R. "Boards Think They're Doing a Good Job ... But CEOs Disagree. What Directors Can Do to Bridge that Disconnect." *Directors and Boards* (Second Quarter 2008).

2   Bogart, R. "The Value of an HR Voice in the Boardroom." *Directorship*, August 24, 2009.

3   Heidrick & Struggles USC/Center for Effective Organizations. "10th Annual Corporate Board Effectiveness Study." 2006–2007.

4   Towers Perrin. "Closing the Engagement Gap: A Road Map for Driving Superior Business Performance." Towers Perrin Global Workforce Study, 2007–2008.

5   Hewitt Associates. "Employee Engagement Higher at Double-digit Growth Companies." Hewitt Associates Study, 2004.

6   Heidrick & Struggles USC/Center for Effective Organizations. "10th Annual Corporate Board Effectiveness Study." 2006–2007.

7   Lorsch, J., & Clark, R. "Leading from the Boardroom." *Harvard Business Review* 86–4 (April 2008): 104–111.

8   Brunswick, R., & Hayes, G. "RX for a Dysfunctional Company: Wake up the Board!" *Directorship* 26–3 (March 2000): 6–7+.

9   Felton, R., & Fritz, P. "The View from the Boardroom." *The McKinsey Quarterly* (2005): 48.

CHAPTER THIRTEEN

1   Deal, T. E., & Kennedy, A. A. *Corporate Cultures: The Rites and Rituals of Corporate Life.* Reading, MA: Addison-Wesley, 1982. p. 4.

2   Kotter, J. P., & Heskett, J. L. *Corporate Culture and Performance.* New York: Free Press, 1992. p. 4.

3   Schein, E. H. *Organizational Culture and Leadership.* San Francisco, CA: Jossey-Bass, 1992. p. 12.

4   Barger, B. "Culture an Overused Term and International Joint Ventures: A Review of the Literature and a Case Study." *Journal of Organizational Culture, Communication and Conflict* 11–2 (2007): 1–14.

5   Hernez-Broome, G., & Hughes, R. "Leadership Development: Past, Present, and Future." *Human Resource Planning* 27 (2004): p. 27.

CHAPTER FOURTEEN

1   Anderson, C., Flynn, F., & Spataro, S. "Personality and Organizational Culture as Determinants of Influence." *Journal of Applied Psychology* 93, No. 3 (2008): 702–710.

2   Kipnis, D., Schmidt, S. M., & Wilkinson, I. "Intraorganizational Influence Tactics: Explorations in Getting One's Way." *Journal of Applied Psychology* 65 (1980): 440–452; Mowday, R. T. "The Exercise of Upward Influence in Organizations." *Administrative Science Quarterly* 23 (1978): 137–156;

Yukl, G., & Falbe, C. M. "Influence Tactics and Objectives in Upward, Downward, and Lateral Influence Attempts." *Journal of Applied Psychology* 75 (1990): 132–140.

3   Anderson, C., Flynn, F., & Spataro, S. "Personality and Organizational Culture as Determinants of Influence." *Journal of Applied Psychology* 93, No. 3 (2008): 702–710.

CHAPTER FIFTEEN

1   Towers Perrin. "Closing the Engagement Gap: A Road Map for Driving Superior Business Performance." Towers Perrin Global Workforce Study, 2007–2008.

2   Ibid. p.12.

3   Towers Perrin. "Communications Effectiveness Consortium." Towers Perrin, 2004.

4   Collins, J. *Good to Great*. New York: Harper Business, 2001.

5   Williams, R., & Williams, T. "Connections with a Purpose." *Communication World* 26–4 (July 2009): 26–29.

6   Meyer, M. "Give More and Get More out of Social Media." *Communication World* 26–6 (November 2009): p. 48.

7   Burrus, D. "The Business Value of Social Networks." *Agency Sales* 39–7 (July 2009): 44–56.

8   Ibid.

CHAPTER SIXTEEN

1   Furlong, G., & Johnson, L. "Community of Practice and Metacapabilities." *Knowledge Management Research & Practice* 1–2 (December 2003): 102–112.

2   Lesser, L. E., & Storck, J. "Communities of Practice and Organizational Performance." *IBM Systems Journal* 40–4 (2001): 831–841.

3   Storck J., & Hill, P. "Knowledge Diffusion Through Strategic Communities." *Sloan Management Review* 41–2 (2000): 63–74.

4   Lesser, L. E., & Storck, J. "Communities of Practice and Organizational Performance." *IBM Systems Journal* 40–4 (2001): 831–841.

5   Lesser, L. E., & Storck, J. "Communities of Practice and Organizational Performance." *IBM Systems Journal* 40–4 (2001): 831–841.

CHAPTER SEVENTEEN

1   Office of the Auditor General of B.C. 2002/2003 Report 1: Building a Strong Work Environment in British Columbia's Public Service: A Key to Delivering Quality Service. April 2002. p. 7.

2   Globoforce Motivation Worldwide. "Great Expectations: Building the Employee Recognition Program Your CEO Wants." Globoforce Motivation Worldwide Study, Issue 9 (January 2009).

3   Office of the Auditor General of B.C. 2002/2003 Report 1: Building a Strong Work Environment in British Columbia's Public Service: A Key to Delivering Quality Service. April 2002. p. 7.

4   Rath, T. "The Best Ways to Recognize Employees." *Gallup Management Journal* 09 (December 2004). http://gmj.gallup.com/content/13888/best-ways-recognize-employees.aspx. (Accessed March 16, 2010.)

5   Globoforce Motivation Worldwide. "Great Expectations: Building the Employee Recognition Program Your CEO Wants." Globoforce Motivation Worldwide Study, Issue 9 (January 2009).

6   Ibid.

7   Globoforce Motivation Worldwide. "Measuring Recognition: How to Build the Business Case for Strategic Recognition in a Recession." Globoforce Motivation Worldwide Study, Issue 10 (May 2009).

8   Williams, M. "Will You Make One of These Five Common Employee Recognition Mistakes?" May 19, 2003. HR.Com. (http://www.hr.com/sfs?t=/contentManager/onStory&e=UTF-8&i=1116423256281&l=0&ParentID=1120248810940&StoryID=1119651662828&highlight=1&keys=Inergy1%2BMarketing1%2BGroup&lang=0&active=no. (Accessed February 20, 2010.)

9   Daniels, A., "Management Practices That Spell Doom." *Business Week,* August 11, 2009.

10 BNET Business Dictionary. http://dictionary.bnet.com/.

CHAPTER EIGHTEEN

1   Hogan, R., Raskin, R., & Fazzini, D. "The Dark Side of Charisma." In Clark, Kenneth E., Clark, Miriam B. (Editors). *Measures of Leadership.* Leadership Library of America, Inc, West Orange, NJ, USA. (1990): 343–354.

2   Ibid.

3   Gladwell, M. "The Talent Myth: Are Smart People Overrated?" *The New Yorker,* July 22, 2002.

4   Wagner, R. "Intelligence, Training, and Employment." *American Psychologist* 52–10 (October 1997): 1059–1069.

5   London, M., & Smither, J. "Can Multisource Feedback Change Perceptions of Goal Accomplishment, Self Evaluations, and Performance Related Outcomes? Theory Based Applications and Directions for Research." *Personnel Psychology* 48 (1995): 803–839.

6   Folkman, J., & Zenger, J. *The Extraordinary Leader.* New York: McGraw-Hill, 2002.

CHAPTER NINETEEN

1   Kotterman, J. "Leadership Versus Management: What's the Difference?" *The Journal for Quality and Participation* 29–2 (2006): 13–17.

2   Nutt, P. "Surprising But True: Half the Decisions in Organizations Fail." *The Academy of Management Executive* 13–4 (1999): 75–90.

3   Rogers, P., & Blenko, M. "Who Has the D? How Clear Decision Roles Enhance Organizational Performance." *Harvard Business Review* 84–1 (January 2006): 52–61.

4   Brousseau, K., Driver, M., Hourihan, G., & Larsson, R. "The Seasoned Executive's Decision-making Style." *Harvard Business Review* 84–2 (February 2006): p. 118.

5   Business Development Bank of Canada. "Strategic Planning Demystified." www.bdc.ca/en/my_project/Projects/articles/strategic_planning.htm?context=%7B2CE16A35-5040-4F1C-9DA0-E4D911FDFDC9%7D. (Accessed January 27, 2010.)

6   Huber, A. "Die Grundlage jeder Basis ist das Fundament." *Strategische Planung in der Klemme*, Phius, Berlin (2006).

7   Rothschild, P., Duggal, J., & Balaban, R. "Strategic Planning Redux. But This Time Linked to Funding and Everyday Execution." *MMC Viewpoint*, Number 1 (2004): p. 35–46.

8   Recklies, O. "Problems and Barriers to Strategic Planning." *Economics and Organization of Enterprise* 1, No. 1 (2008): 3–11.

9   Farrel and Associates. "Mastering Change & Planning for the Future. An Introduction to the Concepts of StrategyManagement and S3 Analysis." Farrel and Associates Article. (2002) p. 2.

10 Thommen, J., & Achleitner, A. *Allgemeine Betriebswirtschaftslehre. Umfassende Einführung aus anagementorientierte Sicht*. Fifth Edition. Gabler, Wiesbaden, (2006) p. 920.

11 Kearns, M. "The Big Problem with Most Strategic Planning in the Nonprofit Sector." www.network-centricadvocacy.net/2005/03/the_big_problem.html. (Accessed January 27, 2009.)

CHAPTER TWENTY

1   Bridges, W. *Managing Transitions: Making the Most of Change*. Third Edition. Cambridge: Da Capo Lifelong Books, 2009.

2   Lewin, Kurt. *Resolving Social Conflicts: And, Field Theory in Social Science*. Washington: American Psychological Association, 1997.

3   Kotter, J. *Leading Change*. First Edition. New York: Harvard Business School Press, 1996.

BIBLIOGRAPHY

Amason, A. "Distinguishing the Effects of Functional and Dysfunctional Conflict on Strategic Decision Making." *Academy of Management Journal* 39–1 (1996): 123–148.

Anderson, C., Flynn, F., & Spataro, S. "Personality and Organizational Culture as Determinants of Influence." *Journal of Applied Psychology* 93, No. 3 (2008): 702–710.

Argyris, C., & Schon, D. *Organizational Learning: Theory, Method, and Practice.* First Edition. Reading, MA: Addison-Wesley, 1978.

Arnold, J., & MacKenzie Daveys, K. "Self-Ratings and Supervisor Ratings of Graduate Employees' Competences during Early Career." *Journal of Occupational and Organizational Psychology* 65 (1992): 235–250.

ASTD. "Learning's Role in Employee Engagement." An ASTD Research Study, 2008.

Bandura, A. *Self-efficacy: The Exercise of Control.* San Francisco: Freeman 1997.

Barger, B. "Culture an Overused Term and International Joint Ventures: A Review of the Literature and a Case Study." *Journal of Organizational Culture, Communication and Conflict* 11–2 (2007): 1–14.

Baron, R. S. "So Right It's Wrong: Groupthink and the Ubiquitous Nature of Polarized Group Decision Making." In Zanna, Mark P. (Ed.) *Advances in Experimental Social Psychology*, 37. San Diego: Elsevier Academic Press. (2005): 219–253.

Bass, B. *Bass & Stogdill's Handbook of Leadership: Theory, Research, & Managerial Applications*, 3 ed. New York: Free Press, 1990.

Berry, L. *Discovering the Soul of Service: The Nine Drivers of Sustainable Business Success.* New York: The Free Press, 1999.

BlessingWhite. "The State of Employee Engagement 2008." BlessingWhite Study.

BNET Business Dictionary. http://dictionary.bnet.com/.

Bogart, R. "The Value of an HR Voice in the Boardroom." *Directorship*, August 24, 2009.

Bridges, W. *Managing Transitions: Making the Most of Change*. Third Edition. Cambridge: Da Capo Lifelong Books, 2009.

Britt, T. "Black Hawk Down at Work." *Harvard Business Review* 81, (January 2003): 16–17.

Brousseau, K., Driver, M., Hourihan, G., & Larsson, R. "The Seasoned Executive's Decision-making Style." *Harvard Business Review* 84–2 (February 2006): 110–121.

Brown. S., Jones, E., & Leigh, T. "The Attenuating Effect of Role Overload on Relationships Linking Self-efficacy and Goal Level to Work Performance." *Journal of Applied Psychology* 90–5 (September 2005): 972–979.

Brunswick, R., & Hayes, G. "RX for a Dysfunctional Company: Wake up the Board!" *Directorship* 26–3 (March 2000).

Bryman, A. *Charisma and Leadership in Organizations*. London: Sage Publications, 1992.

Burrus, D. "The Business Value of Social Networks." *Agency Sales* 39–7 (July 2009): 44–56.

Burruss, J., Hackman, J., Nunes, D., & Wageman, R. *Senior Leadership Teams: What It Takes to Make Them Great (Center for Public Leadership)*. New York: Harvard Business School Press, 2008.

Business Development Bank of Canada. "Strategic Planning Demystified." www.bdc.ca/en/my_project/Projects/articles/strategic_planning .htm?context=%7B2CE16A35-5040-4F1C-9DA0-E4D911FDFDC9%7D. (Accessed January 27, 2010.)

Cashman, K. "Being a Leader." *Leadership Excellence*, 26–1 (January 2009).

Cherniss, C., & Goleman, D. *The Emotionally Intelligent Workplace: How to Select For, Measure, and Improve Emotional Intelligence in Individuals, Groups, and Organizations*. San Francisco: Jossey-Bass, 2001.

Collins, J. *Good to Great*. New York: Harper Business, 2001.

Collins, J., & Porras, J. *Built to Last: Successful Habits of Visionary Companies*. New York: Harper Business, 1994.

Conway, J., & Huffcutt, A. "Psychometric Properties of Multisource Performance Ratings: A Meta-analysis of Subordinate, Supervisor, Peer, and Self-ratings." *Human Performance* 10 (1997): 331–360.

Cook-Greuter, S. *Transcendence and Mature Thought in Adulthood*. Lanham: Rowman & Littlefield Publishers, Inc., 1994.

Conger, J. A. *Learning to Lead: The Art of Transforming Managers into Leaders*. San Francisco: Jossey-Bass, 1992.

Covey, S.R., Merrill, A.R., & Merrill, R.R. *First Things First: To Live, to Love, to Learn, to Leave a Legacy*. New York: Free Press, 1996.

"Creating Leaders." *The Economist* Supplement: "A Survey of Corporate Leadership." October 25, 2003.

Cummings, B. "Sales Ruined My Personal Life." *Sales and Marketing Management* 153 (November 2001): 44–51.

Daniels, A. "Management Practices That Spell Doom." *Business Week*, August 11, 2009.

Deal, T. E., & Kennedy, A. A. *Corporate Cultures: The Rites and Rituals of Corporate Life.* Reading, MA: Addison-Wesley, 1982.

Denning, S. "Telling Tales." *Harvard Business Review* 82, No. 5 (May 2004).

Donlan, J.P. "Best Companies for Leaders," Chief Executive Group, December 2007.

Edmondson, C., Roberto, M., & Watkins, M. "A Dynamic Model of Top Management Team Effectiveness: Managing Unstructured Task Streams." *The Leadership Quarterly* 14–3 (June 2003): 297–325.

Eisenhardt, K. "Making Fast Strategic Decisions in High-velocity Environments." *Academy of Management Journal* 32–4 (1989): 543–576.

Eisenhardt, K. M., & Schoonhoven, C. "Organizational Growth: Linking Team Founding, Strategy, Environment, and Growth Among U.S. Semi-conductor Ventures, 1978–88." *Administrative Science Quarterly* 35–3 (1990).

Farrel and Associates. "Mastering Change & Planning for the Future. An Introduction to the Concepts of Strategy Management and S3 Analysis." Farrel and Associates Article. (2002).

Felton, R., & Fritz, P. "The view from the boardroom." *The McKinsey Quarterly*, 48 (2005).

Folkman, J., & Zenger, J. *The Extraordinary Leader.* New York: McGraw-Hill, 2002.

Furlong, G., & Johnson, L. "Community of Practice and Metacapabilities." *Knowledge Management Research & Practice* 1–2, (December 2003): 102–112.

Gallup Inc. "Employee Engagement: What's Your Engagement Ratio?" Gallup Inc. Study, 2008.

Gladwell, M. "The Talent Myth: Are Smart People Overrated?" *The New Yorker*, July 22, 2002.

Globoforce Motivation Worldwide. "Great Expectations: Building the Employee Recognition Program Your CEO Wants." Globoforce Motivation Worldwide Study, Issue 9 (January 2009).

Globoforce Motivation Worldwide. "Measuring Recognition: How to Build the Business Case for Strategic Recognition in a Recession." Globoforce Motivation Worldwide Study, Issue 10 (May 2009).

Hallowell, E. "Overloaded Circuits: Why Smart People Underperform." *Harvard Business Review* 83–1 (January 2005): 54–62.

Hambrick, D. C., Cho, T. S., & Chen, M. J. "The Influence of Top Management Team Heterogeneity on Firms' Competitive Moves." *Administrative Science Quarterly* 41–4 (1996): 659–684.

Harmon, F. *Playing for Keeps.* New York: John Wiley & Sons, Inc., 1996.

Harris, M., & Schaubroeck, J. "A Meta-Analysis of Self-Supervisor, Self-Peer, and Peer-Supervisor Ratings." *Personnel Psychology* 41 (1988).

Harthill Consulting Ltd, The Grange, Hewelsfield, Lydney, Gloucestershire, England, GL15 6XA., www.harthill.co.uk.

Harthill Leadership Development Framework, Harthill Consulting Ltd. June 2009.

Hay Group. "Brighter Skies Ahead: How Employee Engagement and Enablement Can Improve Performance During the Economic Storm and Beyond." The Hay Group Report, May 2009.

Hay Group. "The War for Leaders: How to Prepare for Battle." Hay Group Report, 2007.

Heidrick & Struggles USC/Center for Effective Organizations. "10th Annual Corporate Board Effectiveness Study." 2006–2007.

Heifetz, R., & Laurie, D. "Learning to Lead: Real Leaders Say, 'I Don't Have the Answer.'" *Ivey Business Journal* 67–3 (January 2003):1–7.

Hernez-Broome, G., & Hughes, R. "Leadership Development: Past, Present, and Future." *Human Resource Planning* 27 (2004).

Hewitt Associates. "Employee Engagement Higher at Double-digit Growth Companies." Hewitt Associates Study, 2004.

Hoffler, D. "Organic Organizations." *Encyclopedia of Management*, Ed. Marilyn M. Helms. Gale Cengage, eNotes.com. 2006. January 23, 2010. www .enotes.com/management-encyclopedia/organic-organizations.

Hoffman, C., Nathan, B., & Holden, L. "A Comparison of Validation Criteria: Objective versus Subjective Performance Measures and Self- versus Supervisor Ratings." *Personnel Psychology* 44 (1991).

Hogan, R., Curphy, G., & Hogan, J. "What We Know about Leadership." *American Psychologist* 49-6 (June 1994): 493–504.

Hogan, R., Raskin, R., & Fazzini, D. "The Dark Side of Charisma." In Clark, K. E., & Clark, M. B., editors, *Measures of Leadership*. West Orange, NJ: Leadership Library of America. (1990): 343–354.

Holzbach, R. "Rater Bias in Performance Ratings: Superior, Self-, and Peer Ratings," I, 63-5 (1978): 579–88.

HR Agenda. "Managers Recognize Heavy Workloads." *HR Briefing*, May 1, 2002.

Huber, A. "Die Grundlage jeder Basis ist das Fundament." *Strategische Planung in der Klemme*, Phius, Berlin (2006).

Intagliata, J., Ulrich, D., & Smallwood, N. "Leveraging Leadership Competencies to Produce Leadership Brand: Creating Distinctiveness by Focusing on Strategy and Results." *Human Resource Planning* 23.4 (Winter, 2000): 12–23.

Janis, I.L. "Groupthink: The Desperate Drive for Consensus at Any Cost." *Psychology Today* 12 (1971).

Janis, I. L. *Victims of Groupthink*. Second Edition. Boston, MA: Houghton-Mifflin, 1982.

Jex, S., *Stress and Job Performance: Theory, Research, and Implications for Managerial Practice.* Thousand Oaks, CA: Sage, 1998.

Jex, S., & Adams, G. (in press). "Organization-based Self-esteem as a Moderator of Reactions to Role Stressors: The Influence of Employee of Job Involvement." *Journal of Social Behavior and Personality.*

Kahn, R., Wolfe, D., Quinn, R., & Snoek, J. D. *Organizational Stress: Studies in Role Conflict and Ambiguity.* New York: Wiley, 1964.

Kaplan, R. "What to Ask the Person in the Mirror." *Harvard Business Review* 85–1 (January 2007): 86–95.

Kearns, M. "The Big Problem with Most Strategic Planning in the Nonprofit Sector." www.network-centricadvocacy.net/2005/03/the_big_problem. html. (Accessed January 27, 2009.)

Kegan, R. *The Evolving Self: Problem and Process in Human Development.* Cambridge: Harvard University Press, 1982.

Kipnis, D., Schmidt, S. M., & Wilkinson, I. "Intraorganizational Influence Tactics: Explorations in Getting One's Way." *Journal of Applied Psychology* 65 (1980): 440–452.

Kotter, J. "What Do Leaders Really Do?" *Harvard Business Review,* May–June 1990.

Kotter, J. *Leading Change.* First Edition. New York: Harvard Business School Press, 1996.

Kotter, J. P., & Heskett, J. L. *Corporate Culture and Performance.* New York: Free Press, 1992.

Kotterman, J. "Leadership Versus Management: What's the Difference?" *The Journal for Quality and Participation* 29–2 (2006): 13–17.

Kouzes, J., & Posner, B. *Credibility: How Leaders Gain It and Lose It, Why People Demand It.* San Francisco: Jossey-Bass, 2003.

Knowles, H., & Saxberg, B. *Personality and Leadership Behavior.* Reading, MA: Addison-Wesley, 1971.

Lax, D., & Sebenius, J. *The Manager as Negotiator: Bargaining for Cooperation and Competitive Gain.* New York: Free Press, 1986.

Lesser, L. E., & Storck, J. "Communities of Practice and Organizational Performance." *IBM Systems Journal* 40–4 (2001): 831–841.

Lewin, K. *Resolving Social Conflicts: And, Field Theory in Social Science.* Reprinted Edition. Washington: American Psychological Association, 1997.

Locke, E. *The Essence of Leadership.* New York: Lexington Books, 1991.

Locke, E., & Latham, G. *A Theory of Goal-setting and Task Performance.* Englewood Cliffs, NJ: Prentice Hall, 1990.

Loehr, J., & Schwartz, T. *The Power of Full Engagement: Managing Energy, Not Time, Is the Key to High Performance and Personal Renewal.* New York: Free Press, 2004.

Loevinger, J. *Ego Development: Conceptions and Theories*. San Francisco: Jossey-Bass, 1976.

London, M., & Smither, J. "Can Multisource Feedback Change Perceptions of Goal Accomplishment, Self Evaluations, and Performance Related Outcomes? Theory Based Applications and Directions for Research." *Personnel Psychology* 48 (1995): 803–839.

Longenecker, C.O., & Fink, L.S. "How Top-level Managers Develop: A Field Study." *Development and Learning in Organizations* 20–5 (September 2006): 18–20.

Lorsch, J., & Clark, R. "Leading from the Boardroom." *Harvard Business Review* 86–4 (April 2008): 104–111.

Low, J., & Seisfeld, T. "Measures That Matter: Wall Street Considers More Than You Think." *Strategy and Leadership* (March–April 1998): 24–30.

Lucia, A., & Lepsinger, R. *The Art & Science of Competency Models*. San Francisco: Jossey-Bass, 1999.

Martin, D. R. "Death of Heroic Leadership." *Rotman Management*, Fall 2000.

Meyer, K., & Rollo, R. "Boards Think They're Doing a Good Job . . . But CEOs Disagree. What Directors Can Do to Bridge that Disconnect." *Directors and Boards* (Second Quarter 2008).

Meyer, M. "Give More and Get More out of Social Media." *Communication World* 26–6 (November 2009).

Mowday, R. T. "The Exercise of Upward Influence in Organizations." *Administrative Science Quarterly* 23 (1978): 137–156.

Murmann, J. P., & Tushman, M. "The Effects of Executive Team Characteristics and Organizational Context on Organizational Responsiveness to Environmental Shock." Working Paper, Columbia Business School. (1997).

Murray, A. "Top Management Group Heterogeneity and Firm Performance." *Strategic Management Journal* 10 (1989): 125–141.

Nadler, D. "High Performance Executive Teams." *Corporate Board* 13–75 (July 1992).

Nadler, D., & Spencer, J. *Executive Teams*. First Edition. San Francisco: Jossey-Bass, 1997.

Nutt, P. "Surprising But True: Half the Decisions in Organizations Fail." *The Academy of Management Executive* 13–4 (1999): 75–90.

Office of the Auditor General of B.C. *2002/2003 Report 1: Building a Strong Work Environment in British Columbia's Public Service: A Key to Delivering Quality Service*. April 2002.

O'Reilly, C., Snyder, R., & Boothe, J. "Executive Team Demography and Organizational Change." In: G.P. Huber & W.H. Glick, Editors, *Organizational Change and Redesign: Ideas and Insights for Improving Performance*. New York: Oxford University Press, 1993.

Ott, B., & Killham, E. "Would You Fire Your Boss?" *Gallup Management Journal*, 2007.

Pearce, C.L., & Conger, J.A. In C.L. Pearce & J.A. Conger, Editors, *Shared Leadership: Reframing the Hows and Whys of Leadership*. Thousand Oaks, CA: Sage, 2003.

Piaget, J. *The Psychology of the Child*. New York: Basic Books, 1966.

Rath, T. "The Best Ways to Recognize Employees." *Gallup Management Journal* 09 (December 2004). http://gmj.gallup.com/content/13888/best-ways-recognize-employees.aspx . (Accessed March 16, 2010.)

Recklies, O. "Problems and Barriers to Strategic Planning." *Economics and Organization of Enterprise* 1 Number 1 (2008): 3–11.

Rogers, P., & Blenko, M. "Who Has the D? How Clear Decision Roles Enhance Organizational Performance." *Harvard Business Review* 84–1 (January 2006): 52–61.

Rooke, D. "Organizational Transformation Requires the Presence of Leaders Who Are Strategists and Alchemists." First published in *Organizations and People* 4.3 (1997). Amended October 2001.

Rooke, D., & Torbert, W. "Seven Transformations of Leadership." *Harvard Business Review*, April 2005: 66–76.

Rooke, D., & Torbert, W. "The CEO's role in organizational transformation." *The Systems Thinker* 10, no. 7 (1999): 1–5.

Rosen, R., & Adair, F. "CEOs Misperceive Top Teams' Performance." *Harvard Business Review* September 2007: 1–2.

Ross, J., & Staw, B. "Expo 86: An Escalation Prototype." *Administrative Science Quarterly* 31–2 (1986): 274–297.

Ross, J., & Staw, B. "Organizational Escalation and Exit: Lessons from the Shoreham Nuclear Power Plant." *Academy of Management Journal* 36–4 (1993): 701–732.

Rosen, R., & Adair, F. "CEOs Misperceive Top Teams' Performance." *Harvard Business Review*, September 2007: 1–2.

Rothschild, P., Duggal, J., Balaban, R. "Strategic Planning Redux. But This Time Linked to Funding and Everyday Execution." *MMC Viewpoint*, Number 1 (2004).

Rutledge, T. *Getting Engaged the New Workplace Loyalty*. Toronto: Mattanie Press, 2005.

Schein, E. H. *Organizational Culture and Leadership*. San Francisco, CA: Jossey-Bass, 1992.

Senge, P. *The Fifth Discipline: The Art & Practice of the Learning Organization*. New York: Currency, 2006.

Smith, R. "A Born Leader?" *Management Accounting* 71–4 (1993).

Stewart, J. "Intervention and Assessment: The Ethics of HRD." *Human Resource Development International* 1–1 (1998): 9–12.

Storck, J., & Hill, P. "Knowledge Diffusion Through 'Strategic Communities.'" *Sloan Management Review*, 41–2 (2000): 63–74.

Thommen, J., & Achleitner, A. *Allgemeine Betriebswirtschaftslehre. Umfassende Einführung aus anagementorientierte Sicht.* Fifth Edition. Gabler Wiesbaden, (2006).

Tichy, N. *The Leadership Engine: How Winning Companies Build Leaders at Every Level.* New York: HarperCollins, 1997.

Torbert, W. *Action Inquiry: The Secret of Timely and Transforming Leadership.* San Francisco, CA: Berrett-Koehler Publishers, 2004.

Towers Perrin. "Closing the Engagement Gap: A Road Map for Driving Superior Business Performance." Towers Perrin Global Workforce Study, 2007–2008.

Towers Perrin. "Communications Effectiveness Consortium." Towers Perrin, 2004.

Ulrich, D., Smallwood, N., & Snyder, S. "Leadership Brand." *Executive Excellence* (March 2001): 14.

Van der Heijden, B., & Nijhof, A. "The Value of Subjectivity: Problems and Prospects for 360-degree Appraisal Systems." *International Journal of Human Resource Management* 15–3 (May 2004): 493–511.

van Hooft, E., van der Flier, H., & Minne, M. "Construct Validity of Multi-Source Performance Ratings: An Examination of the Relationship of Self-, Supervisor-, and Peer-Ratings with Cognitive and Personality Measures." *International Journal of Selection & Assessment* 14–1 (March 2006): 67–81.

Wagner, R. "Intelligence, Training, and Employment." *American Psychologist* 52-10 (October 1997): 1059–1069.

Wagner, W., Pfeffer, J., & O'Reilly, C. "Organizational Demography and Turnover in Top Management Teams." *Administrative Science Quarterly* 29–1 (1984): 74–92.

Wheatley, M. *Leadership and the New Science: Learning About Organization from an Orderly.* San Francisco, Berrett-Koehler, 1992.

Williams, K., & O'Reilly, C. "Demography and Diversity in Organizations: A Review of 40 Years of Research." In B. Staw & R. Sutton (Eds.), *Research in Organizational Behavior.* Greenwich, CT: JAI Press, 1998.

Williams, M. "Will You Make One of These Five Common Employee Recognition Mistakes?" May 19, 2003. HR.Com. www.hr.com/sfs?t=/contentManager/onStory&e=UTF-8&i=1116423256281&l=0&ParentID=1120248810940&StoryID=1119651662828&highlight=1&keys=Inergy1%2BMarketing1%2BGroup&lang=0&active=no. (Accessed February 20, 2010.)

Williams, R., & Williams, T. "Connections with a Purpose." *Communication World* 26–4 (July 2009): 26–29.

Wooldridge, B., & Floyd, S. W. "The Strategy Process, Middle Management Involvement, and Organizational Performance." *Strategic Management Journal* 11(3) (1990): 231–241.

www.hewittassociates.com/Intl/NA/en-US/Consulting/ServiceTool. aspx?cid=2256. (Accessed February 13, 2010.)

www.storytellings.com/power.htm. ©2004–2009 StoryTellings™ Consulting.

Yukl, G. *Leadership in Organizations*. Seventh Edition. Alexandria, VA: Prentice Hall, 2009.

Yukl, G., & Falbe, C. M. "Influence Tactics and Objectives in Upward, Downward, and Lateral Influence Attempts." *Journal of Applied Psychology* 75 (1990): 132–140.

INDEX